BEHAVE
AS A
CHURCH
MEMBER

DR. CHRISTOPHER POWERS

WESTBOW
PRESS®
A DIVISION OF THOMAS NELSON
& ZONDERVAN

WestBow Press books may be ordered through booksellers or by contacting:

WestBow Press
A Division of Thomas Nelson & Zondervan
1663 Liberty Drive
Bloomington, IN 47403
www.westbowpress.com
844-714-3454

ISBN: 978-1-6642-9468-4 (sc)
ISBN: 978-1-6642-9469-1 (hc)
ISBN: 978-1-6642-9467-7 (e)

Library of Congress Control Number: 2023904487

Print information available on the last page.

WestBow Press rev. date: 03/27/2023

CONTENTS

Introduction.. vii

Chapter 1   How to Experience the Heart of Real Christianity............ 1
Chapter 2   Filled with the Spiritual Gifts of the Spirit..................... 16
Chapter 3   What does the Spirit Give?.. 31
Chapter 4   The Leader Meets the Lord.. 47
Chapter 5   Crisis Management.. 60
Chapter 6   The Beginning of Discipleship...................................... 73
Chapter 7   What is Discipleship?... 86
Chapter 8   What is Wisdom?... 98
Chapter 9   The Importance of Prophecy 113
Chapter 10 Defend My Sheep 125
Chapter 11 Stirring Up God's People 142
Chapter 12 Be Strong and Courageous...156
Chapter 13 The Power of Biblical Faith...169
Chapter 14 Can They See Jesus in Me 182
Chapter 15 Royal Ambassadors..198
Chapter 16 Becoming a People of the Towel.................................210
Chapter 17 Love Mercy... 222
Chapter 18 God's Jubilee.. 238
Chapter 19 The Lost Art of Hospitality 248
Chapter 20 Why Attend Church?.. 260

References 269

INTRODUCTION

The Birthday of the Chruch

And in those days Peter stood up in the midst of the disciples (altogether the number of names was about a hundred and twenty) … (Acts 1:15 NKJV)

"Church members ought not to behave that way." That is a phrase that has been said or thought at the end of a Wednesday night business meeting, Sunday gatherings, or even out in public. What is it, that causes church members to behave in such a way that is unbecoming of a follower of Christ? There are a number of reasons: feelings get hurt because something was said towards them, about them, or against them. Maybe they didn't get their way in a decision that was made in the church. However, the majority of the time is the fact that they have not been taught, trained, or discipled on how to behave as a church member. Whose fault is that? Why are we not making disciples? Why are we not fulfilling the discipleship part of the great commission? What is interesting is that most church members tend to believe that discipleship is the job of the pastor and/or deacons of the church; when in fact it is the job of all mature Christian church members. There was this young woman, who was a member of a small church, who was so thrilled of the fact that she had completed a course in First Aid. One Wednesday night during Bible study, they were having a time of testimony. She gets up and begins to give her testimony. She said, "Let me tell you what happened to me. Out in front of my very own home there was a horrible automobile accident. An elderly man lost control of the vehicle he was driving, and went over the curb and hit a big oak tree head-on. He was thrown out of the vehicle onto the ground. He was unconscious and his pulse was thready. It was terrible site to behold." But then she said, "I was the first one on the scene, and all I could remember from my First Aid training was to put my head between my knees so I wouldn't faint."

I am afraid in the church today, there are many members that have been trained to do the work and ministry of the great commission and yet have their head between their knees. However, there could be a number of church members that are attending church and just don't know how to do ministry, share the gospel, or make disciples. They don't know about the inner workings of the church, or all the essentials for being a church member. The world around us is in pain, suffering, economic chaos, evil at every turn, plagues and pestilence, and there are church members who are behaving as though they have their head between their knees. Listen, if you are behaving as a follower of Christ, then you will want to behave as a church member, because God has anointed, empowered the followers of Christ, members of the bride of Christ, to rescue the perishing, and to care for the dying; to lift up the fallen ones, the weak and erring ones, to tell them that Jesus is mighty to save. If we are going to behave as church members then we don't need to be going around in our neighborhoods, work places, school, or everyday activities moaning and groaning or talking about living in the last days as if God were dead! If we are going to behave as church member, we don't need to go around gossiping about the church you are a member of, nor about the pastor, deacons, Sunday School teacher, or other church members. If you are going to behave as a church member you need to remember why you go to church. A church member goes to church to gather with fellow believers in Christ, to gather in His name, in the presence of the audience of the One to worship Jesus Christ. However, this lack of discipleship, not being trained or just not knowing how to behave as church member is not the first time.

Take the early church for instance, they did not have all the things we find essential for success as a church. The did not have buildings, the early church began in an upper room, in Jerusalem, on the Day of Pentecost. Think about what they were doing, they were being obedient. Notice what is going on before Jesus ascended into heaven, "And being assembled together with them, He commanded them not to depart from Jerusalem, but wait for the Promise of the Father, "which," He said, "you have heard from Me; for John truly baptized with water, but you shall be baptized with Holy Spirit not many days from now."" (Acts 1:4-5 NKJV).

So, the followers of Jesus Christ on the Day of Pentecost, are in the upper room praying, waiting, on the Promise of the Father. They did not have money or political power or social influence, they didn't even know about church traditions. The early church had not been formed yet. I'm sure they didn't even know how to behave as a church member. All they knew at this point was to behave as a follower of Christ; and Jesus said to go to Jerusalem and wait on the Holy Spirit. Then on the Day of Pentecost the Holy Spirit came and the church was born. After the that day the church began to grow. Notice what is said, "So continuing daily with one accord in the temple, and breaking bread from house to house, they ate their food with gladness and simplicity of heart, praising God and having favor with all the people. And the Lord added to the church daily those who were being saved." (Acts 2:46-47 NKJV). Listen, there is nothing wrong with a small church or a big church, however, there is something wrong with any church and its members when the church and the members are not behaving in an area where there is a lot of lost people, and not growing. There is something wrong when the church and church members are not fulfilling the entire Great Commission.

This newly born church was perhaps the largest church in the church history. Take a look at these facts. First of all, the newly born church started with just one hundred and twenty members (Acts 1:15). Then in Acts 2:41 it says, "Then those who gladly received his word were baptized; and that day about three thousand souls were added to them." So, now the early church was at three thousand one hundred twenty. Then we read in Acts 2:47, that the early church was, "praising God and having favor with all the people. And the Lord added to the church daily those who were being saved." Theologians don't know how many this was, but just think, every day (day by day) souls were get saved and that was not just in a Sunday service. Another fact to consider is found in Acts 4:4, "However, many of those who heard the word believed; and the number of the men came to be about five thousand." You have five thousand men, not including their wives and children, which is very possible that they were added as well. Now for argument's sake let say each man had a wife and two children that would be 20,000 souls' beings saved and added to the church. Let's tally up to this point, the church went from one hundred twenty to three thousand one hundred and twenty, plus let's say 20,000 the Lord was adding every day, plus we add the 20,000 from Acts 4:4 that comes to a total of 43,120 in just a few days after the Day of Pentecost. One last fact to consider, in Acts 6:47 it says, "Then the word of God spread, and the number of the disciples multiplied greatly in Jerusalem, and a great many of the priest were obedient to the faith." One time we are talking about adding (Acts 2:47) and now we are talking about multiplying. The early church was growing because the church members were behaving as church members. One theologian said that the membership of this early church was around 65,000 members in the first six months, while another theologian says it was more like 250,000 in the first six months. Either way it was because of the power of God when the church members behave as church members. And to think that it was these one hundred and twenty followers of Christ, once they received the Promise of the Father, went out and won multitudes of people to Jesus Christ and started many churches in the Roman empire.

How? Simple, the Holy Spirit! "And suddenly there came a sound from heaven, as of a rushing might wind, and it filled the whole house where they were sitting." (Acts 2:2 NKJV). The Holy Spirit birth, gave life to, and empowered the early church to do the ministry of the Great Commission (Matt. 28:18-20). Can you imagine what it was like to be in that upper room, to be able to experience that mighty day? What must it have been like to feel, hear that rushing might wind, or see the "divided tongues, as of fire" that "sat upon each one of them" (Acts 2:3 NKJV)? Everybody says that a tornado sounds like a freight train. And if you think that a tornado sounds awesome outside, then what would it sound like inside? The rushing of the might wind took place inside that upper room where they were sitting. This wind is symbolic of the Holy Spirit as were other thing that was going on during the Day of Pentecost.

The Day of Pentecost was a special feast day in the life of Israel. For they had kept this feast for fifteen hundred years, however, this Pentecost was special. Furthermore, there would be no other Pentecost like this Pentecost feast. All of the feast in the Jewish religion was a picture of the Lord Jesus Christ. So, if you think about it when you invite someone to come to Jesus, you are not inviting them to come to a funeral, you are inviting them a feast. Now Pentecost means "fiftieth", and according to Leviticus 23:15-22 Pentecost happened fifty days after the Feast of Firstfruits. Here are how these feasts display the work of Jesus Christ.

Passover represent His death as the Lamb of God (John 1:29), the Feast of Firstfruits represents His resurrection from the dead (1 Cor. 15:20-23) and Pentecost represents the formation of the church. The Jews celebrated Pentecost as the day the Law was given, and Christians celebrate it as the day the Holy Spirit was given to the church; the birthday of the church.

The Day of Pentecost was a feast day where many things were happening. For example, the priest would take some grain, crush it, sift it, purify it, and bake two loaves of bread, pour oil (symbolic of the Holy Spirit) on them, and present them on the Day of Pentecost. The two loaves of bread represented the Jews and the Gentiles and on this Day of Pentecost the Holy Spirit baptized the Jews into one body, and the Gentile believers would be baptized by the Holy Spirit in the home of Cornelius (Acts 10). The fact that there was leaven in the bread represents the fact that there was sin in the church on earth. Now these believers, both Jews and Gentile, are no longer individual grains, they have been blended and baked together. Then the priest would take seven perfect lambs, one bull, and two young calves, and offer up a blood sacrifice. These all speak of the perfect shed blood of the Lord Jesus Christ and His completed work on the cross at Calvary. Pentecost was the birthday of the church. The fire that sat upon the heads of the one hundred and twenty followers represents the Holy Spirit. Think about the uniqueness this implies. Fire spreads, consumes, warms, purges, illuminates, energizes, and purifies and this is exactly what the was happening as the church began and then began to minister throughout the entire known world.

They didn't know how to behave as a church member, because the early church was just an infant at this time. And yet, the early church, on the Day of Pentecost, was in the upper room in "one accord" (Acts 1:15 NKJV). In other words, the one hundred and twenty followers of Christ all had one mind; they were there in unity with a desire to seek the face of the Lord (Acts. 1:14). Acts 2:4 (NKJV) says that when the Holy Spirit came, "they were all filled with the Holy Spirit." This how the early church began to reach a multitude of lost sinners and see many churches started. The filling of the Holy Spirit gave them power to witness and serve Jesus as they began to behave as church members. Remember this is the fulfilling of a promise the Jesus made forty days early, before He ascended into heaven. "But you shall receive power when the Holy Spirit has come upon you; and you shall be witnesses to Me in Jerusalem, and in all Judea, and Samaria, and to the end of the earth." (Acts 1:8 NKJV). Understand, we are not encouraged to seek to be baptized by the Holy Spirit again, because this is something that God does once and for all when we accept Jesus Christ as our Lord and Savior. However, we are encouraged to be filled with the Spirit (Eph. 5:18) because in the day and age we live in, we need His power in order to behave as church members and effectively serve Him.

But what kind of power was this? Was it physical power? Economic power? Political power? No, it was spiritual power. This spiritual power was used to speak all of creation into existence. It is the same spiritual power that flooded the earth, brought the plagues upon Egypt, parted the Red Sea, made a virgin girl name Mary pregnant, healed the lame, gave sight to the blind, raised Jesus from the dead, and was given to every believer that places their faith in the Lord Jesus Christ. This same power that was given to the early church members is given to every genuine born-again church member today in order to make us more effective witnesses for Christ. This spiritual power was what caused Peter, who previously had cowered in front of a little girl, to preach (Acts 2:14-39). Notice his transformation; he is not denying Jesus, nor is he swearing and saying, "I never knew the man." But now, he is standing up and he says, "Men of Judea and all who dwell in Jerusalem, let this be known to you, and heed my words." (Acts 2:14 NKJV). There is spiritual power that has moved upon this man and taken up residence in his heart.

The early church did not know how to behave as church members; no one had ever been there before. There wasn't any precedence or traditions, except for the examples of worship found in the Old Testament. All they had was the teachings of Jesus and the apostles' doctrine. It took time before they could fully behave as church members, they had to learn how to behave as church member. And yet, we expect babes in Christ to instantly know how to behave as church members; or worse we expect lost sinners to know how to behave while in church. If you are reading this book and you are a child of God, do you remember what it was like to become a Christian, little lone a church member? Do you know how to behave as a church member? It is my prayer that as you read this book you will learn of the power of the Holy Spirit that God has given you as a mighty gift and learn how to behave as a church member.

CHAPTER ONE

HOW TO EXPERIENCE THE HEART OF REAL CHRISTIANITY

Then Jesus said to His disciples, "If anyone desires to come after Me, let him deny himself, and take up his cross, and follow Me." (Matthew 16:24 NKJV)

When seeking to behave as a church member there are some things that a church member must know and learn in order to grow in your walk with Christ and behave as a follower of Christ. Do you know what the church is? According to the *Baptist Faith and Message 2000* "A New Testament of the Lord Jesus Christ is an autonomous local congregation of baptized believers, associated by covenant in the faith and fellowship of the gospel; observing two ordinances of Christ, governed by His laws, exercising the gifts, rights, and privileges invested in them by His Word, seeking to extend the gospel to the ends of the earth. Each congregation operates under the Lordship of Christ through democratic processes. In such a congregation each member is responsible and accountable to Christ as Lord. Its scriptural officers are pastors and deacons. Both men and women are gifted for service in the church; the office of pastor is limited to men as qualified by Scripture. The New Testament speaks also of the church as the Body of Christ which includes all of the redeemed of all the ages, believers from every tribe, and tongue, and people, and nation." (The Baptist Fatih and Message 2000).

You see the church member is a part of the church, the body of Christ, however there is a prerequisite to becoming a church member of the church. To be a church member, you must have accepted Jesus Christ as your personal Lord and Savior. Have you done that? The Bible says "For all have sinned and fall short of the glory of God." (Rom. 3:23 NKJV). Every person who is born into this world is a sinner and needs to repent and call upon Jesus to save them. Because everything we do falls short. The punishment for not accepting Jesus is death but there is a gift to escape the punishment. "For the wages of sin is death, but the gift of God is eternal life in Christ Jesus our Lord." (Rom. 6:23 NKJV). Therefore, if you want to be a follower of Christ, if you want to be saved from your sin, then you must confess with your mouth and believe in your heart that Jesus is Lord (Rom. 10:9-10). "For whoever calls on the name of the Lord shall be saved." (Rom. 10:13 NKJV). If you have not asked Jesus to come into your heart, then I challenge you right now to stop reading and pray, ask Jesus into your heart to save you.

Now, once you have asked Jesus into your heart the next step is the step of obedience, which is baptism. Baptism does not save you, but it identifies you as a follower of Christ. "Christian baptism is the immersion of a believer in water in the name of the Father, the Son, and the Holy Spirit. It is an act of obedience symbolizing the believer's faith in a crucified, buried, and risen Savior, the believer's death to sin, the burial of the old life, and the resurrection to walk in newness of life in Christ Jesus. It is a testimony to his faith in the final resurrection of the dead. Being a church ordinance, it is prerequisite to the privileges of church membership and to the Lord's Supper. The Lord's Supper is a symbolic act of obedience whereby members of the church, through partaking of the bread and the fruit of the vine, memorialize the death of the Redeemer and anticipate His second coming." (The Baptist Fatih and Message 2000).

What does it mean to be a Christian? The answer you get to that question depends on the person you ask. Some people believe that just being a church member makes you a Christian. Others believe that baptism is what makes you a Christian. Still there are those who believe that being religious and morally clean is enough to allow a person to wear the name Christian. So, what does it mean to be a Christian? The word Christian literally means "the Christ Ones." This name was first given to the followers of Christ in a place called Antioch (Acts 11:26). However, this word Christian was actually given as a byword, slang word, a term for contempt! The people of Antioch, who were pagans, were offended by the clean lifestyles and the preaching of the believers and gave them the name "Christian" as an insult. Instead of insulting these believers, it perfectly summed up the image they were attempting to project to their lost neighbors. So, from then on, a Christian is a "Christ one" or "one who is like Jesus." You see, just going to church and claiming to be a church member cannot make you a Christian. Being a good moral person cannot make you a Christian. Just claiming the name Christian for yourself does not make you a Christian. To be a Christian means that you become like Christ. We tend to lump all saved people under the title Christian bur real Christians are people who live and behave like Jesus Christ.

Therefore, if you are a genuine Christian then you are going to have desire to join a local church and become a member of that church. While a member of that church, a genuine Christian should want to behave as a church member. Which means that you "let your light so shine before men, that they may see your good works and glorify your Father in heaven." (Matt. 5:16 NKJV). To behave as a church member means that you experience the heart of real Christianity with your fellow believers of the local church, doing the Kingdom work that Jesus left us here to do (Acts 1:8). Take Matthew 16:21-24 for instance, in that passage of Scripture, Jesus is talking to His disciples about His impending death (vs. 21). He is immediately rebuked by Peter (vs. 22). Giving Jesus the opportunity to use this event to teach His disciples about the heart of real Christianity. Listen to what Jesus says in verse 24, "If anyone desires to come after Me, let him deny himself, and take up his cross, and follow Me." If we are going to behave as a church member then we need to get down to the heart of what it means to experience real Christianity.

But why is this important? Because as individual Christians, members of a local church, there are many who have no idea what it means to behave as a church member. Not to mention as the Body of Christ, the church, we have left the heart of our faith behind in an effort to be found pleasing in the sight of the world. Jesus calls mature believers and babes in Christ to return to the heart of what it means to behave as followers of Christ and start behaving as church members. Let me point some of the simple ideas Jesus gives us and if we will hear His voice and heed His words, then we can behave.

WE MUST FIND OUR HEART

Notice the first part of verse 24, "If any many will come after Me…" Jesus, and Jesus alone is to be the heart of who we are and all we do as believers. If we are going to experience the power of real biblical Christianity in our lives and in our church, then we are going to have to find our heart! That simple means, we are going to have to discover what makes us tick! We can begin this process by asking ourselves some amazingly simple questions.

Why do you go to church? There is an old saying, "you always get what you come for". If you go to church with some kind of expectations, then you are going to get your expectations met. There was this preacher who went to a church to try out, to see if the church wants him as their pastor. He took his son that Sunday. As they enter the lobby of the church the preacher was looking around and saw a box marked collections. The preacher was intrigued and reached into his pocket and pulled out two dimes. The boy watched as his dad took those two dimes and placed them into the box, and two waked on into the sanctuary. After the service had concluded, the chairman of deacons went back to the lobby and retrieved the box. He came to the preach and told him, "Pastor, we don't have a lot of funds at this time to pay visiting preacher. But what we do is put this box of collections out for people to put money in to pay our visiting preachers." The deacon reached in and pulled out the two dimes and handed to the preacher. The boy witnessed all of this and look to his dad and said, "See dad, if you would have put more in, you would have got more out." Needless to say, if you come to church out of a sense of duty then you will not receive a blessing. If you come out of habit then you will leave every service out of habit. If you come to see and be seen then you will get an eye full. If you come out of love for the church and its traditions then your traditions will leave you empty. However, if you come because of your personal relationship with Jesus Christ, your desire to focus your worship upon Him and only Him, then you have come with the only valid reason to attend church. You will always benefit from coming to church, but every church member needs to reach the place where Jesus is the sole reason, we attend church. "Blessed are those who hunger and thirst for righteousness, for they shall be filled." (Matt. 5:6 NKJV).

Why does the local church exist? Churches exist for lots of reasons. Too often, they exist only because someone started it a long time ago and the reason why has been long forgotten. Let me share three valid reasons for any local church to exist. The reasons are easy to remember each one starts with the letter E. First: Exalt the Savior. "Therefore, by Him let us continually offer the sacrifice of praise to God, that is, the fruit of our lips, giving thanks to His name." (Heb. 13:15 NKJV). Second: Edify the saints. "Therefore, comfort each other and edify one another, just as you also are doing." (1 Thess. 5:11 NKJV). Third: Evangelize the sinners. "But you shall receive power when the Holy Spirit has come upon you; and you shall be witnesses to Me in Jerusalem, and in all Judea and Samaria, and to the end of the earth." (Acts 1:8 NKJV). All three reasons are represented in the Great Commission found in Matthew 28:18-20 and all three reasons are clearly seen in the life of the early church Acts 2:41-47. Therefore, if these are valid reasons as to why the local church exist, then who makes up the local church? The answer, church members; genuine born-again, Christ following church members. If we are to behave as church members then clearly, we need to be fulfilling the duties of the church member by participating in the ministry of the church set forth by these reasons for the existence of the church. I read a survey taken by the Southern Baptist Convention that they had done over the years as to why people join Southern Baptist churches. What was shocking is only three percent joined because the pastor visited them and that fifty-six percent joined because a member of the congregation invited them to come! Now as a pastor, I am a church member and so are other pastors, I should be setting the example of how to behave a church member in fulfilling these reasons the local church exists. However, when you add the pastor, the beauty of the facilities, prior denominational ties, and the variety of other reasons people join a Southern Baptist church or any church for that matter; it doesn't compare to the effectiveness of the church member in the pew evangelizes the lost by inviting them to church. The pastor along with his fellow church members should be working together to equipping the saints. During the worship service the pastor, and his fellow church member are to be exalting the Savior. We need to find our heart for God, for our fellow saints, and sharing the Gospel to the lost.

WE MUST FOCUS OUR HEART

If we are really in love with Jesus and He is the central love of our hearts, there will be a desire to be where He is! Jesus said, "For where two or three are gathered together in My name, I am there in the midst of them." (Matt. 18:20 NKJV). When church members gather together on Sunday morning, Sunday evening, Wednesday night service, or whenever they gather majority of the time they gather in the name of Jesus and as promised He is there. To behave as a church member, we should have a hunger to be in the presence of Jesus. We need to have the same hunger to be in the presence of the Lord as David had. He said, "As the deer pants for the water brooks, so pants my soul for You, O God. My soul thirst for God, for the living God. When shall I come and appear before God? My tears have been my food day and night..." (Ps. 42:1-3a NKJV).

The disciples that day heard the call in that phrase "come after" (Matt. 16:24 NKJV). For the disciples to hear Jesus call them to follow Him, meant they were to forsake everything else (Matt. 19:27-30; Mark 1:16-20). For us, it may come to mean the very same thing. "And whoever does not bear his cross and come after Me cannot be My disciple" (Luke 14:27 NKJV). Bottom line is that when your heart is focus upon Jesus, the Author and Finisher of your faith, then nothing is more important. Think about, you go where you want to go; you do what you want to do; you follow who and what you want to follow; you do what you love to do. All Jesus is doing is call us to focus our hearts upon Him, come after Him, and go with Him wherever He leads us! The Psalmist said it this way, "O God, my heart is steadfast..." (Ps. 108:1 NKJV). David said it like this, "One thing I have desired of the Lord, that will I seek: that I may dwell in the house of the Lord all the days of my life, to behold the beauty of the Lord, and to inquire in His temple." (Ps. 27:4). Paul said, "Brethren, I do not count myself to have apprehended; but one thing I do, forgetting those things which are behind and reaching forward to those things which are ahead, I press toward the goal for the prize of the upward calling of God in Christ Jesus." (Phil. 3:13-14 NKJV). All three individuals are examples of a single-minded person whose heart is focused upon following the Lord wherever He leads.

What has your heart today? Who is on first in your life? Are you behaving as a church member? Are you behaving as a follower of Christ? May the Lord help you to come to the place where nothing in your life means more to you that Jesus Christ and His leadership. May He become and remain the central focus of your heart as you strive to behave as a church member.

WE MUST FOLLOW OUR HEART

If Jesus has our heart, and if we are in love with Him more than anything else in this world, and if we are focused on His will for us and upon His leadership in our lives then we need to take whatever steps necessary to see that we follow our heart. If Jesus is our everything, then let's follow Him, however, I must warn you to behave as a church member it is going to cost you. There in Matthew 16:24, Jesus explains the three cost that it will take to behave as a church member.

DENY HIMSELF

We are called to lay our lives down at the feet of Jesus. The phrase "deny himself" literally means, "To completely disown, to utterly separate oneself for someone." (Webster n.d.). It is same word used to describe Peter's denial of Jesus outside the high priest home (Matt. 26:34-35). The disciple is to utterly disown himself, refuse to acknowledge the self of the old man. We are to count the old nature as being dead. "Likewise, you also, reckon yourselves to be dead indeed to sin, but alive to God in Christ Jesus our Lord." (Rom. 6:11 NKJV). We are to make no provisions for the flesh. "But put on the Lord Jesus Christ, and make no provisions for the flesh, to fulfill its lust." (Rom. 13:14 NKJV). To deny yourself means to follow the example set forth by the Lord Jesus Himself in coming to this world. Paul writes, "Let this mind be in you which was also in Christ Jesus, who, being in the form of God, did not consider it robbery to be equal with God, but made Himself of no reputation, taking the form of a bondservant, and coming in the likeness of man. And being found in appearance as a man, He humbled Himself and became obedient to the point of death, even the death of the cross." (Phil. 2:5-8 NKJV). We are to live our lives as one alive to God, but dead to sin and the world (Gal. 2:2). I know it sounds hard that is because it is hard! Self does not like to be denied, but until self is, we cannot possibly follow Christ and behave as a church member like He desires for us.

TAKE UP HIS CROSS

When His disciples heard Jesus speak about the cross, every in His audience knew what He was referring to. It has been estimated that over 30,000 Jews were crucified during the lifetime of Jesus alone. When Jesus says that we are to take up our cross, He is saying that we are to live as dead men! In those day, to take up one's cross was to start upon a death march. Their walk under that cross, always ended up with them on that cross. They began a process from which there was no retreating and no turning back. To take up your cross was to embrace the death of self! This is just what Jesus did when He came to this world. Jesus said, "For even the Son of Man did not come to be served, but to serve, and to give His life a ransom for many." (Mark 10:45 NKJV). He set the example that we are to follow.

To understand what this cross Jesus refer to is, we need to talk about what it isn't. It isn't your lost husband or wife. It isn't your wayward children. It isn't your in-laws. Your cross isn't your difficulties or the bad situation you face in life. The cross is not just a place of suffering; it is a place of death! To take up one's cross means to willingly pick up and carry the shame, the rejection, the suffering, and the death that Jesus Himself willingly carried for us. To take up your cross means that you are willing to identify personally, publicly, and/or financially! That's not a side of Christianity you hear very often! It isn't popular to talk about sacrifice, death, and suffering but that Christianity is all about! That is what it means to behave as a church member. The sooner we learn that truth, the sooner God can and will send revival to the hearts of His children and use us for His glory!

FOLLOW ME

After laying down our lives at the feet of Jesus, and picking up His cross; we are now expected to live something out. We are called upon to carry that cross and go after Jesus. We are not to back out, turn around, or lay down the cross. We are to die on that cross, giving our all for His glory! This phrase has the idea of being willing to go all the way for Jesus; no holds bar and no turning back; just a steady, humble walk that follows His footsteps and His path through this world, where ever He leads (Hab. 2:4). Jesus said it as simply as it could possibly be said, "If anyone serves Me, let him follow Me; and where I am, there My servant will be also. If anyone serves ME, him My Father will honor." (John 12:26 NKJV).

The simple truth is if you want to behave as a church member then you must first must be saved by placing your faith in Jesus Christ. "If anyone desires to come after Me, let him deny himself, and take up his cross, and follow Me." (Matt. 16:24 NKJV). If you want to be saved, you can be, but there's only one way that will ever happen. That is through faith in the finished work of Jesus Christ. God is inflexible and firm on that point. In fact, He has stated it this way, "I am the way, the truth, and the life. No one comes to the Father except through Me." (John 14:6 NKJV). God had made up His mind about that matter. If you want to be saved, you can be but only on His terms.

Just like God is inflexible when it comes to salvation, He is just as inflexible when it comes to this matter of being a follower of Christ. If you want to experience the real heart of Christianity, then you will have to meet His terms. You can have as much or as little of God as you want. The question is what do you want? If you want to behave as a church member, then I invite you to hear and heed the words of the Savior. Why not just bow your head and come before Him, deny yourself, take up your cross and follow Him. Until you make that commitment in your life, you will never experience all God has for you.

WE MUST REST OUR HEARTS

Do you ever get weary? Do you ever get tired? Do you feel like you have reached the end of your rope and there simply isn't enough rope left with to tie a knot? Life is full of burdens, full of weariness especially if you are trying to behave as church member following Christ carrying your cross. But praise God, we don't have to wait until we go to heave to find rest for our hearts. The fact is, when you rest your spirit, then the body seems to get along pretty well. Think about your lawnmower, or washer and dryer, or your vehicle or any other type of machine they all have one thing in common; Revolutions Per Minute or RPM for short. But it is not those RPMs that wear out your machine, it's the revolutions. In other words, the friction that is caused by the revolutions is what wears the machine out. Did you know that many people do not really wear out because of hard work? As matter of fact, a laboring man who is spiritually resting has the greatest vitality of any man.

Jesus said it this way, "Come to Me, all you who labor and are heavy laden, and I will give you rest. Take my yoke upon you and learn from Me, for I am gentle and lowly in heart, and you will find rest for your souls. For My yoke is easy and My burden is light." (Matt. 11:28-30 NKJV). Men try to find peace and spiritual rest in just about anything. For example, man thinks that money can purchase the rest they need. Isaiah says, "There is no peace," says my God, "for the wicked."" (Isa. 57:21 NKJV). There is none for the wicked. They cannot find peace in their possessions. Money can buy most things but happiness, and they cannot take it with them when they die. There are some people who try to find rest in a bottle, some pill, some pleasure, or they think that a doctor can write them a prescription and some turn to a psychiatrist to help them into peace. However, this is not the peace that Jesus is talking about, because this peace the world cannot give nor can the world take away.

THERE IS REST IN SALVATION

Here in Matthew 11:28-30, Jesus is giving an invitation to whosoever may come. In Christ alone you will find salvation. There is no other place to find true saving grace that in Jesus Christ. That is why He said, "If anyone desires to come after Me, let him deny himself, and take up his cross, and follow Me." (Matt. 16:24 NKJV). This invitation is extended to "all" people, the whosoever will may come; not just a select few but the whole world. He invites those who labor and are heavy laden. The word "labor" refers to those who are absolutely worn out from effort. (Webster n.d.) While the word "heavy laden" calls to mind those who have been pressed down by a great weight, similar the grapes in a wine press. (Strong's Concordance 1984) Basically, the reference here is those who are struggling with sin and those who are laboring under the bondage of religion and vain attempts at self-righteousness. Jesus describes their situation this way, "For they bind heavy burdens, hard to bear, and lay them on men's shoulders; but they themselves will not move them with one of their fingers." (Matt. 23:4). Jesus is calling out to all those who are trying to behave their way and trying to be good enough to go to heaven. Jesus knows, just as those sinners who do not accept Jesus will find out one day, that every effort to save oneself is a foolish waste of time.

Jesus opens the door of salvation wide enough to allow the "whosoever will" (Rom. 10:13 NKJV) to pass through. And if you will put your faith in Jesus Christ, He promise to give you His salvation and eternal life. When pick up your cross, and put on His yoke He promises to give your "rest". This word "rest" speaks of "quietness, calmness, and refreshment." (Dictionary 1828) He promises to allow them to rest from their labors and their attempts at self-righteousness. He promises to save them fully and freely by grace alone in Christ alone, without any works whatsoever. When we grasp this truth, we come to understand that when we come to Jesus for salvation, we truly are given rest. Let me give you some of the areas we find this rest. First, we can find peace with God (Rom. 5:1). Second, there will be rest from our attempts to please God (Eph. 1:6). Third, we have assurance, a calmness concerning our salvation (Rom. 8:16). Next, you will have a quietness about your future (John 6:37; 10:28). Then finally, Jesus gives us refreshment as we carry our cross and wear His yoke in our life's journey (Isa. 40:31). These are glorious promises that we have been given (note: not necessary in that order) by our Lord and Savior so that we can behave as church members as we follow Him.

THE SECRET OF HIS REST

Jesus moves from talking about rest in Matthew 11:28, to talking about work in verse 29. Notice what He says, "Take My yoke upon you and learn from Me, for I am gentle and lowly in heart, and you will find rest for your souls." (Matt. 11:29 NKJV). What is the "yoke" that He is referring to? Well, a yoke is a wooden bar, carefully fashioned and carved with a harness on it, that would fit across the shoulders of an ox. That ox was then connected to another ox on the side of the yoke, with the same bar and harness across its shoulders. The two oxen would then be able to pull the load that they were required to pull. So, it is apparent that Jesus expects His followers to serve Him by taking the spiritual counter part of that wooden beam upon us, and learning to wear the yoke if we are going to find rest. Sadly, this is a foreign concept to many believers, but in truth, no believer will ever be fully satisfied until he or she finds themselves engaged in the Lord's work, which involves behaving as church members. To do anything less is to deny our destiny as Christians. We are not saved by works, but work is surely expected for us after we are saved (Eph. 2:10; Titus 2:14, 3:8; Jam. 2:18). When we put on His yoke, it as if Jesus is like that ox on one side and you are on the other. He becomes your yokefellow and He is pulling with us, however, Jesus doesn't need to be on the other side and even though it may look empty and seem like you are pulling alone you are not. Because once you accept Jesus as your personal Lord and Savior, that is when the Holy Spirit has taken up residence in your heart and now gives you the power and strength to pull the load that Jesus calls you to bear. This can also be a beautiful picture of behaving as a church member when it comes to discipleship. We are to called upon through the Great Commission to make disciples, we are to mentor other believers by coming along side of them and sharing the load. As a church member you are to work, serve alongside your fellow brothers and sisters in Christ for the work of the ministry in the strength and spiritual gifts that Christ through the Holy Spirit give you.

The yoke of Jesus is a symbol of submission and service. That's what is meant by the phrase "Take My yoke upon you", you are to yield your life to His control, put your will under the will of Christ. When a believer yields his or her life to Jesus in service, they will find that they have truly become satisfied in their hearts and souls. Jesus does make a difference and the difference should always be lived out by behaving as church member.

So many people think that rest comes by taking the yoke off; but rest for the ox comes at the end of the day. That is when the battle is over and the work is done. He takes the yoke off and then he rests. It is not a rest from service; it is a rest in service. I know that it is a strange rest that comes by putting on the yoke rather than taking it off. However, rest does not come from mere inactivity. Yes, you need to rest your body; and yes, as we get older, we cannot do physically what we used to do, but that does not mean we drop out, sit back, soak, and sour. Think of it like this, the moment you take of the yoke of Jesus is the moment you pick back up your burdens. The most miserable people on this earth are those searching and trying to find peace in their lives by going to the pleasure palaces of this world. If you could look into the faces of those people, who are carrying around their own burdens, who are searching for happiness, joy, and peace you will find the most exhausted, weary-looking people you have ever seen in your life. That is why we need to yield ourselves to Jesus in service. In the yoke of Jesus, we will find satisfaction and rest for our hearts and souls. Jesus does make a difference and that difference is lived out by behaving as a church member.

So, notice the words of command that Jesus gives: come, take, learn (Matt. 11:28-29). All those words are verbs (Dictionary 1828). These words anticipate some action on the part of the hearers. They are words given by Jesus to produce a response from every person who heard them. When we talk about surrender what do we mean? Surrendered is defined as: "yield to the power, control, or possession of another upon compulsion or demand." (Dictionary 1828). It means to give up completely or agree to forgo in favor of another. It means to give (oneself) up to another into the power of another or give (oneself) over to another. When we come to Jesus we are to surrender to (take) His yoke upon us with absolute confidence that He will place us first in His considerations. Notice that word "learn," This is the same word from which we get the word disciple (Strong's Concordance

1984). What Jesus is asking us is to surrender to Him and become His disciples. This is accomplished by taking up your cross and following Jesus (Matt. 16:24). Simply stated, we are to surrender everything we are, have, and ever hope to be, to the will of the Lord. We are to place ourselves at His disposal and allow Him to be the absolute Lord and ruler of our lives. When we do, we will find genuine satisfaction for our heart and soul.

As you look at what Jesus is saying by these commands it is plain to see that He has a plan for your life and it is apparent that Jesus expects us to get into the "yoke." As I stated earlier, the yoke was a wooden instrument that is place around the neck of the ox and was then attached to the plow, the wagon, or whatever burden needed to be moved. Now, I couldn't help but notice what Jesus said, "For My yoke is easy and My burden is light." (Matt. 11:30 NKJV). Does that mean that life lived under His will is going to be a life of ease and perfection? Well, no! Each yoke was carved in such a way that it perfectly fit the shoulders of the ox for which it was designed. Each yoke was as different form every other yoke as were the oxen who wore them. So, what is implied here is that "His yoke fits." When we surrender to the Lord and to His will for our lives, we can be confident that He has perfectly and individually designed your yoke just for you. He has made your life to be a perfect fit. That is why the phrase "My burden is light" (vs. 30) is made. When we are surrendered to the Lord's yoke and are pulling the burden, He has designed for us, there will be satisfaction even in the midst of trials and afflictions.

When you put first put a yoke upon an ox, the ox is going to rebel against the yoke. It doesn't quiet feel right to the ox. However, when the ox gives in and surrenders and them puts his shoulder to the task of pulling his burden, he finds that the yoke makes the job of pulling the burden much easier. Here the lesson, we should all strive to yield to the yoke of Jesus which He has designed for us to wear. It may not feel right at first, we may want to buck and kick against it, but if we surrender to it, we will find that it may actually make our lives easier and it will be easier to behave as church member. There is a bunch of followers of Christ who are not behaving as church member because they are trying their best to wear another's yoke. Some followers of Christ are trying to wear the yoke of worldliness and they find that yoke doesn't fit. Some try to wear a yoke that is designed for someone else and they try to do things they aren't gifted for, because that yoke doesn't fit. When we wear the wrong yoke, we bring even more burdens upon ourselves that causes unnecessary pain and bruising that could have been avoided by merely surrendering to our own individual yoke of service.

If you will remember, Jesus was a trained carpenter. In those days, carpenters didn't build houses and bookshelves. Carpenters usually spent their time building farm implements. In other words, Jesus must have carved out a lot of ox yokes as He was growing up in Nazareth. As our Savior, He is still carving out individualized, perfect fitting yoke for each of His children. We need to surrender to the yoke of Jesus, because nothing fits our lives so well as the plan which Jesus has designed for us. When we surrender to His will, we can rest assure that Jesus will not allow anything to harm us, however, every burden that Jesus asks us to pull, He has placed it there for our good (Rom. 8:28).

Does the yoke of Jesus seem easy and His burdens light in your life? If the answer is yes, then you are a satisfied person. If the answer is no, then maybe you need to spend time in prayer with Jesus. Asking Him to help you stop kicking and fighting against the yoke. Maybe you need to surrender to your yoke so you can behave as a church member.

CHAPTER TWO

FILLED WITH THE SPIRITUAL GIFTS OF THE SPIRIT

And they were all filled with the Holy Spirit and began to speak with other tongues, as the Spirit gave them utterance. (Acts 2:4 NKJV).

The early church members didn't start right off the bat behaving as church members. Yes, it is true that immediately after being filled with the promise of the Holy Spirit (Acts 1:8), they were given to the power to proclaim the Gospel message and "three thousand souls were added to them." (Acts 2:41 NKJV). Yes, they were filled with the spiritual gifts of the Holy Spirit, but it still took time to know how to use and fully understand those new spiritual gifts they were given. That is why "they continued steadfastly in the apostles' doctrine and fellowship, in the breaking of bread, and in prayers." (Acts 2:42). When I get a new gadget, new computer, a new app, or new anything; it takes some time before I am familiar with that item. It is the same way with the spiritual gifts of the Holy Spirit (Rom. 12:6-8; 1 Cor. 12:8-10, 28-30; Eph. 4:11; and 1 Pet. 4:9-11). Every child of God is equipped with these spiritual gifts because the moment we accept Jesus Christ as our Savior and Lord, we are filled with the Holy Spirit. These spiritual gifts are individualized traits given to us by the grace of our Heavenly Father for the purpose of enabling the church member, the follower of Christ, to serve Him and do the work of the ministry of the great commission (Matt. 28:18-20) and the church.

The early church member of the early church was able to work in unity and harmony because they were filled with the Holy Spirit. The results of the spiritual gifts caused them to be able to preach the same message (Acts 2:11); believe the same things (2:41-44); carry the same burdens (2:44-45; 4:34-35); and love the same things. You see, the fact that there are problems in the modern church is the fact that church members are at different stages of their spiritual walk with Christ. Some are saved but are still babes in Christ; some are saved and growing; some are saved and Spirit-filled; and some are not saved. This diversity makes it difficult for church members to behave as church members. There is no way around this diversity, however, God has uniquely woven each church with diverse unique church members. It is God's will that every single child of God, "be filled with the Spirit." (Eph. 5:18 NKJV). To be filled means to be controlled and when Jesus controls me and you, we will walk together in His power for His glory!

Now notice what happened after they were filled with the Holy Spirit it says, "and began to speak with other tongues, as the Spirit gave them utterance." (Acts 2:4b NKJV). That means every church member began to behave as a church member, everyone was busy doing their part. Think about it, God did not save you or me to sit on our "do nothings" and do nothing! He saved us to serve! "For we are His workmanship, created in Christ Jesus for good works, which God prepared beforehand that we should walk in them." (Eph. 2:10 NKJV). If you are not behaving as a church member then you don't have a faith that is real. "But someone will say, "You have faith, and I have works." Show me your faith without your works and I will shou you my faith by my works." (Jam. 2:18 NKJV). These early church members began to do the work which God gave them to do. They "began to speak with other tongues," (Acts 2:4b NKJV), which the Holy Spirit gave them as a gift. Please understand, the other tongues mean they were using known languages. According to Luke in Acts 2, there were fifteen different geographical locations; and each resident of those places heard Peter and the others declare God's Word in a language that they understood. My point is this: every person in that upper room on the Day of Pentecost, ALL were filled with the Holy Spirit, ALL began to speak, and everyone who was nearby got to hear the message in their own language. Therefore, no task is unimportant or small; every area of church ministry is vital to the success of the church when the church members behave as church members. That means to behave as a church member you must use the spiritual gifts that the Holy Spirit has given you.

ARE YOU SATISFIED WITH GOD'S GIFTS?

Do you know what once was the most despised gift that was given at Christmas? It was fruitcake. Lots of people gave those nasty things to a lot of other people who hated them. Those who received them would take them hide them in their closets, use them to scotch their car's tires, use them as doorstops, save them up and use them to brick their homes, throw them at stray dogs, or best of all, the really mean ones would re-wrap them and give them to some other poor sap. Now let's be honest, when you receive a present from someone that you really despised, you took it, didn't you? You even were polite and said, "Thank You!" And even though you didn't like the gift, you were thankful for the expression of love from the giver, because that is what grateful people do.

But have you ever been around someone who received a gift from someone else and rudely rejected it in front of the giver? I have seen it happen and it is an awful thing to watch or hear. For the giver, I'm sure their heart is broken. But it is amazing how cruel some people can be. Take the people of Israel and their behavior in Numbers 11. They were behaving with ungrateful hearts towards the generous gift of God. Ultimately, they rejected Him and His gift! The story in Numbers 11 is a sad tale of pride, arrogance and foolishness. Yet, I fear there are many church members who are and have rejected God and the gracious gift of salvation. As you examine this chapter it teaches us about people who were not satisfied with the Gift of God and shows us what it means for the church members.

THEY ENCOUNTERED A GRAVE DILEMMA

Before we dive into the events in Numbers 11, we need a little background. Over in Exodus 16:2-3 (NKJV) it says, Then the whole congregation of the children of Israel complained against Moses and Aaron in the wilderness. And the children of Israel said to them "Oh, that we had died by the hand of the Lord in the land of Egypt, when we sat by the pots of meat and when we ate bread to the full! For you have brought us out into this wilderness to kill the whole assembly with hunger."" As the children of Israel journeyed toward Canaan, they were met with legitimate needs. They needed food! Did you know there are three basic physical needs for mankind? Mankind needs food, water, and shelter. These people had shelter, but they lacked water and food and there were two million people at this time that needed them. This was not a small problem, due to the fact that they were pilgrims and could not raise any crops. Their livestock could never reproduce at a rate sufficient to sustain them. They were helpless and the future, at least to them, appeared bleak. They could not help themselves! What they needed was a divine intervention in order to stay alive. So, when faced with a legitimate need instead of trusting in God, they murmured and complained against Moses and Aaron.

The children of Israel are a good picture of lost humanity, as lost people live their day to day lives, they have needs. In the United States, most people can take care of the basic physical needs of life for themselves. Most folks can provide themselves with food, water, and shelter. However, they have other needs that they can never meet on their own! Food, water, and shelter may get you through this life, but they can never help you in the afterlife! Lost people need spiritual bread and spiritual water. They need a spiritual shelter for their souls and they, out of their own resources, can never meet that need. Just like the children of Israel, lost people seek to meet the legitimate need of their souls through illegitimate means. People try to scratch the itch within their souls by moving deeper into sin. They try to fill the void in their hearts with money, good times, friends, sex, drugs, alcohol, and many other things that can never satisfy. What they all need is divine intervention! They need the scales removed from their eyes (2 Cor. 4:4)! They need the quickening power of the Spirit of God to operate within their hearts (Eph. 2:1). They need the provisions that only God can provide.

THEY EXPERIENCED A GRACIOUS DELIVERANCE

In Exodus 16:4-7, we see that God did intervene. God was merciful to them, and He tells Moses that He will rain bread from heaven for them (vs. 4). Even though they were looking for help in the wrong way, God still moved in power to meet their need! What a beautiful picture of grace and mercy! These people deserved judgment and wrath, yet God reached out to them in love, grace, and compassion. He extended divine grace to them, when they deserved something far different! Every person in this world whether they are a child of God or not has received something far better than we deserved! In fact, the Bible is clear the we all deserve to be in a place called Hell (Ps. 9:17; Rom. 6:23). However, God is a God of grace and love! Therefore, in spite of our sinful condition, God loved us anyways (Jer. 31:3; John 3:16). He proved this love by the gift of His Son, Jesus, on the cross at Calvary (John 3:16; Rom. 5:6-9). He demonstrated His grace toward us when He sent conviction to our hearts (John 6:44). The fact that Jesus Christ went to Calvary, died in agony, arose in victory three days later, and ascended to heaven as our Great High Priest is a promise to save all, the whosoever will, who come to Him by faith (Rev. 22:17; Rom. 10:13; Matt. 11:28; John 6:37)!

God moved in response to the children of Israel's need and sent them exactly what they needed. He sent them bread from heaven and this bread is called manna! This bread would lay upon the ground every morning for the forty years of wandering around in the wilderness and even while they were conquering the Promised land until they were settled in the land (Josh. 5:11-12)! This manna was given to sustain them every day, it was what they needed for good health and satisfaction. The manna is a good picture of Jesus Himself. He even compares Himself to the manna in John 6:35.

But notice the ways the manna points ahead to Jesus, the Bread of Heaven. It was small which speaks of Christ's humanity (Ex. 16:14). It was round (Ex, 16:14) which speaks of Christ's eternal nature (John 1:1). It was white (Ex. 16:31) this reminds us of the sinless, holy nature the Lord Jesus Christ (1 Pet. 2:22; 2 Cor. 5:21). It came at night (Ex. 16:13-14), and as we know Jesus came to a world lost in spiritual darkness and gave them light and life. The manna was misunderstood by those who found it

(Ex. 16:15). The name manna means "What is it?" (Strong's Concordance 1984) Jesus was misunderstood by the very people He came to save (John 1:11; 10:20). The manna was sufficient for every man's need (Ex. 16:17-18) and reminds us that Jesus is the all-sufficient Savior. He meets the need of man's soul. The manna was sweet to the taste and satisfying (Ex. 16:31). By the same token, all who accept Jesus Christ as their personal Lord and Savior will find Him to be sweet to the soul and satisfying in life. David encourages us this way, "taste and see that the Lord is good." (Ps. 34:8). The manna was to be kept and passed on to others (Ex. 16:32). Jesus is the same way; He is to be shared with those who cross our path. There is more that could be said about the manna, but that is enough to let us see that it is an excellent type of the Lord Jesus. Just as He did for Israel, God has provided us everything we need for good spiritual health and perfect satisfaction. Jesus, and Jesus alone, can save and satisfy the soul (Acts 4:12).

They Exhibited a Great Disappointment

This brings us to Numbers 11 and this point the people had been eating manna for nearly two years. Every day except the Sabbath, the manna was there on the dew when they awoke every morning. The manna had fed them, sustained them, and had met their need for food. Some has said that it would have taken approximately 240 boxcar loads of manna per day to feed two million people. Yet, God sent it every day, faithfully, sufficiently, and graciously. However, Israel did not appreciate the gracious gift of God! Listen to what it says, "Now the mixed multitude who were among them yielded to intense craving; so, the children of Israel also wept again and said: "Who will give us meat to eat? We remember the fish which we ate freely in Egypt, the cucumbers, the melons, the leeks, the onions, and the garlic; but now our whole being is dried up; there is nothing at all except this manna before our eyes!"" (Num. 11:4-6 NKJV). There was a mixed multitude that wanted more which caused the children of Israel to look back on their days in Egypt and the foods they had. They began to esteem the provisions of Egypt superior to the gift of the Eternal God! They literally compared the manna to nothing, and began to despise it and wanted no more of it. They wanted meat to satisfy their lust and they were ungrateful for the manna which God, in His grace, had given them. According to verse 8 they even went as far trying to tamper with the manna in many ways to make it more appealing to their taste, but their efforts only robbed the manna of its sweetness and left it tasting like oil and losing its ability to satisfy.

When the Gospel is accepted and taken in just as God gave it, it has the power to bring life out of death. It has the power to convert the sinner and save the soul. It has the power to alter one's eternity and make all the difference in the world! However, when it is tampered with, it loses its power to save! When the Gospel is added to, or when parts are taken away from it, it cannot save the soul! Yet, so many people, church members, and churches today are guilty of tampering with the Gospel. They grind it, they beat it, they bake it; all in an effort to make it more appealing to the flesh! But it will never work! The Gospel was never sent to make man feel better about himself. The Gospel was given to show man that he is a sinner in need of a Savior! The Gospel was given to show man that he is guilty before God and is in danger of the judgment of God in the fire of hell. The Gospel is not pleasing to the flesh. It is openly opposed to the flesh and stands in sharp contrast to the world. The demands of the Gospel are clear: "repentance toward God, and faith toward our Lord Jesus Christ." (Acts 20:21 NKJV). If you want what the salvation God has to give, then you will come to Him on His terms. Salvation is a lost sinner turning from his sins and placing his faith in Christ Jesus alone for the saving of his soul (Acts 16:31).

Because they judge His gift, God was not pleased by what they did. He answered their request for meat according Numbers 11:18-20, however, He judged them severely for they lack of gratitude for His gracious provisions. Here is what God did; He sent quail (meat), so much in fact that they spent all that day and night and the next day gathering the quail (vs. 31-32). "But while the meat was still between their teeth, before it was chewed, the wrath of the Lord was aroused against the people, and the Lord struck the people with a very great plague." (vs. 33 NKJV). It may seem harsh to us, but what these people were saying was, "We don't like how God is treating us! We would be better off without Him! We don't want His manna and we don't want Him!" Their rejection brought a high price. Many of the people perished because they rejected Him and His precious gift! What this says to us, is you can have another plan if you want it. You don't have to receive Jesus. You don't have to be satisfied with Him. You can modify God's Gospel any way you wish. But know this, everything you try will fail and, in the end, you will still face the judgment of Almighty God! There is only one way to avoid facing God in judgment, you must receive His gift, the Lord Jesus Christ. He is the Bread of Life (John 6:36). He is the water for your soul (John 4:13-14; 7:37-38). He is the only shelter from the wrath of God (1 John 5:12; Phil. 3:9).

JESUS THE GREAT GIFT GIVER

God gave His only begotten Son. Jesus, the Great Gift Giver, gave us the Holy Spirit. How do we know? Well, the Holy Spirit is a fulfillment of the promise of Jesus in John 14:16-18. Jesus even goes on to tell His disciples about the Holy Spirit in John 16:7-15. And then repeats this promise for us in Acts 1:8. And as we know the Holy Spirit came on the day of Pentecost in Act 2. So, in John 14-16, as Jesus and His disciples made their way from the upper room to Gethsemane, Jesus taught them many valuable truths. Jesus had openly taught His disciples that one day persecution would come. This should not have surprised His disciples when Jesus brought up persecution, because they had heard Him warn them about it plus, they had seen Him face men's hatred throughout His ministry.

Therefore, until Jesus returns, or until we die, we must behave as church member, followers of Christ, in this hostile world and face continued opposition. How can we do it? What is the secret to a victorious Christian life? How can we behave as church members? Because of their distress, Jesus gave them the truths that would encourage them and comfort them concerning the future. The answer to all these questions is the fact that we are given the presence and power of the Holy Spirit of God in our lives.

THE WORTH OF THE GREAT GIFT

"Nevertheless, I tell you the truth. It is to your advantage that I go away; for if I do not go away the Helper will not come to you; but if I depart, I will send Him to you." (John 16:7 NKJV). Jesus told His men that it was to their advantage for Him to leave. How would that be possible? Well, to understand the worth of this great gift, we must first understand Who the Holy Spirit is.

The Hoy Spirit of God is a person. Jesus referred the Spirit of God as a "He" and not an "it" (John 16:7-8, 13-14; John 14:16-18). The Holy Spirit is co-equal with the Father and the Son and is as much God as they are (1 John 5:7) and all three make up the Triune God. Just think for a moment, that the moment you receive Jesus Christ into your heart that is when the Holy Spirit comes in to your heart to dwell. Meaning that you know you have God the Father, God the Son, and God the Holy Spirit living in you! "You are of God, little children, and have overcome them, because He who is in you is greater than he who is the world." (1 John 4:4 NKJV). The Holy Spirit is a person with a mind (Rom. 8:27), a will (1 Cor. 12:11), and emotional feelings (Gal. 5:22-23; Eph. 4:30). If we do not have the Holy Spirit within, we would not be able to serve the Lord in this present and evil world. We are to walk in the Spirit (Gal. 5:16), worship in the Spirit (Phil. 3:3), and witness in the Spirit (Acts 1:8). The Holy Spirit can be "quenched" (1 Thess. 5:19), which means "to put out a fire" (Dictionary 1828). He can be lied to (Acts 5:1-11). In John 14:16, Jesus referred to the Spirit as "another Comforter." There are two words for "another" (Strong's Concordance 1984). One means "another of a different kind" and the other word means "another of the same kind". So, here in John 14:16, Jesus is not telling us that He is going to send another comforter of a different kind. What that means is He is going to send another Comforter of the same kind; some just like Him. The Holy Spirit will never promote Himself according to John 15:26 and John 16:13-14. He is in the sole business of pointing men, women, boys and girls to Jesus.

The Holy Spirit is given the name "Comforter." This name means "an assistant, a helper. One who comes alongside of another to offer aid. It can refer to a defense attorney." (Strong's Concordance 1984) In reference to the Spirit, it refers to Him as One Who comes alongside the saint of God to offer help for the journey. The Comforter comes to empower the church member for life and witness. He comes to our aid, our encouragement, and teaches us those things we need to know. The Holy Spirit is the child of God's best friend on earth! The Holy Spirit comes to the Christian not the world which means that He works through the church member. It would absolutely be impossible to live the Christian life without the presence of the Holy Spirit. If He did not live in the heart of the child of God and give direction minute by minute, we would never be able to do the work of the Lord nor behave as a church member. Please bear in mind that even the Lord Jesus Christ lived His life solely in the power of the Holy Spirit (Matt. 3:16-17; Phil. 2:5-8). Jesus did not come into this world live as God in a man's suit. He came to live as a man, fulfilling all the demands of God's righteousness. He came to live the kind of life that is possible only through the power of the Spirit of God.

According the Bible, the Spirit of God comes into a life at the moment of conversion (1 Cor. 12:13), and then He just never leaves (John 14:16). The fact that He comes into the life of the believer and dwells in Him is a remarkable thing. For Jesus, in his body, it is impossible for Him to dwell in you, however, in the Person of the Holy Spirit, He is able to dwell in every child of God at all times! That is a Great Gift of great value!

THE WORK OF THE GREAT GIFT IN THE LIVES OF SINNERS

In relation to those without Jesus, the Holy Spirit performs a two-fold work. He performs conviction, where he points out wrong and sin in a sinner's life. The Holy Spirit also performs convincing where points to the truth; and the truth is revealed to the heart of the sinner that has been opened through the ministry of conviction. Notice how Jesus puts it, "And when He has come, He will convict the world of sin, and of righteousness, and of judgment: of sin because they do not believe in Me; of righteousness, because I go to My Father and you see Me no more; of Judgment, because the ruler of this world is judged." (John 16:8-11 NKJV).

The areas that the Holy Spirit works conviction and convincing are sin, righteousness, and judgment. When comes to sin, the Holy Spirit convicts the lost sinner of the fact of his sinfulness. He makes Romans 3:23 and Romans 3:10 real to the heart of the sinner. Men may try and deny their personal sin, however, when it comes to the convicting power of the Holy Spirit the sinner will know he is guilty! Conviction may not be pleasant, but it is essential plus it is a blessing from the Lord. Not only does the Holy

Spirit convict of unbelief, but He is convincing men of the foolishness of not believing in Jesus Christ. He does this by show the sinner it is wrong to even have unbelief. In fact, there is a classification of sin committed. Sins like murder, blaspheme, abortion, adultery, lying, lust, any known sin against God are all lumped into the same classification and are ranked on the same level as sin; except one. The worst sin a person can commit is the sin of unbelief. This is the only unpardonable sin that wills send a sinner to hell. Jesus said, "Therefore I said to you that you will die in your sins; for if you do not believe that I am He, you will die in your sins." (John 8:24 NKJV). Thankfully, the Holy Spirit doesn't just convince us by show us the bad side and then leaving us to twist in the wind, but He points out to where salvation can be found. Verses like John 3:16 have been sprinkled throughout the Bible to give hope and direction to every sinner seeking rescue.

Second, the Holy Spirit convicts the lost person of the need to get right with God; righteousness. The Holy Spirit produces in the heart of the lost a deep-seated feeling of filthiness, because remember we are absolutely unrighteous in and of ourselves. Plus, Isaiah 64:6 says the very best we can produce in and of ourselves is nothing more than a filthy, stinking, rotting rags. Mankind, without Jesus, is totally defiled and absolutely wretched. Yet, the Holy Spirit's convincing ministry points us to the truth that Jesus has paid the price for sin and that He has been accepted by the Father. Now, anyone who places their faith in Jesus Christ for salvation will be saved and declared righteous by God in Heaven. The righteousness of Jesus will be "imputed" to anyone who receives Him (Rom. 4:24)!

The last area that the Holy Spirit works conviction and convincing is that of judgment. The Holy Spirit convicts the heart of the sinner about the reality of approaching judgment and condemnation. Men may joke about hell, and they may even use the word as a by word in everyday language, but deep in the soul of man he knows that when he leaves this world without Jesus, he is headed to a Christless eternity. He convinces the sinner of the great truth that the price of judgment has already been paid in full! He teaches us that when Jesus went to Calvary and died, that Jesus satisfied the demands of a just God for sin and the judgment has already been passed over for those who receives the blood of Jesus Christ. Just think, Satan and sin have already been judged; all that remains is for the death sentence to be carried out.

THE WORK OF THE GREAT GIFT IN THE LIVES OF THE SAINTS

God the Father sent God the Son to us. God the Son sent God the Holy Spirit to us. But what does the Holy Spirit give us? Jesus said, "I still have many things to say to you, but you cannot bear them now. However, when He, the Spirit of truth, has come, He will guide you into all truth; for He will not speak on His own authority, but whatever He hears He will speak; and will tell you things to come. He will glorify Me, for He will take of what is Mine and declare it to you. All things that the Father has are Mine. Therefore, I said that He will take of Mine and declare it to you." (John 16:12-15 NKJV). So, while the Holy Spirit is active in the lives of unbelievers, He is also very active in the lives of God's people. Now there are several ministries that He conducts in our lives that help us behave as followers of Christ, which in turn aide us to behave as church members. One of the ministries that Holy Spirit works or gives us is spiritual gifts, (listed in Ephesians 4, 1 Corinthians 12, and Romans 12), and in the rest of this book we will examine these spiritual gifts one by one. We will see how they minister to us in our daily walk with Christ, which teaches us to behave as church members.

The next ministry that the Holy Spirit works in us is that of Indwelling. Jesus tells very plainly that the Holy Spirit lives inside each believer. He said, "the Spirit of truth, who the world cannot receive, because it neither sees Him nor knows Him; but you know Him, for He dwells with you and will be in you." (John 14:17). That little word "in" is very significant, for it tells us that within the heart of every child of God lives the Triune God. It tells us that the child of God is full of the power of God. The same power that spoke the world into existence, parted the Red Sea, walked on water, turn water into wine, fed the five thousand, and raised Jesus from the dead is in the person of the indwelling Holy Spirit. Sometimes you often hear of people talking about the men and women of the Old Testament, and they say, "Oh, how great it would be to be living during those times and see all the wonders that took place during those days." They even go as far as to say, "What would it have been like to hear God's voice and see Him move in such powerful ways? I'm so jealous of those Old Testament people. When I get to heaven, I cannot wait to ask David,

Daniel, Elijah, or Moses what it was like." However, let's look at it from a different perspective and how the opposite will happen. When we get to heaven, before you can ask David what it was like to slay the giant and win those battles, David will say, "Tell me what it was like on earth to have the Holy Spirit living inside of you, giving you strength when you were weak." Then we ask Elijah what it was like to call down fire from heaven before the prophets of Baal and to raise that boy from the dead? Elijah interrupts and says, "Yeah, well the boy actually ended up dying again. But you have to tell me what it is like to have God living inside you. What is it like to live life on earth with the Holy Spirit giving you joy when you are depressed or giving you the power to overcome that sin in your life?" We might ask Moses, "What was it like to follow a cloud by day and the fire by night? What was it like to meet with God on that mountain?" Moses might say, "I had to climb that mountain in order to meet God. But you got to tell me what it was like to have him dwell within you every day. What was it like to have the Holy Spirit giving you direction when you didn't know what to do or where to God?"

You see, the Holy Spirit is a gift, not a reward nor can be earned, sent by God to dwell in the hearts of only the true believer. The early church, even though they were turning the world upside because of the power of the Holy Spirit within them, still had to be reminded from time to time of this truth (1 Cor. 3:16; 6:19). There are some church members that behave as though the Holy Spirit comes and goes because of the behavior of the child of God. The truth of the matter is that the indwelling of the Holy Spirit is not based upon our behavior and there are passages that teach this. Romans 5:5 (NKJV) says, "Now hope does not disappoint, because the love of God has been poured out in our hearts by the Holy Spirit who was given to us." 2 Corinthians 5:5 (NKJV) says, "Now He who has prepared us for this very thing is God, who also has given us the Spirit as a guarantee." You see, neither of these verses say that the Holy Spirit was given only to some believers nor was there any sin or reason that would cause God to take the Holy Spirit back. Therefore, we can conclude that the Holy Spirit is a gift that takes up permanent residence in the heart of a true believer. If there is an absence of the Holy Spirit in a person then that means the individual is in an unsaved condition (Rom. 8:9). That is what it means to have the Holy Spirit indwelling in you.

The next ministry of the Holy Spirit is that of instructing. In John 16:13 we understand that when the Holy Spirit comes into the heart of the believer He will guide/teach us about all truths concerning Jesus Himself based on the Word of God. This ministry of instructing results in Christ being glorified and Christians being edified, because Christ is being glorified when the Word of God is expounded upon through the power of the Holy Spirit for the edification of the believer. Therefore, it is through the ministry of instructing that child of God never has to walk around in total spiritual blindness. The child of God has the freedom to ask and receive guidance, direction from the Holy Spirit.

The next ministry of the Holy Spirit is Infilling. Paul writes, "…but be filled with the Spirit." (Eph. 5:18 NKJV). The Holy Spirit desires to fill our lives with His presence and power so we might be able to serve the Lord in an abundant and glorious manner. This is the most important aspect of the doctrine of the Holy Spirit. The infilling ministry is what brings about the spiritual gifts, the teaching, the guiding, the enabling, and encouraging as we strive to behave as church members in order to serve and live for Christ. The fact that we are commanded to be filled means that we are to be continually filled each and every day as we yield our lives to the control of the Holy Spirit.

The next ministry of the Holy Spirit is Enabling. What was it that transformed those disciples hiding in an upper room on the Day of Pentecost, that caused them to take the world by storm? It was the power of the Holy Spirit. In Acts 1:8, Jesus tells the disciples that the Holy Spirit will empower them to carry out the mission work the He was leaving them to do. And they wouldn't have to do that work alone. Plus, He promised them His power, His touch, and His blessing as they went out to share the Gospel to the ends of the earth. Today, God's mission work has not changed. God has commanded each and every believer/church member to go out and share the Gospel of our Lord and Savior Jesus Christ. And because of the indwelling, infilling of the Holy Spirit we are empowered by the Holy Spirit to do the work. We have the same power the early church has, the same power that raised Jesus from the dead living in us! We need to behave as church members.

One last ministry of the Holy Spirit I would like to mention is the ministry of Encouraging. Jesus said, "I will not leave you orphans; I will come to you." (John 14:18 NKJV). As the Holy Spirit is indwelling in you, He is always living in you to encourage you. He knows every trial you face and He is able to support you, abide with you, and keep you during all of life's difficult times. This promise that Jesus told to Philip is a promise He makes to us. He repeats this promise in Matthew 28:20 as part of the great commission. The writer of Hebrew even reminds us of this promised ministry, "For He Himself has said, "I will never leave you nor forsake you."" (Heb. 13:5 NKJV). This ministry of encouragement even spills over into our prayer life. Paul puts it this way, "Likewise the Spirit also helps in our weaknesses. For we do not know what we should pray for as we ought, but the Spirit Himself makes intercession for us with groanings which cannot be uttered. Now He who searches the hearts knows what the mind of the Spirit is, because He makes intercession for the saints according to the will of God." (Rom. 8:26-27). You see with faith in Jesus we are more than conquers, we are overcomers (1 John 5:4). Paul told the young Timothy, "For God has not given us a spirit of fear, but of power and of love and of a sound mind." (2 Tim. 1:7 NKJV). There is no doubt that we can be encouraged, strengthened through the ministry of encouragement by the Holy Spirit.

The fact the Holy Spirit is a wonderful gift should be abundantly clear and we have even begun to discuss the gifts of the Holy Spirits nor have we even gone into depth about these ministries of the Holy Spirit. But just think, every child of God is a living, breathing, Temple of God that is amazing in and of itself (1 Cor. 6:19). Listen, there is nowhere we can go or do that can separate us from the presence of God. Everywhere we go, He goes in us! The key to experiencing all of this; we must learn to yield to Him so that He won't just be in us, but that He will also be able to live through us. Think about how much we have because of Christ Jesus. Then think about how you are behaving as church member or a follower of Christ.

CHAPTER THREE

WHAT DOES THE SPIRIT GIVE?

Now concerning spiritual gifts brethren, I do not want
you to be ignorant. (1 Corinthians 12:1 NKJV)

God sent us His only Begotten Son, Jesus Christ. Jesus Christ sent us the Holy Spirit on the Day of Pentecost. What does the Holy Spirit give us? The Holy Spirit gives spiritual gifts to the believer as part of His ministry in the believer. These spiritual gifts are given to empower and strengthen the child of God to serve the body of Christ in the church which helps him or her behave as a church member. Spiritual gifts are given to benefit the whole church body. At the very least, one spiritual gift is given to every church member of the body of Christ and therefore we have been uniquely woven together with other believers with different spiritual gifts for the purpose of advancing the Gospel of Jesus Christ. Spiritual gifts are not for personal enjoyment, but for corporate employment.

The doctrine of spiritual gifts is mostly taught by Paul and the majority of his teaching can be found in Ephesians 4:7-11; 1 Corinthians 12:8-10, 28-30; and Romans 12:6-8. Peter does give a list of a few of the spiritual gifts in 1 Peter 4:9-11. However, when you combine all of Paul's list of Spiritual gifts, you get a total of nineteen different gifts. These gifts are suitable for the ministry of the church, provided that the church members are behaving as church members. However, God is not limited to just this list and He may give other gifts if He wants to. There is a Greek word that is used for "spiritual gift" it is the word "charisma." (Strong's Concordance 1984). The synonym for this word charisma is the word behavior, which helps us understand that these spiritual gifts effect our walk with Christ. However, we don't want to take away from the meaning of this word charisma because the word relates to grace; therefore, a spiritual gift is due to grace. We don't deserve these spiritual gifts but the Holy Spirit gives them to believers by grace for the service to the body of Christ. You could think of these spiritual gifts as a God-given ability for service.

Over the rest of this book, we will be spending time looking at each one of the spiritual gifts that is given to the believer for the work in the body of Christ. In other words, we are talking about behave as a church member. However, something to keep in mind is not every believer will possess every spiritual gift, but every believer has at least one spiritual gift. Can a person have more than one spiritual gift? Yes, there are many people who are multi-gifted with one predominant spiritual gift. Let me caution you, do not get wrapped up or overwhelmed by the individual gifts that you forget why Paul writes about them in the first place. Paul writes about spiritual gifts to remind us that they are given to teach us behave as a church member, which in turn aids in uniting the church and fulfill the ministry of the church as one body. Something else to keep in mind is the fact that spiritual gifts are not exercised in just one place. They can be exercised anywhere, at any time. Furthermore, a spiritual gift is not an office, meaning, just because you possess a spiritual gift does not mean you get to hold an office in the local church. For example: the pastorate is an official position in the church reserved for men called of God, however, the spiritual gift of pastor could be exercised by a man or a woman because there are not any restrictions on where or to whom such gifts are given to. A mother or father could have the gift of a pastor and serve her or his family and friends. Understand, there are qualifications for the position of pastor in a church (2 Timothy 3) and these qualifications should be considered to fill the position of the pastorate. There is more that can be said about the gift of pastor and we will discuss that when we get to that gift. But, before we start looking at the different spiritual gifts, there are some principles we need to look at because when it comes to spiritual gifts there are some misconceptions that need to be clarified.

SPIRITUAL GIFT DOES NOT USUALLY MEAN YOU ARE SPIRITUAL

The first principle is, spiritual gifts does not usually mean you are spiritual. Spiritual gifts are not primarily a particular technique like the gift of wood work, nor are they a natural talent like playing the piano by ear. Spiritual gifts are not limited to a particular age. Whatever the age of the believer, whether a child, teenager, college age, or an older adult; every believer can benefit from spiritual gifts. Spiritual gifts are the ability to serve and edify the church and Christ. Spiritual gifts and spiritual people are not necessarily linked together. In 1 Corinthians 12:1, Paul is concerned about the Corinthian church members who are not behaving. Because they were trying to use their spiritual gifts in the wrong manor. They were using their spiritual gifts to promote themselves and not edify the church. If you want to behave as a church member, you need to accept your spiritual gift(s) with humility, then can promote unity and harmony within the church, and edify (build up) the church. "Now concerning spiritual *gifts*, brethren, I do not want you to be ignorant:" (1 Cor. 12:1 NKJV). Now in the original Greek it says "the spiritualities" which the Greek word is "pneumatica" and has to do with the spirit or breath. (Strong's Concordance 1984) Everybody is probably heard of pneumonia which is a breathing disease, but that is not what this word relates to. If you have a pneumatic tire what you have is a tire that has air in it. In the Bible, the words that are often used for the Spirit of God or the breath of God the Bible often uses the words wind or air. Therefore, Paul uses the word pneumatica, not necessarily to talk about spiritual gifts, but to talk about spiritual matters. Because up until chapter 12, Paul had been talking about the carnalities of the church and he uses these spiritual gifts to spring board into talking about spiritual matter.

As a pastor, I have heard people say, even preachers say, "Oh, we need a New Testament church." But the thing of it is, they are not very specific when they make that statement. What they need to say is. "We need to have a church that is like Philadelphia or like the church at Ephesus." But if you are not specific then someone might think that you want a church like the church at Corinth. But let me show just how the members of the church at Corinth were not behaving as church member and were very carnal.

Think about the first eleven chapters of the book of 1 Corinthians, he been telling the members of the church at Corinth about their carnality. In 1 Corinthians 1:7, Paul writes, "so that you come short in no gift, eagerly waiting for the revelation of our Lord Jesus Christ" (NKJV). The church at Corinth was not lacking in spiritual gifts. They were saturated with them and had a full knowledge of the spiritual gifts. Therefore, they made a big deal about having spiritual gifts within the church. However, they were not behaving as church members when it came to using those spiritual gifts. You might be thinking, "If they had spiritual gift and they were clearly seen, then shouldn't they behave as spiritual people?" The answer is no, because they were carnal people instead of being spiritual people. As you look at the church at Corinth you begin to see a division in the church. When you have division in the church you are going to have contentions (1 Cor. 1:10-11). In other words, they were arguing among one another, there were disputes, back biting, friction; just to name a few. This is not how to behave as a church member. When you have a carnal Christian, you have someone who is not behaving and the church at Corinth was full of carnal Christians. For example, Paul struggled to speak to the church at Corinth, because of their carnal behavior. As a matter fact, Paul just comes out and just says, "And I, brethren, could not speak to you as to spiritual people but to carnal, as to babes in Christ" (1 Cor. 3:1 NKJV). Now compare this verse with what he said earlier in 1 Corinthians 1:7, here you see that a child of God can have spiritual gifts and act all spiritual but in truth they are not. Paul could not speak to this church body because of the division and the contentions, because they were not spiritual, they were still babes in Christ and they were carnal (1 Cor. 3:3). In other words, they were still learning how to behave as a church member.

So, because they were acting as though they were spiritual, Paul writes this first letter to them to correct them. "I do not write these things to shame you, but as my beloved children I warn you" (1 Cor. 4:14 NKJV). But then, he gives by what authority he has to warn them in verses 15-16. Just think, Paul had to explain to these church members that he was an apostle of Christ and had to tell them "Imitate me" (1 Cor. 4:16 NKJV). The church members of Corinth were not behaving and it was because they were hardheaded, mulish, and stubborn, therefore, they didn't have enough sense to recognize the authority of Paul. So, all through this letter and the next letter, 2 Corinthians, he still defends his apostleship.

These church members were acting all spiritual, but when a serious sin was committed in the church they behave as though it did not bother them. "It is actually reported that there is sexual immorality among you, and such sexual immorality as is not even name among the Gentiles; that a man has his father's wife! (1 Cor. 5:1 NKJV). What happened was that a son had an incestuous relationship with his father's wife, his stepmother. Now if these church members were behaving as church members they would have been on their face before God, at the altar, weeping about this terrible sin. However, because of their proud behavior of acting like they were spiritual, looking the other way and tolerated this sin (1 Cor. 5:2). But again, with all this division in the church it is no wonder that this tolerance of this sin was accepted. What is worst is the fact that the division and contention in this church was so bad, they were taking their fellow church members to court, to judges that were not Christians (1 Cor. 6:1). Since they were not behaving as church members within the walls of the church, they were taking their disputes out into the public where everybody could see (1 Cor. 6:6-7). They were tearing down the testimony of the church and bringing to a halt the ministry of the Gospel of Jesus Christ. But this was not the only public thing that ruined their testimony. At Corinth, there was a mountain called Acrocorithus, and on the top of that mountain was a temple devoted to goddess of sex, Aphrodite. In that temple there were prostitutes, and the way that you worshipped the goddess of sex was to go to that temple and have sexual intercourse with the temple prostitutes. (Wood, Marshall and Millard 1996) Therefore, Paul has to warn these church members against this immorality (1 Cor. 6:15-16).

Then in 1 Cor. 8:1-2, the stronger more mature Christians were offending the weaker babes in Christ, thus bringing more division and contention into the church body. What was going at this time was their difference about where to buy meat. There was meat being sold at the regular markets at a higher price, and then there was meat being sold at the local temples. Meat that was sold at these pagan temples was meat that had been sacrificed to idols and sold at a cheaper price. So, the more mature Christians had come to the knowledge that the sacrifices to the idols did not contaminate the meat, and would go to these temples and purchase the much cheaper meat. This offended the weaker Christians, because they could not understand why their fellow believers would have anything to do with meat sacrificed to idols. What Paul is telling us in verses 1-2 is that just because you think you know everything, you don't. When we behave with a know-it-all behavior we are actually behaving in ignorance. Because it is possible to grow in knowledge and not behave as a church member because you have not grown in your relationship with God.

In 1 Corinthians 9:1, Paul again has to defend his apostleship; followed by a strong warning that God is going to judge them if they didn't repent (1 Cor. 10: 5-7). In the rest of chapter 10, Paul describes for us the terrible behavior that was happening among the church members. He tells us how they were trying to drink from the cup of the Lord and the cup of the devil at the same time (1 Cor. 10:21). In chapter 11, their behavior seems to have gotten worse. Apparently, they were drinking from the cup, the Lord's Supper cup, and getting drunk (1 Cor. 11:21). I point all this out to ask, what do you mean when you say, "We need to have a New Testament type of church again"? Do you mean this New Testament church at Corinth? You see, with all that was going on in this church certainly the believers were not behaving as church members; and the way they were behaving it might cause you to ask, "Were they saved? Were they born again? Did they know anything about Jesus?" Yes of course they were saved, however their behavior was so carnal that for eleven chapters in his letter Paul has to deal with their carnal behavior. Now, I didn't cover every carnal behavior that Paul talks about, things like: marriage and divorce; but in those eleven chapters Paul is warning them, begging them, explaining, and urging them to start behaving as church members. He wants them to bring unity and harmony into the church and he wants them to start growing in their walk with Christ, instead of behaving as babes in Christ. So, when you come to 1 Corinthians 12:1, you now understand why Paul begins to change gears and says, "Now concerning your spiritual gifts brethren, I do not want you to be ignorant" (1 Cor. 12:1 NKJV).

YOU ARE IN CONTROL OF YOUR SPIRITUAL GIFTS

Now it is true that the Holy Spirit is the source of spiritual gifts, however, the second principle is, the believer is in control of developing and executing his or her gift(s). The believer is always in control of himself when the Holy Spirit is in control of the believer, for self-control is one of the fruits of the Spirit (Gal. 5:23). Paul writes, "And the spirits of the prophets are subject to the prophets" (1 Cor. 14:32 NKJV). Therefore, we are to behave as a church member by desiring to use our spiritual gifts to the very best of our ability and to do this we need to develop them to be the very best (1 Cor. 10:31) for the purpose of ministering to one another. No church member has any need to complain about his or her gift, neither should they boast. In 1 Corinthians 12:31 Paul writes, "But earnestly desire the best gifts. And yet I show you a more excellent way" (NKJV). The word translated "best" simply means "greater" (Strong's Concordance 1984) There are some spiritual gifts that are greater in their importance than others, however, that does not mean that the lesser is not needed at all. Just think of what the Corinthian church was doing. They were placing the greatest value upon the gift of tongues, while Paul places the greatest value upon the gift of prophecy and put the gift of tongues at the bottom of the list (1 Cor. 14:1-5). So, what is Paul saying in 1 Corinthians 12:31? He is saying that we should desire the best spiritual gifts, because if you desire the best spiritual gifts then you can develop them in your walk with Christ and as you grow you can help edify, build up the church. When the church is edified or built up that means that there is unity and harmony which aids in growing the church. And this unity and harmony, along with diversity of spiritual gifts needs to be balanced with in the church by mature church members who are behaving by developing (growing) their spiritual gifts and serving with their spiritual gifts in love.

The Holy Spirit works through believers to help them develop their spiritual gifts, even with their desires, limitations, ambitions, and abilities.

In Ephesians 4:12-13, Paul states the purpose for the giving spiritual gifts, "for the equipping of the saints for the work of ministry, for the edifying of the body of Christ, till we all come to the unity of the faith and of the knowledge of the Son of God, to a perfect man, to the measure of the stature of the fullness of Christ" (NKJV). Now, if you are going to equip someone, then that means you are going to give them the ability to do something with that training. Therefore, gifts are to be discovered by the believer and developed by active service. As we behave as a church member, we are to do all that we can for the glory of God, this in turn will open other doors of opportunity to do more which will show us the need for additional gifts in our lives. Take Philip for instance. Philip was an evangelist (Acts 21:8), however before he received his evangelist gift (Acts 8:5) he first had the gift of ministry (Acts 6:5). So, as Philip served, developing and growing his gift of ministry, God gave him opportunities to evangelize. Now Philip needs to start developing the gift of the evangelist.

The developing of spiritual gifts was something that church members at Corinth was not doing. As matter fact, listen to what Paul said, "You know that you were Gentiles, carried away to these dumb idols, however you were led. Therefore, I make known to you that no one speaking by the Spirit of God calls Jesus accursed, and no one can say that Jesus is Lord except by the Holy Spirit" (1 Cor. 12:2-3 NKJV). What Paul is getting at concerning spiritual gifts, instead of developing for the edifying of the church for the glory of God, you are being carried away to the lifeless idols. In Corinth there were many Greek mystery religions, which they got from the Egyptians, which the Egyptians got from the Babylonians. The Corinthian's Greek Mythology worshipped demigods that lived on Mount Olympus, who had carnal pleasures and carnal desires. The Corinthians wanted to make sure that they always stayed in favor with these fake gods and the way they did that was to worship them by fasting, deny themselves, pray to them, work themselves up into a particular state of meditation until they make contact with that god or goddess. Plato once described the people of Corinth as people whose hair was unkept, their faces glowing, all while becoming babbling incoherently and just making noises and sounds. After being in a trance they would claim that they had contacted their demigod that lived on Mount Olympus. Paul was reminding the Corinthian church they were once this kind of worshipper.

He is reminding them of their past, and how they were carried away with no control of themselves. His point is this, since the Holy Spirit gives you gifts then you should behave as a church member by being in control of your spiritual gifts, because your spiritual gifts will never carry you away. You will never be in a position where you can't help yourself.

So how do you develop and discover your spiritual gifts? Well to begin with, start by taking inventory. List your abilities that you have and then remind yourself that these are natural abilities that God has given to you specifically. While you are making a list of abilities that you have, why not just make a list of natural abilities that you would like to learn and seek out opportunities to learn them. If you periodically take inventory, much like stores take inventory, it will give you an idea of how you can behave as a church member and help edify the church. After making a list, start preparing yourself for service. That old phrase of practice makes perfect applies here. Put into practice your natural ability by look for doors of opportunity to use your abilities and for those opportunities to learn a new ability. If some of your abilities coincides with spiritual gifts then work on them as well. As you work on your abilities and/or spiritual gifts another spiritual gift may be discovered that you did not know you had. The key to developing and discovering your spiritual gifts is by being active in service where ever God gives you opportunity. Understand, being active and behaving as a church member is the best way to develop and discover your spiritual gifts, but there are resources that can provide a survey that can show you what your spiritual gifts are. You could use the survey to get you started to making your list and help you to improve on, develop those abilities and spiritual gifts. You can do a google search for spiritual gifts; in the search box enter: LifeWay Christian Resources. Once on that page you can then look for spiritual gift resources (LifeWay Christian Resources 2003).

SPIRITUAL GIFTS ARE USED TO HONOR CHRIST

In the first two verses of 1 Corinthians 12, Paul was comparing the Corinthian church members' behavior with that of the unconverted idolaters and reminded them they once worship dead idols, but now that they belong to God, they were to behave different. Through His

Holy Spirit, God speaks to His children, dead idols do not talk they are lifeless objects. Before they became believers they lived under direction of demons (1 Cor. 10:20), and were "carried away" (1 Cor. 12:2 NKJV). Since becoming believers the Holy Spirit takes up residence inside the heart of the believer and gives direction to the believer.

Paul writes, "Therefore I make know to you that now speaking by the Spirit of God calls Jesus accursed, and no one cand say that Jesus is Lord except by the Holy Spirit" (1 Cor. 12:3 NKJV). Paul explains that it is through the Holy Spirit that a child of God can say "Jesus is Lord." Paul had told the Roman Christians "That if you confess with your mouth the Lord Jesus and believe in your heart that God has raised Him from the dead, you will be saved. For with the heart one believes unto righteousness, and with the mouth confession is made unto salvation" (Rom. 10:9-10 NKJV). There are people who go to church, who only pretend to know God. They may mouth the words, but they are not truly praising God. What is worst is when church members half-heartedly give praise to Jesus. Paul is telling the Corinthians that you are not any better than those unconverted idolaters. Some of the church members of Corinth had gotten worked up into frenzy that they were being attacked by a demonic invasion, and were actually cursing the Lord Jesus instead of praising Him. That is why Paul says the were "carried away" (1 Cor. 12:2). Church members need to beware of any spectacle that is claimed to be led by the Holy Spirit or any parades that is said to be led by the Holy Spirit, because of the fact the Holy Spirit does not lead parades. Jesus should be at the center of everything and the Holy Spirit will be standing on the side and point to Jesus, because the ministry of the Holy Spirit is to magnify the Lordship of Jesus Christ. Therefore, the child of God will say that Jesus is Lord because the Holy Spirit is living inside the heart magnifying Jesus.

The church members of the Corinthian church were not behaving as church members because there were division and confusion among them, they were being carried away, they were trying to obtain as many spiritual gifts as possible, and they were competing with other church members. Paul writes, "There are diversities of gifts, but the same Spirit. There are differences of ministries, but the same Lord. And there are diversities of activities, but it is the same God who works all in all" (1 Cor. 12:4-6 NKJV). That means since God is the source of the gifts, the One who gives out the gifts, and the One that provides the power for the gifts; then why were these Corinthian church members in competition with one another? Remember spiritual gifts are given to bless, edify the whole church. They are not given for personal enjoyment, but to be put to work alongside other believer in the church. "For as the body is one and has many members, but all the members of that one body, being many, are one body, so also is Christ. For by one Spirit, we were all baptized into one body; whether Jews or Greeks, whether slaves or free; and have all been made to drink into one Spirit. For in fact the body is not one member but many" (1 Cor. 12:12-14 NKJV). Therefore, since we receive spiritual gifts at conversion, that is the moment we got saved and were baptized by the Holy Spirit and we are all members of body of Christ; then it does not matter what your race, social status, wealth, or even sex (Gal. 3:28) is, because we all fellowship and serve the same Lord Jesus Christ.

Despite our own uniqueness and different spiritual gifts that we have, we are the one. Paul says, "For as the body is one and has many members, but all the members of that one body, being many, are one body, so also is Christ. For by one Spirit, we were all baptized into one body whether Jews or Greeks, whether slaves or free; and have all been made to drink into one Spirit" (1 Cor. 12:12-13 NKJV). The word "were" literally means "an accomplished action, in other words it is done" (Strong's Concordance 1984) Nowhere in the Bible will you ever find a command for a New Testament Christian to seek to be baptized in the Holy Ghost. Think about it, why command us to seek the baptism of the Holy Spirit, for something that has already taken place? Here in Corinthians is the only place that gives a description of the baptism of the Holy Spirit. It is true, before the Day of Pentecost the Bible said it would happen, but after Pentecost, every genuine child of God at the moment they accept Jesus into their hearts is baptized immediately into the body of Christ by the Holy Spirit.

There are people who think and talk about a person should receive a second blessing from Jesus. They imply that once you get save you receive Jesus and then later you are going get something else. Paul writes in Colossians 2:9-10 (NKJV), "For in Him dwells all that fullness of the Godhead bodily; and you are complete in Him, who is the head of all principality and power." All of the fullness of God is in the Lord Jesus Christ, meaning that God the Father, God the Son, and God the Holy Spirit is wrapped in the name of Jesus. Therefore, "you are complete" (Col. 2:10 NKJV) in Jesus and you do not need any more or anything else. When Jesus came into your heart, you get all of Jesus. Therefore since, the Holy Spirit is living in your heart any movement from the Holy Spirit is going to magnify the Lord Jesus; any gift you receive is going to magnify the Lord Jesus.

You do not choose your Spiritual Gifts

Since the child of God is complete in Christ Jesus (Col. 2:10), then every Christian church member has a spiritual gift. Paul writes, "But the manifestation of the Spirit is given to each one for the profit of all" (1 Cor. 12:7 NKJV). Just so you will know, gifts are given to each and every one of God's children, and Paul restates this fact in verse 11. If you are saved, then you have already received your spiritual gift. You don't have to go looking for it, you have already gotten it. Now, it is up to you to discover that gift or gifts, develop that gift, and put it to work "for the profit of all" (1 Cor. 12:7 NKJV). As you are discovering your spiritual gift and develop it and put it work you may discover that you already had more spiritual gifts that was already given to you. However, you do not get to decide what gift you will have. Paul said, "But one and the same Spirit works all these things, distributing to each one individually as He wills" (1 Cor. 12:11 NKJV). Notice that word "individually" in that verse, the Greek word literally means "one of a kind." (Strong's Concordance 1984) What Paul is saying is that every Christian, every church member, is one of a kind. Someone put it like this, "God never makes duplicates, only originals." People are different physically, we have different talents, different interests, and we all are different spiritually. It is the Holy Spirit living inside our hearts that make each of us different. He places in every child of God, every church member, a special blending of spiritual gifts. Then God uses this special blending in each church member to work as a part of a unit.

Every Believer is Part of a Unit

"For in fact the body is not one member but many" (1 Cor. 12:14 NKJV). There hundreds of thousands, multitudes of believers that are in the body of Christ. Yet while we are many, we have one agenda, therefore all members of the body of Christ, church members, are to be committed to one agenda, do what the Head, which is Jesus Christ, says to do. A healthy body is a body that is coordinated, where the members learn to work together at the direction of the Head. Which implies that the church is to be organized. Think of it this way; the human body has many parts, the automobile has many parts; and every part is essential to the unit in order to properly function as a whole, yet the body or the care is thought of as one. This is true for the body of Christ as well. The body of Christ is formed of believer from all walks of life, all cultures, all sections of society, and all levels of wealth. The body is made up of people who have nothing else in common, except the fact that they have received Jesus as their Savior. The body of Christ is a unified diversity and when every church member behaves and fills their purpose that they are assigned by Jesus, the body functions as it should and therefore glorifies Jesus and the work of the Kingdom is carried out.

EVERY BELIEVER IS PLACED BY GOD

Paul uses the human body as an illustration to show us that God places each believer where he wants them to be (1 Cor. 12:15-20). No church member should compare or contrast themselves with any other church member, because each one is different but equally important. Just because these parts of the body do not get the attention, they thing they deserve, they have no right to try and divorce themselves from the rest of the body. Now, I suppose I could walk on my hands, but rather walk on my feet; and not to mention I have yet to master the skill of typing with my toes. Now as kids, I remember the joke that was told about the human body. It goes like this, "The human body is made up side down; your feet smell and your nose runs." All joking aside, what Paul is saying is that God has placed us in the body where He wants us to be. It may not be a high-profile position, it may not be glamorous, it may not even be what we want to do, but it pleases the Lord, then it is the right place for us. Therefore, no matter where you are functioning within the body of Christ, remember that you were placed in that exact position by the will of God and we should behave as church members each doing our part. Furthermore, there is no greater knowledge than to know you are walking in the will of God. If I behave as a church member in the place God put me, then I am do just what God would have me to do. What I am saying is that we need to surrender to our place in Jesus, even if we would like to be something else. God knows us and He knows where we can best function. Who knows maybe God is preparing you in that position for something better, therefore bloom where God puts you until God moves you! When we submit to His will, He is glorified and His Kingdom is advanced in the world!

EVERY BELIEVER PLAYS AN IMPORTANT ROLE

The diversity of church member in a church just shows us the wisdom of God. Church members need other church members, and in the day and age which we live, we cannot afford to be independent of one another. In 1 Corinthians 12:21-24, Paul again tells us that every member is important to the proper function of the entire body. The eye cannot tell the hand that it does not need it. If the eyes were disconnected from the hand, it would never be able to attain the object of its desire. The head cannot tell the feet to get lost, for without them, it has no method of locomotion. What Paul is saying is that every part of the body needs every other part to fully carry out the work of the body. The whole point of this section is to teach us that every member, no matter how insignificant the position or gift may appear, it is essential to the proper operation of the entire body. No one should ever be guilty of believing that he or she is unimportant to the operation of the body. No one should think that they are not needed. No one should ever say to or about another believer, "We do not need you." Every member is vital, every member is important.

YOUR PURPOSE IN THE BODY

There are at least three purposes that a church member has within the body of Christ. The first is to promote unity. Paul says, "that there should be no schism in the body" (1 Cor. 12:25a NKJV). When every member does their part and submits to God doing what they are called to do, then the body of Christ will function in absolute peace and unity. In our day, there are too many feet who want to be hands and too many ears who want to be eyes. When this happens, the body is fractured (division) and chaos is the result! God's plan for His church is that we be united (1 Cor. 1:10; Phil. 1:27). When we are not behaving as church members in unity the body of Christ suffers (1 Cor. 1:10).

The next purpose that a church member has within the body of Christ is to practice mutual care. "…but that the members should have the same care for one another. And if one member suffers, all the members suffer with it; or if one member is honored, all the members rejoice with it" (1 Cor. 12:25b-26). Paul reminds us that we are one unit, with each part of that one unit having responsibilities to the other parts. When another believer is hurting, we need to respond to that need (Gal. 6:2). You may never take the time to think of your fingers. But, just slam the car door on them and watch how the whole body gets involved in responding to their crisis. The nerves will carry the message to the brain. The brain in turn sends a message to the feet which begins to hop around, the eyes begin to water, the mouth now hangs open in surprise, the other hand is reaching franticly for the door handle; therefore, now the whole body is involved to take care of your fingers. When one of those less visible members gets into trouble, everything else responds to the need. What I am saying is this, we are not just to respond to the needs of the high-profile members. We are to practice mutual care that encompasses the entire body. What if the hands refused to give hygiene to the other members? The body would become diseased and have problems. In the church, every church member is called upon to behave as a church member and look after the need of every other member, regardless of their place in the body of Christ.

The last purpose for the church member in the body of Christ is to participate together in the activity of the body. When a member hurts, it affects the entire body. When one is exalted, the entire body should be blessed by it. The idea is this. When everything functions as it should, the body operates efficiently and accomplishes much. There is no "I" in team and the acronym for "team" is Together Everyone Accomplishes Ministry. When parts do not function as they ought, then there are problems and nothing gets done as it should. Paul's goal is to get the church to see that we need one another. Jesus said, "By this all will know that you are My disciples, if you have love for one another" (John 13:35 NKJV). Together, we are a complete body; individually, we are a small but vital component of a very important organism called the body of Christ.

Now, if every believer has a spiritual gift the obvious question is; "Why are they not using them?" The problem is not with the Spirit, who gives the gifts, but with the believer who has buried their gift(s) and talents instead of investing their life in the work of the kingdom of God. Please understand, the church will grow or diminish based on the active work of the Holy Spirit as He flows through the people of God to accomplish the will of God here on earth.

You may not even know what your gift(s) are. Let me encourage you to pray and ask the Lord Jesus to reveal to you what your gift, or gifts may be. At the very moment you received Jesus into your heart as your Lord and Savior, is the moment that God placed you into the body of Christ. When He did, He gave you certain gifts to be used for His glory and for the good of the entire body. But you can't use them until you know what yours are. You may be guilty of seeking some seat or position in the church that you know that you are not gifted for. Or you may be envious of some other believer who has a higher-profile calling than yours. If so, then you are not behaving as a church member. You need to confess to the Lord Jesus that you have been trying to be something you are not meant to be and you need to be willing to accept the place He has especially for you. I encourage you to get to know these spiritual gifts and how they are used within the body of Christ so you can behave as a church member.

CHAPTER FOUR

THE LEADER MEETS
THE LORD

And we urge you, brethren, to recognize those who labor among
you, and are over you in the Lord and admonish you, and to
esteem them very highly in love for their work's sake. Be at
peace among yourselves. (1 Thessalonians 5:12-13 NKJV)

Did you know you can pull a rope behind you, but you cannot push it!
The gift of leadership aids the church by leading and directing members
to reach the goals and ministry of the church, through motivations that
promotes unity and harmony in each member of the church. Take the
church members of Thessalonica, Paul was very appreciative of their
response to the ministry and it was because their leaders were gifted with
the gift of leadership from the Holy Spirit. When it comes to leadership it
takes a unique behavior in order to lead people. For instance, in the movie
Hoosiers, staring Gene Hackman playing the part of Norman Dale. Coach

Dale was a former college coach with a tainted past who is hired to coach a rural high school basketball team from Hickory, Indiana. Coach Dale leads the team all the way to the state finals. On the day of the semifinals, the team arrives at Butler Field house, the huge inner-city arena where they are to play in just a couple of hours. When the players enter the arena, their jaws fall slack and their eyes are large with anxiousness. Gawking at the seats, the stand-alone goals, the suspended scoreboard, and the lights, they are awestruck and intimidated.

Coach Dale breaks the awkward silence by instructing one of the players to take the tape measure and determine the distance between the free-throw line and the goal. "What's the distance?" he asks. "Fifteen feet," the player says. Coach Dale then tells the smallest player on the team to climb on the shoulders of the taller player so they can measure the rim of the goal. "How high is it?" Coach Dale asks. "Ten feet," the player says. Coach Dale then gives some great words of encouragement to his team, "I believe you will find these are the exact same measurements as our gym back in Hickory." The team members share in some nervous laughter, and everybody begins to relax. As they exit the gym, Coach Dale turns to the assistant coach and whispers, "Sure is big; isn't it!" (Anspaugh 1986)

Coach Dale certainly has a unique leadership style, which is calm but confident. When it comes to leadership everybody as some point has experienced great leadership or the lack of leadership. Using one's spiritual gift of leadership can be a difficult job, not to mention, it can be difficult to follow a leader if he or she is unable to lead. Christian leaders can become so discouraged due to the fact that they carry such a heavy burden along with the fear of letting down their people and the Lord Jesus. Their stomach feels as though it is tied in knots because the church is not growing or going anywhere, but on the other hand they are hesitant to leave for a different position. The question that often gets ask, "What can we do for our leaders?" The obvious answer to that question is to pray for your leaders. Be specific in your prayer, ask God to give your spiritual leaders who may, or may not be experiencing the fulness of their potential that God has given them. Pray that God will help develop your leaders to fully understand their spiritual gift of leadership.

Did you know that being a leader in a church in this day and age is totally different than what it was like twenty to thirty years ago? Generations Z and

Generation Alpha brings with it some unique challenges that can prove to be really difficult for leaders today. We live in a digital world where everything is at your fingertips. Men, women, boys, and girls are more concerned with social media and themselves than they are interacting with other people face to face. Teenagers rather text each other while being in the same room than talk. Yes, it is true the Social Media age has given leaders many different avenues to lead their people, however, this has placed a heavy demand on leaders to more creative with their leadership style, than the previous generation.

What is amazing is that people are desperate for leaders to make a difference in their lives. They are in search of spiritual leaders that can bring about a positive change in their lives. Unfortunately, even with a growth in spiritual interest that can be found on social media websites and apps; many churches and denominations are declining. According to George Barna, "the American church is dying due to a lack of strong leadership. In this time of unprecedented opportunity and plentiful resources, the church is actually losing influence. The primary reason is the lack of leadership. Nothing is more important than leadership." (Barna 1997) Pastors today are stressed out from the many different issues and ministries. In order for churches to survive, they are in search of leaders who will overcome their embedded problems and make the church more attractive to bring in more people and income. But please understand this; Christian leaders who know Jesus as their personal Lord and Savior, and know how to use their spiritual gift of leader will know how to behave as a church member. Because of their spiritual gift of leadership, they will be far more exceptional than any skilled or qualified leader who does know Jesus Christ.

But let me clear, the gift of leadership is not restricted to pastors, deacons, and missionaries. All church members have the responsibility to make a difference in their world. The challenge for leaders today is to use gift of discernment and discern between the latest leadership fads and the timeless principles established in God's Word. So, what does a leader do? And what is a leader? How does a church member use his spiritual gift of leadership? Well, did you know that leadership is the most observed and judged position? However, leadership is the least understood. Volumes upon volumes have been written on the subject of leadership and what leaders do. As a matter fact there are over 850 different definitions of leadership. Which explains why most leaders never know how successful they are, because there are too many standards to behave by.

LEADERS ARE TO BE EXEMPLARY PEOPLE

Let me give you a simple definition of a leader and what a leader is to be doing, which shows us how a leader can use their gift of leadership to behave as a church member. A spiritual leader is spirit filled leader, leading God's people to behave as followers of Christ all the while following Christ themselves. Paul writes, "And you became followers of us and of the Lord, having received the word in much affliction, with joy of the Holy Spirit" (1 Thess. 1:6 NKJV). The word "followers" is actually "imitators" (Wood, Marshall and Millard 1996) and as leaders we have people who are following our lead. Therefore, leaders need to know how to be exemplary people. Exemplary means to be a model of something. So, who are Christian leaders modeling for their followers? As Paul looked at the church at Thessalonica, he rejoiced with gratitude as they were behaving as church members. They were imitating Jesus Christ, because of the example they follow from the lives of Paul, Silvanus, and Timothy. They were examples to others in several areas of their lives.

First, they received the word. Paul said, "For our gospel did not come to you in word only, but also in power, and in Holy Spirit and in much assurance, as you know what kind of men we were among you for your sake" (1 Thess. 1:5 NKJV). The gospel came to these church members through the ministry of Paul and his associates. That phrase, "by our gospel", Paul is not implying a different message from that of the other apostles. The content was the same; the difference was in the messengers. The Thessalonians had not treated the message as a mere religious lecture; they had received the word, but not in word only. They also received in power and in the Holy Spirit, and in much assurance that it came to the. In other words, they were spirit-filled leaders. The word "power" means that the message worked in their lives with supernatural energy, producing conviction of sin, repentance, and conversions. "In the Holy Spirit" means that this power was produced by the Holy Spirit. Therefore, because of the power and the Holy Spirit upon their lives they lived lives that was full of assurance of faith.

Second, the church members followed their spiritual leaders according to 1 Thessalonians 1:6. These new believers not only accepted the message and the messengers, but they also imitated their lives. Young Christians should respect their spiritual leadership and learn from mature believers. Just as a newborn baby needs a family, so a newborn Christian needs the local church and the leaders there. That is what discipleship teaches; we are to "Obey those who rule over you, and be submissive, for they watch out for your souls, as those who must give account. Let them do so with joy and not with grief, for the would be unprofitable for you" (Heb. 13:17 NKJV). It is not enough for us as mature believers to win souls; we must also watch out for souls and encourage new Christians to obey God's word through discipleship. And as a church member with this gift of leadership you should set the example. Lead the way, give people good steps to follow in! We need leaders who are exemplary.

THE IMAGE OF A SHEPHERD

The leadership of Joshua is a good example of a leader being exemplary. Before Joshua could ever become the hero or great leader he was; he first had to yield to the Lordship of God. In Joshua 5, Israel is about to attack the city of Jericho. Before that battle, the leader of Israel, Joshua, goes out to inspect the site of the coming battle. On that important day, Joshua came face to face with the real leader of Israel. He had an encounter with One who was far more powerful that he was. On that day, outside the walled city of Jericho, the leader meets the Lord. When he did Joshua's behavior as a leader is fully seen. He was humbled, but was also prepared for the battle that lay ahead. Notice the interaction between Joshua and the Lord. "And it came to pass, when Joshua was by Jericho, that he lifted his eyes and looked, and behold, a Man stood opposite him with His sword drawn in His hand. And Joshua went to Him and said to Him, 'Are You for us or for our adversaries?'" (Josh. 5:13 NKJV).

THE SHEPHERD'S BURDEN

Joshua was the leader of the people and it was God Himself had chosen him for that position. When the Lord called Joshua to lead Israel, the Lord gave Joshua some very precious promises. In Joshua 1:5 (NKJV), the Lord said the following to Joshua, "No man shall be able to stand before you all the days of your life; as I was with Moses, so I will be with you. I will not leave you nor forsake you." Now it was on the basis of this great promise that Joshua had assumed the leadership role in Israel. Now, he has led them over Jordan. He has led them in obedience to the Law of the Lord. He has led them in observing the Passover. He has led them to the place where they are ready to begin their battle for the land of Canaan. On the eve of the battle, Joshua goes out to look at the great walled city of Jericho. Joshua is a military leader, and there can be little doubt that he is out there partially to consider the defenses of the city and to formulate a plan of attack. However, there could be a deeper reason as to why Joshua was there.

Joshua is the leader of a couple of million men, women, and children. Can you imagine being a leader, pastor, or church member in a church with two million people? Every decision Joshua makes will affect the people under his leadership in profound ways. Some will die, others will be injured, families will be torn apart, and lives will be altered based on the decisions Joshua makes. Before those decisions are made, Joshua goes out alone, under the weight of the burden of his office, to seek counsel from the Lord. In Joshua 5:13 (NKJV) it says, "…he lifted up his eyes, and looked." This seems to imply that Joshua has his head bowed and his eyes close in prayer and then he takes the time to look up and just listen; seeking the Lord's help because of the terrible burden that rest upon his shoulders. He needs help in making the right decision. If you want to behave as a church member then pray for your pastor! Pray for the leaders of your church! Because anyone who has ever filled a position of leadership knows, to some degree, how Joshua must have felt. Pastors make decisions in their lives, their ministries, and their preaching that affects the lives of those in the congregation; and we are only talking about congregations of 250 or less. If you are a deacon, the decisions you make can have profound effects on the congregation as well. Teachers, your statements in class and your demeanor shape the hearts and minds of your students. Parents, your decisions regarding your children, what they are allowed to do, what they are not allowed to do, where they can and cannot go; all carry consequences that will follow your children for the rest of their lives.

Leadership and the gift of leadership comes with great responsibility. There is the responsibility to seek the will of the Lord in every matter you face. There is the responsibility to make decisions that honor God above all personal feelings. There is the responsibility to do everything with the understanding that every decision is like tossing a pebble into a pond. There will be ripples from every decision you make. When a preacher, church ministry, father, mother, children, family, deacon, Christian, church member, or testimony fails; sometimes people will understand your motives behind a decision and other times they will not. At the end of the day, it does not matter what people think; all that matters is what the Lord thinks. Because leaders will face Him, not them, with the decisions they have made in life (Rom. 14:12).

If you have been placed in a position of leadership, take it seriously, because the Lord does! If you have a position of leadership, take it seriously, because your decisions effect all those who whom you lead. Behave as a leader, behave as a church member using the gift of leadership that the Holy Spirit gave you.

THE SHEPHERD'S BRAVERY

As Joshua meditates and contemplates the upcoming battle, he sees an unidentified man standing nearby with his sward drawn. This is the posture of battle. It is the picture of a man who is ready to fight. Joshua does not hesitate, but approaches the man and demands to know which side the man is on. Is he on the side of Jericho? Or, is he on the side of Israel? When Joshua first sees this man, he identifies him as a possible threat to Israel. His instincts as a shepherd are aroused and steps up to the defense of his people. Joshua is burdened by the weight of leadership, but he is also consumed with the protection of those under his care. That same behavior should mark all true leaders. The pastor who will not defend his congregation when it is under attack is not much of a pastor! The deacon who will not defend his church is not much of a deacon! The husband who will not defend his wife or the father who will not defend his children is not much of a man. The mother who will not defend her children is not much of a woman. We are living in a time when the church, our doctrines, our Bible, our worship, and all the other things that identifies us as the Lord's people are under attack. We are living in days when the family, the institution of marriage, and our children are under assault. We need men and women who are not afraid to stand up and fight for the things that matter. We need men and women, who will behave as church members, who have been given the gift of leadership. We need people who are not ashamed to take a stand against the rising tide of evil and ungodliness. We need people who are not ashamed of the gospel of our Lord and Savior Jesus Christ (Rom. 1:16). We need people who will stand for the Lord to protect their church, their family, and their community from all those who wish to destroy it. It is time for God's people to awaken, and take a stand!

THE IMAGE OF SOVEREIGNTY

While Joshua was out by himself, he has an interaction with another person. "And it came to pass, when Joshua was by Jericho, that he lifted his eyes and looked, and behold, a Man stood opposite him with His sword drawn in His hand. And Joshua went to Him and said to Him, "Are You for us or for our adversaries?" So, He said, "No, but as commander of the army of the Lord I have not come.""" (Josh. 5:13-14 NKJV). These verses reveal the problems, perils, and the pitfalls of leadership, but it also draws our attention to the idea of lordship. Even though Joshua was a leader of the people, he himself was under the Lordship of God Almighty. These verses identify and clarify the person and the power of the One Joshua encountered outside Jericho that day. The Man that Joshua encounters in none other than the pre-incarnated Lord Jesus Christ and this is just one of the other instances of His appearance in the Old Testament. Jesus appeared to Abraham, who was a pilgrim, as a traveler and shared a meal (Gen. 18:1-8). Then there was Jacob, liked to do a lot of scheming, Jesus appeared to him as a wrestler (Gen. 32:24-32). Of course, there is the popular children's story of the three Hebrew children, Jesus met them in fiery furnace as their companion (Dan. 3:25). What is unique about this encounter that Joshua had is the fact that here he is the leader of Israel's army, a soldier, and Jesus, as the captain of the Lord's armies met with him. From these encounters of these men of the Bible, that let us know that Jesus always meets us when we need him, particularly in the way we need him.

When Joshua encounters Jesus, He is standing, "with His Sword drawn in His hand." This is a picture of a Person ready for battle. This is not the image of some passive observer of events. This is the image of someone who is ready to make something happen. It is the image of someone ready for a fight, ready to take on the enemy. Today God does not react to events that take place in our human world. He is not sitting in Heaven waiting to see what we will do first, so that He can decide how to respond. Instead, He is in control of both the actions and the reactions. He already knows what we are going to do, and He has already made His plans accordingly.

When Joshua encounters this man, he does not know who he is, therefore he asks Him. Joshua asks, "Are you for us, or for our adversaries?" (Josh. 5:13 NKJV). The Lord's answer must have taken Joshua by surprise. The Lord says, "No, but as Commander of the Army of the Lord I have now come." (vs. 14 NKJV). In other words, the man answers Joshua by saying, "I did not come to take sides in this battle; I came to take over." It must have been great encouragement, for Joshua, to know that he was not alone. If you are a leader with the gift of leadership, the tendency is to behave as a church member as though the emotions of discouragement and depression are getting you down. Which this can affect your decision making as a leader of other people. It is possible that Joshua felt as though he was alone. However, it must have brought great comfort to Joshua to know that God, Who had promise to be with him (Josh. 1:5, 9), had kept that promise! By the way, that is a promise God intends to keep to you too. He has promised you that He will be with you as you face the ups and downs of your life, so you can behave as a church member (Matt. 28:20; Heb. 13:5). If you have the gift of leadership the reason you have the strength to lead, because the same Lord Jesus Christ Who stepped out of eternity to move in the lives of His people in the past, is the same God Who intends to do the same thing for you. You are not alone as you lead; the Lord Jesus Christ is with you!

The Lord identifies Himself as "the commander of the Army of the Lord." Joshua could not see them, but there was a vast army of heavenly warriors camped about him, ready to take on the people of Canaan. The implication is clear: Israel would not face their enemies alone; they would face them aided by the armies of Heaven. So, in order for us to behave as church members, those with the spiritual gift of leadership must learn that public victories will be won only when we, as leaders, submit and receive the command of the Lord Jesus Christ. Joshua was learning really quick that he was only second in command. That is what we need to get grip on, because every dad, mom, pastor, deacon, and Christian leader is second in command to the Lord Jesus Christ. Therefore, if we forget this lesson and move forward, our homes and ministries will be heading to failure and collapse. Jesus came that day to Joshua to lead; for the Lord said, "I am the vine, you are the branches. He who abides in Me, and I in him bears much fruit; for without Me you can do nothing" (John 15:5 NKJV).

Then Joshua receives the assurance that the Lord is about to control of this battle and victory is certain. There is a spiritual realm around us that we cannot see. In that hidden spiritual dimension, there are angels and there are demons. Those spiritual beings are continually waging war in the battle of good and evil. Remember that is the invisible host which aided Elisha (2 Kings 6:14-17). The invisible host struck fear in the hearts of the Assyrian army (2 Kings 7:5-7); protecting the city of Jerusalem, then destroying 185,000 Assyrian soldiers in one night (2 Kings 19:35). This is the same power that came to the aide of Israel in Jericho, it is the same power that came to aid Israel time and time again. It is the same power that comes to the aid of each and every Christian that is behaving with dependency upon Him. Our Lord and Savior Jesus Christ is still the Captain of the Lord's host and He still fights battles on behalf of His people. These truths should remind us that our God is a sovereign God, that He is in control at all times. He is Lord of both time and eternity. He is in charge and He can be trusted to take care of you! So, behave as a church member.

THE IMAGE OF A SERVANT

When Joshua realizes just Who is standing before him, he assumes the place of a servant before the Lord. Notice what the Bible says, "And Joshua fell on his face to the earth and worshiped, and said to Him, "What does my Lord say to His servant?" Then the Commander of the Lord's army said to Joshua, "Take your sandal off your foot, for the place where you stand is holy." And Joshua did so." (Josh. 5:14b-15). Joshua's attitude toward the Lord has much to teach us about how we should approach the Lord as well.

SERVANTS SHOULD BE HUMBLE

As leaders we should behave in humility. Joshua comes face to face with the Lord Himself and he falls down before the Lord in worship to Him. This also shows that Joshua is submitting to the will of the Lord and that he knows Who is in control. Then, Joshua wants to know what the Lord would have him to do. He is yielding his role as a leader to the Lord. He is assuming the place of a servant before the Master. In an instant, General Joshua falls before the Commander-in-Chief and yields all authority and power to Him. This is a crucial step on the road to victorious living, victorious ministry, and behaving as a church member as we learn to relinquish leadership to the will of the Lord! The leader had to bow to the True Leader; the one who commanded the people had to yield to the One Who commanded him! Before you can have victory, you must be vanquished. Before you can overcome, you must first be conquered. Many church members today need to do just what Joshua did. Many need to lay down their swords at the feet of the Commander of the army of the Lord's host; surrender their pride and yield to His authority!

SERVANTS SHOULD BE HONEST

Did you catch the strange demand that the Lord gave to Joshua? Joshua is commanded to "take your sandal off your foot." (vs. 15 NKJV). Why did the Lord ask for just one shoe? The answer lies in ancient customs. When a covenant was made between two individuals, in which one person possessed power to keep the covenant and the other did not, the weaker individual handed the other individual one of his shoes. It was his way of saying, "I cannot, but you can." For Joshua, this was a challenge for him to come to the place where he could admit his own weakness and inability to gain the victory. It was a call for him to surrender to the Lord. Something to keep in mind as we behave as a church member: we fight from victory not just for victory. The Christian leader stands in a position of guaranteed victory because Jesus Christ has already defeated every spiritual enemy. Therefore, one has the gift of leadership and/or is in a position of leadership must be honest about his or her ability to lead.

When Joshua discovered that the battle belonged to the Lord, and He already overcame the enemy, all Joshua had to do was be honest by admitting that there was nothing else he could do but listen to the Lord and obey His commands. For us, we need to learn the truth that we cannot, but He can! You might be reading this book and you have been trying to fight your battles in your own power, and because that kind of behavior, you keep getting whipped. What you need to do is take off your shoe, hand it to God and say, "Lord, I cannot fight these battles, but you can! I cannot win the victories I need in my life, but you can!" What that means is that in order for us to behave as church members we need to come to the place of absolute surrender! To that place where we and all we have are at the feet of Jesus. To the place where we are willing to say once and for all, "I cannot Lord, but You can!"

But oh, how hard it is for us to be humble, little lone honest, right? Think about Joshua, he was a soldier, and lot of times we like to think of ourselves a strong soldier. Think about Joshua's example to us; when he bowed before the Lord, he placed himself in a vulnerable position. He exposed his neck. He placed himself in a position where he could not use his own sword. He placed himself in a position of extreme weakness. He was totally yielded to the Lord! Live or die, he placed his all in the hand of the Lord. Have you ever come to that place in your own life? In your ministry? In your family? Have you ever come to the place where you place yourself and your sword on the ground before the Lord and surrendered fully to His will for your life? Ministry? Family? If not, you will have to do just that if you ever want to enjoy absolute victory over all the strongholds and enemies in your life. You will have to do just that if you ever want to behave as a church member. As long as you demand your rights, your will, and your way you will have problems because you are not behaving. When you yield to His sovereignty, His power, and His will you are on the fast track to victory! Romans 12:1-2 sums up what I have been saying about the gift of leadership and behave as a church member. It says, "I beseech you therefore, brethren, by the mercies of God, that you present your bodies a living sacrifice, holy acceptable to God, which is your reasonable service. And do not be conformed to this world, but be transformed by the renewing of your mind that you may prove what is that good and acceptable and perfect will of God" (Rom. 12:1-2 NKJV). If you are in a position of leadership, whether it is in public, or within the family, you need to come before the Lord to ask Him to help you lead as one led. He will enable you to be a blessing to the lives of others as you behave as a church member.

CHAPTER FIVE

CRISIS MANAGEMENT

Let all things be done decently and in order. (1 Corinthians 14:40 NKJV)

The gift of administration is the God-given ability to tend to or manage the affairs of a group of people, or manage an event. A person who has this gift has the ability to lead the church body by steering others to remain on task. The Christian who has this gift has a tendency to be organized, develop strategies or plans to achieve their goals, and assist in ministries making them to become more efficient and effective. Most people on church staff, committee leaders, church leaders, pastors, deacons, administrative assistant, church clerk, event planner will often have this gift of administration.

Please understand, it is not men or women who placed these administrators into the body of Christ for the purpose of enabling the body of Christ to become organize to reach or stay on focus of performing the ministry of the church and fulfilling the Great Commission (Matt. 28:18-20). This is done by God Himself according to 1 Corinthians 12:28a, where it says, "And God has appointed these" (NKJV). These administrators have the spiritual gift of keeping things in order and know that "God is not the author of confusion but of peace, as in all the churches of the saint" (1 Cor. 14:33). This means that we are to behave as church members by "let all things be done decently and in order" (1 Cor. 14:40). This might be the reason why Paul left Titus in Crete. Paul writes, "For this reason I left you in Crete, that you should set in order the things that are lacking, and appoint elders in every city as I commanded you" (Titus 1:5).

Now it is true, all believers have equal standing before God as priests, however, there is an ordered rule in the church. Christ is the Head of the church; the pastor is the under-shepherd, the deacons and associate pastors are helpers under the pastor, and then there is the church members. So, how are we to behave as church member towards those who have the gift of administration and/or are in the position of administrator? "Obey those who rule over you, and be submissive, for they watch out for your souls, as those who must give account. Let them do so with joy and not with grief, for that would be unprofitable for you" (Heb. 13:17 NKJV). Now, if a servant of God is in the will of God, teaching the Word of God, then the church member should behave by submitting and obeying. Let me just say, that this in no way means that a pastor or deacon should be a dictator. As a matter of fact, Peter encourages against pastors being dictators. He says, "Shepherd the flock of God which is among you, serving as overseers, not compulsion but willingly, nor for dishonest gain but eagerly; nor as being lords over those entrusted to you, but being examples to the flock; and when the Chief Shepherd appears, you will receive the crown of glory that does not fade away" (1 Peter 5:2-4 NKJV). There are some church members who behave poorly or rudely towards the pastor and/or deacons. However, there are some pastors, some deacons who behave as though it is their way or the highway. Listen, one day every pastor will stand before God and give an account of his ministry, this goes for a deacon as well. The pastor or deacon should want to fulfill his office with joy. We as a church should behave in such a way that it will bring joy to the pastor, deacon, or those in position of administration. Because, just as the pastor or deacon has to stand before Christ and give an account so do church members have to give an account. A misbehaving Christian will find out on that day the results of disobedience, which will be unprofitable, not for the pastor or deacon, but for that church member.

Why should pastors, deacons, and church staff behave with this gift of administration? Should it be important to them in their role as an administrator? Many administrators, especially pastors, will have a greater stewardship responsibility for people, money, and property, than many business owners and manager in America. However, pastors will normally be well trained in worship and pastoral care for their congregation, and lack training in church administration and financial issues. Yes, it is true that pastors can delegate this to other church staff, but the brunt of the responsibility lies with the pastors. What are the main concerns that the administration should be concerned with? What is involved in being an administrator and using the gift of administration? The main concern for administration in a church should be to use the vital resources available to effectively achieve the work of the church. That means the administration knows how to use human resources, church money, and property wisely.

When it comes to human resources, those in administration must see people as the greatest resource a church has. Because nothing can get done unless there are committed church members doing kingdom work. Whether we like to hear it or not, and I know it sounds strange, people need to be managed in church if we are going to behave a church member. Think about it, in order fill church staff positions or volunteer positions in a church; people need to be carefully chosen for the task or position at hand. Then they need to be trained and guided through the task they are called upon to do. They must be led, while giving them freedom to fulfil that position and allowing them to succeed. We should not forget that progress toward more effective use of people's talents, which means from time to time we must assess, evaluate, and communicate the goals.

When dealing with church financial business the one who has the gift of administration, must keep in the front of his or her mind is: it is God's business. Those in the administration position naturally will be involved in the financial aspects of the church when comes to funding the church and the ministry of the church. Those in administration need to know the potential of the members' stewardship and their habits, not necessarily individually but corporately as a whole. That is why is important for pastors, deacons, others in leadership to set the example when it comes to giving. Then as the funds are coming in, those in administration must manage the funds received by the church and be good stewards of the finances of God's church. Because nothing undermines the mission of the church and the ministry of church than poor behavior of those who handle the finances of the church and bring about reproach upon the church. Those with the gift of administration need to be very sensitive with the knowledge of accounting principles and the ability to recognize when the church is in trouble financially and then know when and how to seek help and make changes. For pastors the specific involvement in detailed budget transaction might be minimal, it would be a good idea that you have a working knowledge of how the budget works.

Church property must be prayed for and realistically planned out when obtaining it for the church's ministry. The decision of obtain new property will ultimately involve the whole church. However, those in administration need to behave in this process by challenging the congregation to move forward all the while keeping everything in perspective that is more realistic. More than likely the church will form a property committee or a buildings and grounds committee to manage the properties of the church. This could also include trustees, custodial staff, or other volunteers. These committees would then maintain the church property, by making sure there is an established maintenance schedules and delegated responsibilities. Why should this be important? Well, if you have newcomers for the first time the first impression these will notice is the appearance of the church. That will let the first-time guest know how the congregation feels about their place of worship. Therefore, it is important for those with the gift of administration lead out when it comes to church property. So, as the pastor and the administration team figure out how to behave in their roles and manage the resources entrusted to them, it is only natural that they would want to know how to start and where to begin. The elements that are involved in management include planning, organizing and staffing, and assessing and reporting these elements are vital to the ministry and mission of the church. But what is expected of them? And what is their responsibilities?

ADMINISTRATIVE RESPONSIBILITIES AND EXPECTATIONS

It is hard to pin down or even define the job requirements of the pastor and administrative team, especially when there are hundreds of viewpoints of these responsibilities and expectations. Let me just give you a small list of responsibilities and expectations that are just put on pastors, who are expected to behave as pastors. The list includes: advocate for the local in the community, always available, biblical interpreter, budget analyst, conflict resolver, counselor, encourager, friendly, mentor, model of integrity, preacher, teacher, spiritual leader, someone who visits everyone, and the list goes one.

Theses expectation also include every element of management. Most congregation naturally want their pastor to be the administrator, preacher, and teacher; which places a great deal of demand upon the pastor. Therefore, if a pastor does not have the gift of administration, he would struggle to lead the congregation, care for the congregation, and fail to fulfill his duties as a pastor. It is easy to see after thinking about the expectations and responsibilities placed on pastors, that Jethro was right in saying to Moses, "The thing that you do is not good. Both you and these people who are with you will surely wear yourselves out. For this thing is too much for you; you are not able to perform it by yourself" (Ex.18:17b-18 NKJV). Pastor do tend to wear many hats in churches; however, pastors cannot perform all the functions of the church by themselves. They need to behave as church members by overseeing and administering the church by delegating to qualified and creative church members.

JOSEPH THE ADMINISTRATOR

A good example of an administrator who had it all together is Joseph. When you look at the story of Joseph, we can see that he had his act together. He is a man who knew how to behave in all kinds of situations, including family matters. In Genesis 47:13-26, we find Joseph right in the middle of dealing with his father and brothers, all while managing a crisis in Egypt. When you think upon Joseph's life up to this point, you realize that everything he has faced was just preparing him for this crisis management. Joseph's lessons in life taught him how to behave as an administrator and become the master of crisis management. Here are the trials he had to face and overcome. His mother died while he was young (Gen. 35:16-18). He family was in a state of constant turmoil where there was jealousy, hatred, and fighting (Gen. 37:1-22). He was betrayed and sold into slavery by his brothers (Gen. 37: 23-36). He was lied on and falsely accused in Egypt and imprisoned (Gen. 39). The butler, who promised to help him, forgot about him for two years (Gen. 40). He was suddenly promoted to a position of prominence, power, and responsibility (Gen. 41). In very crisis he faced, Joseph displayed exceptional wisdom and faith.

The passage of Scripture found in Genesis 47:13-26, we are allowed to see how the Lord used Joseph to prevent a nation from descending into starvation and anarchy. We get to see Joseph use all his administrative skills of crisis management. Over in Genesis 41:53-57, we see the people are hungry and they come to Pharaoh for help. His advice to them is clear, "Go to Joseph; whatever he says to you do" (Gen. 41:55 NKJV). That is what the people did, and they survived that family as a result of Joseph behaving as an administrator. The people were brough to the end of themselves and of their own resources. They turned to Joseph because they knew there was no future apart from him. When church members behave as they should and obey the Lord, trust in the Lord, they will be able to overcome the most severe crisis moments.

But what steps did Joseph take to save the nation? He took every necessary step to bring everything in Egypt under the authority of the throne. Notice how he exercised his administration skills in Genesis 47. First, he took from their purses. "Now there was no bread I all the land; for the famine was severe, so that the land of Egypt and the land of Canaan languished because of the famine. And Joseph gathered up all the money that was found in the land of Egypt and in the land of Canaan, for the grain which they brought; and Joseph brought the money into Pharaoh's house" (Gen. 47:13-14 NKJV). Joseph took control of all the money in the land. All of the people were place on the same level. There were no longer rich people and poor people, there were just people. Every dime was brought under the control of the throne. That is where our money needs to be as well. We should strive to bring every cent we possess under the control of the Lord. Let Him use it in His work as He sees fit.

Second, Joseph took control of their possessions. "So, when the money failed in the land of Egypt and in the land of Canaan, all the Egyptians came to Joseph and said, "Give us bread, for why should we die in your presence? For the money has failed." Then Joseph said, "Give your livestock,

~~and~~ I will give you bread for your livestock, if the money is gone." So, they brought their livestock to Joseph, and Joseph gave them bread in exchange for the horses, the flocks, the cattle of the herds, and for the donkeys. Thus, he fed them with bread in exchange for all their livestock that year" (vs. 15-17 NKJV). Here we see, when the money ran out, the people traded their livestock and their possessions for food. Everything they possessed was brought under control of the throne. Should not the same thing be true in our lives? Everything we have should be dedicated to the glory of the Lord. If you possess anything that cannot be dedicated to the Lord to be used for His glory, it has no place in your life.

Not only did Joseph take control of their possessions, but he also took control of their property. "When the year had ended, they came to him the next year and said to him, "We will not hide from my lord that our money is gone; my lord also has our herds of livestock. There is nothing left in the sight of my lord but our bodies and our lands. Why should we die before your eyes, both we and our land? Buy us and our land for bread, and we and our land will be servants of Pharaoh; give us seed, that we may live and not die, that the land may not be desolate"" (vs. 18-20 NKJV). When their money was exhausted and their possessions were all gone, they gave Joseph their land. He bought that under the control of the throne. Again, everything we possess should be relinquished to God for Him to use as He sees fit. After all, it all came from Him anyways (James 1:17).

Talk about crisis management! One problem after the next, and each one revolves around the same overall problem, a famine in the land. Thankfully, Joseph had good administrative skills given to him by God. If pastors, deacons, and staff want to behave as church members then they need to use the gift of administration that the Holy Spirit has given them. The fact that the people of Egypt were giving everything they had in order to survive, reminds me of the first church. I mean, if you look at what Joseph was doing, he was setting a good example of, not only an administrator, a good steward. He was taking care of the resources in the nation. Pastors, deacons, staff, and church members should behave as church by being good stewards of God's resources that He gives the church. Look a what the early church was doing, "Then fear came upon every soul, an many wonders and signs were done through the apostles. Now all who believed were together, and had all things in common, and sold their possessions and goods, and divided them among all, as any had need" (Acts 2:43-45 NKJV). What the Egyptians and the early church members were doing is similar but under different circumstances. The Egyptians were doing it to survive while the early church members were freely giving of their possessions as people had need. Please understand, the early church had a major crisis, the early church was facing was that of persecution. The early church needed those who had the gift of administration as well. Especially when all these items started coming in. The church members were behaving as good stewards, by their actions they were saying, "Lord, if you want my possessions, you can have it."

Now there are some people that will look at what Joseph did to save a nation and what was going on in the early church and say, "Well, that is talking about communism. These two stories are a picture of communism." Listen, this was not communism in either situation for a number of reasons. Number one: in both situations they were temporary. Number two: It was based on belief in God; Joseph believed in the leading of God and the church put their faith Him. Number three: Joseph controlled the solution to survive the famine, and the church controlled how to meet the needs with the resources given. And number four: It was voluntary. Think about it, the Egyptians did not have to give their money, possessions, and property. They could have kept it. The church members did not have to give their money, possessions, and property. They could have kept it. Listen the point is this, that everything that they owned was at the disposal of the Lord Jesus Christ. Let me ask you a question, is everything you own at the disposal of Jesus? If He were to ask you for your last two pennies, would you give Him all that you had?

Now when the people's money ran out, when all their possessions were gone, and they own no more property, what was the people to do for food? Well, that is when Joseph took control of the people. Therefore, the people willingly gave themselves up to be the servants of Pharaoh in exchange for food to eat. Sometimes we are able to give the Lord everything we own; however, we keep ourselves back for our own use. God wants us to fully surrender our all on the altar for His glory, that includes ourselves as well. "I beseech you therefore, brethren, by the mercies of God, that you present your bodies a living sacrifice, holy, acceptable to God, which is your reasonable service" (Rom. 12:1 NKJV). After all, if you are a true child of God, saved by grace through faith, then He already owns you. "Or do you not know that your body is the temple of the Holy Spirit who is in you, whom you have from God, and you are not your own? For you were bought at a price; therefore, glorify God in your body and in your spirit, which are God's" (1 Cor. 6:19-20 NKJV).

There are two more areas that Joseph took control of. He took control of their position. "And as for the people, he moved them into the cities, from one end of the borders of Egypt to the other end" (Gen. 47:21 NKJV). Joseph moved the people from the country and other outlying areas and brought them into the cities, where work and food distribution could be more easily managed. Think about something: you and I really have no say in where we go and what we do. We belong to Him and He chooses where we serve; how long we serve; and what happens while we serve there. He is the Lord of His people. The last area that Joseph took control of is their production. According to Genesis 47:23-26, at the end of the famine, everything in Egypt was under control of the throne. Joseph was in absolute control over everything and over every person in the land of Egypt. He graciously gave the people seed to sow the land and allowed them to keep eighty percent of everything they raised. Everything they produced was subject to a twenty percent tax. This is what Joseph did to be sure there was grain during the famine. This what he did to ensure the people would succeed after the famine. Everything Egypt produced was brought under the authority of the throne.

Some people criticized Joseph for his administrative tactics in these verses. They see him creating a feudal system where everything is controlled by a central power. No one owns land, no one owns houses, and no one can get ahead in a system like that. Some people have a hard time believing that he instituted a twenty percent income tax on the people. I wish twenty percent tax is all I paid! With all the taxes we pay here in America it is hard for us to get ahead today. Think of our taxes today, income tax, Social Security, gas tax, road tax, county tax, city tax, sales, tax, plus there are assorted user fees. The people of Egypt did not see this as problem, nor did they criticize Joseph. In fact, they credited him with saving their lives. They saw him as a savior of their nation. When you get to thinking about Genesis 47, one can see Joseph as a picture of the Lord Jesus Christ. The same advice that Pharaoh gave to Egypt regarding Joseph is given to us regarding Jesus. The advice comes from Mary the mother of Jesus, "His mother said unto the servants, "Whatever He says to you, do it"" (John 2:5 NKJV).

In Egypt, Joseph's desire was to bring everything under his control. He knew that unless he could consolidate power in Egypt, the country would tear itself apart when the famine came. He knew the rich would oppress the poor. He knew the nation would be ripped to pieces by rebellion, revolution, and turmoil. To stop this from happening. Joseph took control of everything and brought it under his control. So, how does apply to us behaving as a church member. Because we don't have the luxury to know when the next problem is going to take place. When someone's feelings are going to get hurt. When there is not going to be enough money in the bank. That is why the Holy Spirit gives the gift of administration. They have the capability to organize people, property, and money. "Let all things be done decently and in order" (1 Cor. 14:40 NKJV). We can help those in the position of administration of the church by behaving as church members when we bring all these areas of our life under the control of the Lord Jesus Christ. So does God have your money, your possessions, your person, and your position? So, with all of Joseph's dealing with the people, let me point out a few important principles for behaving as a church member towards those in the position of administration or using your gift of administration. These principles can make all the differences when a crisis come into your life. These principles teach us the real value of the crisis we face in our lives.

CRISES ARE NO RESPECTER OF PERSON

When the famine came to Egypt, it came to everyone; the poor, the rich, even royalty was affected by the crisis of the moment. The same is true in this life, every person in the world is affected by crisis from time to time. No one gets out of this world without facing moments of crisis. If we are going to behave as church members then we must see; pastors, deacons, and staff as humans being. They may not understand what you are feeling as you go through your crisis, but that does not mean they do not understand going through a crisis. They have their own crisis in their life. Pastors move from one crisis to the next. Job says, "Man who is born of woman is of few days and full of trouble" (Job. 14:1 NKJV). Jesus took it a step further and explained that followers of Christ would have tribulations. He said, "These things I have spoken to you, that in Me you may have peace. In the world you will have tribulation; but be of good cheer, I have overcome the world" (John 16:33 NKJV). So, again no one is immune to crisis. The secret is knowing how to handle a crisis. With the gift of administration, in a family or church, you would have the strength, knowledge, and wisdom to get to get through the crisis. Listen to how Solomon felt when came to life and problems in life. He said, "Therefore I hated life because the work that was done under the sun was distressing to me, for all is vanity and grasping for the wind" (Eccl. 2:17 NKJV). By Solomon saying "I hated life" does not mean he was contemplating ending his life because of all the problems he had to face in life. To Solomon death was something he wanted to avoid, and life was better even though it seemed unreasonable and vain. As church member we might get disgusted with life, but we should never behave as though we hate life; no matter how hard the crisis we are called upon to face. By the way, there were men in the Bible that wanted to die, for example: Job (Job 3:21-7:15), Moses (Num. 11:15), Elijah (1 Kings 19:4), and Jonah (Jonah 4:3). However, these men later changed their minds concerning death. We should behave as church members who loves life. "For "He who would love life and see good days, let him refrain his tongue from evil, and his lips from speaking deceit. Let him turn away from evil and do good; let him seek peace and pursue it. For the eyes of the Lord are on the righteous, and His ears are open to their prayers; but the face of the Lord is against those who do evil" (1 Pet. 3:10-12 NKJV). The child of God should be seeking to put the most into life and getting the most out of life, all for the glory of God (1 Cor. 10:31). We may not be happy with everything in our life, or be able to explain why bad things happen to good people, those things are not important. We behave as church member when we live by the promises of God and not by explanations. We behave as followers of Christ because we know that our "labor is not in vain in the Lord" (1 Cor. 15:58 NKJV).

CRISIS CAUSE US TO RETHINK OUR PURPOSES

When this crisis came to Egypt, the people were told to do one thing, "Go to Joseph; whatever he says to your do" (Gen. 41:55 NKJV). From that moment on, the people of Egypt had just one purpose. They had just one duty. They were to obey Joseph and do exactly what he said do. Sometimes it may take a crisis moment in our lives to remind us of our purpose in life. Sometimes, we lose focus in life. We may find ourselves doing thing the Lord does not want us to do; going places He does not want us to go; and behaving in a way that the Lord does not want us to behave. The writer of Hebrews says, "looking unto Jesus, the author and finisher of our faith" (Heb. 12:2a NKJV). If we are saved, our first and foremost duty as church members is to do exactly what the Lord tells us to do. That should be our sole purpose before the Lord. There is nothing like a crisis to cause us to rethink our purpose in life. Whether we are in a crisis or not, we need to ask ourselves a few questions. What am I doing? What does God want me to do? Am I responsible and obedient to Him?

CRISIS CAUSE US TO REEVALUATE OUR PRIORITIES

When the crisis came to Egypt, suddenly things like money, possessions, land, and power meant nothing. What good are these things when there is no food? These people wanted to survive and they knew their possessions would not see them through. As people move through life, they sometimes focus on things that do not truly matter. When that happens, they might just lose the things that really do matter. Consider this: people put their jobs head of their families; they put recreation ahead of their marriages; they put their plans ahead of God's plans for their lives. A crisis has the power to cause us to rethink the things that are most important in life. When a crisis comes, you are reminded just how valuable your relationship with your spouse is; you are reminded just how important family is; you are reminded how valuable church family is; and you are reminded of just how important your relationship with the Lord is. Listen, if you want to behave as a church member, then why wait for a crisis? Look at your own priorities now. Who really comes first, you or the Lord? What is your real priority in life, you or others? Reevaluate your priorities.

CRISIS CAUSE US TO REESTABLISH OUR PRINCIPLES

You will notice that all the land in Egypt came under the authority of the throne, except for the lands that belong to the priests (Gen. 47:22). The priests were cared for by Pharaoh and their needs were met by decree of the king. Joseph was unwilling to take over sacred things, for they were more important than the immediate crisis. When we are thrown into a crisis moment, we will learn what is truly sacred to us. We will find out what we cannot live without. We will discover that many of the things we love and cling to so tightly are mere stuff. When hard times come, we will find out what truly matters in our lives. 2020 begin with a crisis moment for the entire world, we were all effected, what were the things you were not willing to give up under any circumstances? Did we really behave as church members during that crisis moment?

Someone once said, "The hardest part of the Christian life was living it." It is a real struggle for me to bring all of my life under His authority. How about you? It is a real struggle for me to keep my purpose, my priorities, and my principles in life in line with His will for me. How about you? But I find that it is all worth it to behave as a church member during a crisis moment. When my life lines up with His will for me, I can live in confidence and power, and that is how He wants me to live. Do you have a crisis you want to bring to Him? Do you need to get your life lined up with His will? Behaving as church member mean you know how to use the organizational skill found in the gift of administration especially when you have a crisis moment.

CHAPTER SIX

THE BEGINNING OF DISCIPLESHIP

For though by this time, you ought to be teachers, you need someone to teach you again the first principles of the oracles of God; and you have come to need milk and not solid food. (Hebrews 5:12 NKJV)

Paul had been discipling Titus and his mentoring of the young pastor did not stop just because he was not in Titus's presence. Paul writes to teach him about a few things that Titus needed to be aware of. He says, "But as for you, speak the things which are proper for sound doctrine" (Titus 2:1 NKJV). Paul was getting ready to teach Titus about several different areas of ministry in the local church. He starts off by explaining what it means for teachers to teach. The gift of teaching is instructing members about the doctrines of God's Word, the precepts, and the truth found within God's Word, all for the purpose of edifying the saints, evangelizing the lost, and exalting the Lord Jesus Christ. The gift of teaching has the ability to unify the saints which in turn matures the body. So, if you have the gift of teaching then you need to behave as a teacher, teaching and making disciples. The writer of Hebrews implies that there is a purpose for teaching. Those with the gift of teaching should not want the pupil to become lazy, sluggish, or slothful, "but imitate those who through the faith and patience inherit the promises" (Heb. 6:12 NKJV).

The ability to teach the truth of the Bible with others would mean that the teacher is a mature Christian. However, not all Christians have the gift of teaching, that does not mean that all Christians cannot share their testimony, share what they have learned from God's Word, or train someone to do what they are doing. Now the problem is, one of the most difficult lessons for a child of God to learn is that of sharing the Gospel, their testimony, or leading someone to Christ. Take for instance, the recipients of the book of Hebrews; they were saved and they have the ability to share Christ and His truth to others from God's Word. However, they were not behaving like church members. They did not help one another to grow in Christ neither were they teaching the thing that they had learn. In essence, they need to learn again what it means to behave as a follower of Christ (Heb. 5:12). As a matter of fact, the writer of Hebrews had much that he wanted to teach them, but it was hard to explain because they were not listening (Heb. 5:11).

This goes back to what Paul was telling Titus about one of the areas of ministry in the church which is teaching (Titus 2:1). There is a tendency with young pastors or even the younger adults in a church to neglect the older members. It seems now days young pastors, who are right out of seminary, are only looking for churches that has a majority of young people. What they and others need to understand is that it takes both young and old to behave as a church. Therefore, if both the young and the old church members were behaving as church members, they would be ministering to one another. Paul says, "That the older men be sober, reverent, temperate, sound in faith, in love, in patience" (Titus 2:2 NKJV). "Likewise, exhort the young men to be sober-minded, in all things showing yourself to be a pattern of good works; in doctrine showing integrity, reverence, incorruptibility, sound speech that cannot be condemned, that one who is an opponent may be ashamed, having nothing evil to say of you" (vs. 6-8 NKJV). Paul's instructions are not just for men but also for the women. He says, "the older women likewise, that they be reverent in behavior, not slanderers, not given to much wine, teachers of good things; that they admonish the young women to love their husbands, to love their children, to be discreet, chaste, homemakers, good, obedient to their own husbands, that the word of God may not be blasphemed" (vs. 3-5 NKJV).

It is through the grace of God which empowers us to bridge the gap, make the connection, and make disciples within the church. What Paul is getting at, and when you apply Hebrews 5:12, that we should be making disciples and someone else should be making a disciple out of you. Just because you are a teacher or preacher, and have the gift of teaching, "you need someone to teach you again the first principles of the oracles of God" (Heb. 5:12 NKJV). For example, just because you teach calculus, somebody should be teaching you how to add and subtract. If you are a grammar teacher, someone needs to teach you how to read. This is what the writer of Hebrews saying spiritually. Children, babes in Christ they do not know how to share the gospel, give a testimony, or explain the truths of the Word of God. They do not have the ability to teach and help other believers, they have to be helped; they have to be discipled.

When you are making disciples that means you have to teach. If you are teaching that means you are sharing, training, and explaining the truths and doctrines of the Word of God, as well as setting the example by putting into practice and living the Christian life before others. Think about this, discipleship is more than just teaching believers how to present the gospel of our Lord Jesus Christ. A disciple is a learner; a scholar; one who receives or professes to receive instruction from another. A disciple is a follower; a believer of the doctrines of another. The work of salvation was accomplished only by Jesus and He did it upon the cross of Calvary, when He cried out "It is finished!" (John 19:30 NKJV). However, the witness of this salvation is accomplished by His people, those who have trusted Him and have been saved. The King needs ambassadors to carry the message of the Gospel to a lost and dying world. Isaiah asked a question, "Whom shall I send, and who will go for us?" (Isa. 6:8 NKJV). Jesus commanded us to pray for laborers (Matt. 9:36-38), however, it is not enough to just pray, unless we make ourselves available to serve Him.

Now some link the gift of pastor and the gift of teaching together. Pastors can and should be distinguished from teachers. Pastors should have the ability to teach even though they may not possess the gift of teaching. Teachers have a special work of instruction and not an office in the local church. Teachers are those who clearly explain the doctrines of the church as found in the Bible. Teachers are able to give systematic instructions from the Bible and doctrine of the Bible for the development of disciples which helps them to grow into mature believers. Here are some reasons for teaching in the church and how the gift of teaching can be used. First, teaching builds up the church through the ministry of teaching the members. This is where teachers equip the saints and disciple them. Ephesians 4:12 says, "for the equipping of the saints for the work of ministry, for the edifying of the body of Christ" (NKJV). Second, teaching promotes unity and harmony of the faith and knowledge of our Lord and Savior. That means that teach should be to exalt the Savior. Ephesians 4:13 says, "till we all come to the unity of the faith and the knowledge of the Son of God" (NKJV). Third, teaching is used to foster spiritual growth of church members, helping them to behave as church members, and showing them how to reach out to the lost. We call this evangelizing the lost. Ephesians 4:14-16 says, "that we should no longer be children, tossed to and fro and carried about with every wind of doctrine, by the trickery of men, in the cunning craftiness of deceitful plotting, but, speaking the truth in love, may grow up in all things into Him who is the head; Christ; from who the whole body, joined and knit together by what every joint supplies, according to the effective working by which every part does it share, causes growth of the body for the edifying of itself in love" (NKJV).

Teaching and the making of disciples is so vital to the ministry of the church, however, while churches do a good job of teaching, discipleship has been neglected in the church. Could it be that we have failed to disciple our teachers on how to disciple, or could it be that we have become so complacent that we do not disciple allowing the devil to prey on the weak Christians, babes in Christ, to be set aside within the church. We have a responsibility to help new or weak Christians to grow in their walk with Christ and to help them learn biblical truths by discipling them to behave like Christ through the providing of spiritual food on a regular basis. If we are going to behave as church members then we need to prepare the new and weaker souls so they will not be preyed upon by our enemies: the world, the flesh, and the devil.

THE MASTER

Jesus is the perfect teacher and perfect example of a teacher; He never made a mistake. And though He became like us, partaking in our life, and being tempted in all points as we are, He was not bound by the limitations of the flesh which He had accepted for our sake. Even when He chose not to exercise His divine knowledge, His mind was clear. He always knew what was right, and as the perfect man, He lived as God would live among humans. His life was ordered by His objective; to seek and to save that which was lost (Luke 19:10). This was the motivating vision governing His behavior. Not for one moment did Jesus lose sight of His goal. That is why we can learn from Him on how He achieved His objective. Jesus revealed to us God's strategy of world conquest. He had confidence in the future precisely because He lived according to that plan in the present. There was nothing haphazard about His life; no wasted energy, not even an idle word. He was on mission for God (Luke 2:49). He lived, He died, and He rose again according to schedule. Like a general plotting His course of battle, the Son of God calculated to win. He could not afford to take a chance. Weighing every alternative and variable factor in human experience, He conceived a plan that would not fail.

So, how did Jesus handle discipling or teaching His followers? According to Mark 3:13a, Jesus stepped aside from His public work for a time of solitude. Mark writes, "And He went up on the mountain…" (Mark 3:13 NKJV). He did this so He could call "to Him those He Himself wanted" (Mark 3:13 NKJV). Jesus wanted a special communion time with God. Luke gives us a little clearer detail in Luke 6:12. He writes, "He went out into a mountain to pray, and continued all night in prayer to God" (Luke 6:12 NKJV). Jesus was about to ordain twelve men who will be His spokesmen, His representatives to people of Israel. This is a big decision and Jesus wants to be sure that He knows the mind of the Father. Thus, He sought a private place and spent the night in prayer seeking His Father's will. That should be a great lesson for teachers, preachers, and for all of us! Jesus took time out of His busy schedule to spend time in prayer. Jesus saw the great need of reaching up to the Father for the help He needed day by day. The fact that Jesus made prayer a priority in His life highlights our own need to seek the Lord in prayer.

MEN WERE HIS METHOD

Jesus had many disciples some of them were truly converted (John 6:66), however, Jesus only called a few men to follow Him. What this shows us is the discipleship plan that Jesus was going to use to evangelize the world. His concern was not with programs to reach the multitudes, but with men teaching God's Word, whom the multitudes would follow and continue that teaching. What is unique about this approach is the fact that Jesus called these men before He even preached a sermon in public. Men were to be His method of winning the world to God. In Jesus' plan of discipleship, it was to enlist men who could bear witness to His life and carry on His work after He returned to the Father.

Here are the twelve men that Jesus began with, notice a little something about each of them. There was Simon, and his Hebrew name means "a rock or a stone". (Strong's Concordance, 1984) Jesus changes his name to "Peter" in Matthew 16:18 and he was the leader of the group. He was a fisherman with a family. Next is James, who was a fisherman and a member of Jesus' inner circle. James was a great leader in the early church serving as the first pastor. James is the first Apostle to be put to death. Then there is John, the brother of James and a member of the inner circle. John was known as the Beloved Disciple. He was a mighty influence in the early church, writing five books of the New Testament. John was the only Apostle not put to death for his faith, but was persecuted, imprisoned, and banished to a desert island. Then we have Andrew, the brother of Peter. He had been a fisherman before he came to Christ and every time he appears in the gospel record, he is bringing someone to Jesus. Philip in the next disciple to consider but not much in known about him, only the fact that Jesus calls him in John 1:43. Bartholomew, also known as Nathaniel, seems to be a man with some issues of prejudice (John 1:45-46). However, he is a man of honesty and deep religious conviction (John 1:47). Matthew was a Jew, who name is also Levi, and had been a tax collector for Rome. Thomas, also known as Doubting Thomas, was loyal to Jesus even to the point of dying with Jesus (John 11:16). He was the only disciple not cowering in fear in the upper room on the day Jesus arose from the dead (John 20:25). He was a doubter of the unseen, but he was willing to accept the truth when it was revealed to him (John 20:28). James the son of Alphaeus is another disciple that we do not know much about, other than the fact that his mother was at the cross when Jesus was crucified (John 19:25). Thaddaeus is the last of the disciples that we do not have enough information on. Then there is Simon the Canaanite or Simon the Zealot. Simon was a revolutionary man. He was a Jew sworn to the over throw of the Roman government and was probably idealistic, proud, radical, outspoken, fiery, and fearless. Finally, Judas Iscariot; who was the only disciple to come from Judea. He was the treasurer of the group, but he was a thief and a miser (John 12:5-6). Judas was never truly saved and would eventually betray Jesus into the hands of the Jews for thirty pieces of silver (Matt. 26:7-15). He died lost and went to hell. Now some wonder why Jesus chose this man, however the answer is not quite clear. We do know that he played an important role in God's redemptive plan.

It is always hard to get something started, and as one might expect this early effort of soul winning had little or no effect upon the religious life of Jesus day, but that did not matter greatly. For as it turned out these few early converts of the Lord were destined to become the leaders of His church that was to go with the gospel to the whole world to teach and make disciples. Here is what we need to understand, today it is still hard to get something started. Today when it comes to ministries in the church, mission projects, evangelism outreach programs, church growth, or discipleship programs it going to take time. That is why it is necessary for teacher or those with the gift of teaching to lay down a solid foundation upon which the church can build up the church. Anything that is done in the church, there must be faithful members behaving as church members.

MEN WILLING TO LEARN

Once Jesus called them unto Himself, Mark says "and they came to Him" (Mark 3:13 NKJV). Now what is obvious about these men is the fact that none of them are really key men. None of them were leaders in the synagogue, none of them were priest, and none of them had professional training beyond the necessary training of their jobs. In other words, these were nothing more than common labor men. That is why the gift of teach is unique when it comes to teaching and making disciples. Some of them might have come from rich families like the sons of Zebedee, but none of them were considerably wealthy. They did not have academic degrees, no formal education; most of them, like Jesus, were raised in the poor section of the country around Galilee. There was only one exception to the twelve, Judas. He came from the more refined region of Judea. So, when looking at these twelve on cannot help but wonder how in the world could Jesus ever use them? They were impulsive, temperamental, easily offended, and had all the prejudices of their environment. In short, these men selected by the Lord to be His assistants, represented an average class of society in their day.

Yet, Jesus saw in these men the potential of leadership for the kingdom. They were indeed unlearned and ignorant according to the world's standards (Acts 4:13) and yet they were teachable. Although they were often mistaken in their judgments and slow to comprehend spiritual things, they were honest men willing to confess their need. Their manners may have been poor, but with the exception of the traitor, their hearts were big. What is perhaps the most significant about these men is the fact that they were sincere in their yearning to learn more about God and the realities of His life. They were fed up with the hypocrisy of the religious leaders of their day and that is why we see them joining the revival movement of John the Baptist. These men were looking for someone to lead them in the way of salvation. Such men, pliable in the hands of the Master, could be molded into a new image; Jesus can use anyone who wants to be used.

The Lord called these men to follow Him in a relationship of personal fellowship. He wanted to teach them His ways, learn from Him, and train them by personal example and that required closeness. Most of all, He wanted them just to be with Him because He loved them, and He desired their fellowship. Being with Jesus should be the first priority in each of our lives. If we would behave like Christ behaving as church members, then we must spend time with Him. If we would serve Him like He desires, then we must spend time with Him. There is nothing as important in your life as time spent with Jesus! When you spend time with Jesus and allow Him to use your gift of teaching there is nothing better in the world. The time you spend with Him in the closet of prayer is worth more than all the gold in the world. The time spent feeding in the green pastures of His Word is worth more than all the diamonds in the world. The time spent in His presence as you walk through your day will strengthen you to behave as a church member. Nothing compare to being with Him!

MEN WHO ARE MOLDED

So, here is the beauty of His method of discipleship which He used to evangelize the world. Remember that Jesus had many disciples; therefore, as the company of followers of Jesus increased, it became necessary by the middle of His second year of ministry to narrow the select company to a more manageable number. Mark writes, "Then He appointed twelve, that they might be with Him…" (Mark 3:14 NKJV). Accordingly, Jesus "called His disciples to Himself; and from them He chose twelve whom He also named apostles" (Luke 6:13 NKJV). Regardless of the symbolical meaning we put on the number twelve, it is clear that Jesus intended these men to have unique privileges and responsibilities in the Kingdom work. Now, this does not mean that Jesus' decision to have twelve apostles excluded others from following him, for as we know, many more were numbered among His associates, and some of these became very effective in the church.

Jesus was just devoting most of His remaining life on earth to just these twelve disciples. The was His strategy to disciple these men in evangelizing and disciplining the whole world. The world could be indifferent towards Him and still not defeat His strategy. It did not even bother Him when His followers who were on the fringes of things gave up their allegiance when confronted with the true meaning of the Kingdom (John 6:66). But He could not bear to have His close disciples miss His purpose. They had to understand the truth and be sanctified by it (John 17:17), else all would be lost. That is why He did not pray for the world but for the few God gave Him out of the world; His disciples (John 17:6, 9). Everything depended on their faithfulness if the world would believe in Him through their word. That is why He discipled them, molding them into His image. That is why the church and its members must behave by fulfilling the great commission.

MEN THAT ARE EQUIPPED

Jesus called the twelve so they would be with Him, but why did Jesus deliberately concentrate His life on just a few people? Had He not come to save the world (Matt. 18:11)? Jesus was simply demonstrating discipleship in its simplest form, plus He was reminding Israel of the duties of the

Levitical priesthood which was to teach them God's Law (Deut. 33:10). However, with the glowing announcement of John the Baptist ringing in the ears of the multitudes, Jesus could have easily had an immediate following of thousands if He wanted. Why then did He not capitalize on His opportunities to enlist a mighty army of believers to take the world by storm. To answer this question brings us to the real purpose of His plan for discipleship, which leads to evangelism. Jesus was not trying to impress the crowd, but to usher in a kingdom. This means that He needs people, who were equipped, trained, and had the ability to lead the multitudes. What good would it have been for the masses to follow Him if these people had no supervision or instruction in their walk with Christ?

Jesus was a realist. He fully realized the fickleness of humanity, as well as the satanic forces of this world against humanity. And because of this knowledge, Jesus formed the plan of evangelism by starting with discipleship to mee the need. This was the divine brilliance of His strategy. Jesus called these men "that He might send them out to preach" (Mark 3:14 NKJV). The word "preach" means "to act as a herald; to sound forth the message of the King" (Dictionary, 1828) Jesus handpicked these men and called them to take His message to the nation of Israel. What was the message they were to preach? It was the same message that Jesus Himself had been preaching. It was the good news that God had sent His Son into the world to be the Savior of sinners. It was a message of hope, peace, and blessing. The disciples were to take this message to the people and call them to come to Jesus.

So, what were the disciples to do with those who answered the call of evangelism? They were to disciple them, teach them how to behave like Christ and behave like a church member. Now, we all know that not everyone is called to be a preacher. In fact, some of the people who claim to be preachers have never been called by God to that position. Some have called themselves; others have been called by their mom, dad, or grandparents; and yet others have been called by the church because of their popularity in the church. Listen, you can tell when God calls a man to preach. When God calls a preacher three things will be true: first, God will use that man by opening doors for him to preach; next, God will speak through the preacher to feed His sheep; and lastly, God will make the preacher fruitful by saving souls under his preaching. That is how you will know.

A WARNING ABOUT THE TONGUE

Apparently, James was having trouble with the Christians he was writing to, because everyone in the assembly was wanting to teach and be a spiritual leader. Therefore, James had to write them and warn them about this. James writes, "My brethren, let not many of you become teachers, knowing that we shall receive a stricter judgment" (Jam. 3:1 NKJV). This warning can be paraphrased like this: do not become overly ambitious to be a teacher. Please understand that this is not a prohibition against the use of one's spiritual gift of teaching. James is simply saying that type of teaching ministry should not be taken lightly. Those who teach, preach, and/or pastor from God's Holy Word face a stricter judgment if they fail to practice what they teach. It is a great responsibility to teach the Bible. Teachers must use their tongues to share God's truths, and it is easy to commit sins of the tongue. Just think of the damage that can be done by a teacher who is unprepared, or whose spiritual life is not up to par. However, it is not only teachers who are tempted to sin; every Christian must admit that "we all stumble in many things" (Jam. 3:2 NKJV). If we could exercise control in speech then we should be able to have self-control over other areas of life as well. Of course, there has been only one man who has ever completely exercised this kind of control. James implies that we should stride to be Christ-like, that we are to try to be as perfect as Christ was (Jam. 3:2). When James says perfect, he is meaning one who is mature, one who is complete, and one who is thoroughly disciplined. This should be our aim as we try to behave as church members, because the church member who is able to discipline his tongue gives evidence that he can control his whole body. Therefore, proving that he is a mature Christian.

Never under estimate the power and guidance you give by the words you speak or do not speak. Jesus spoke to the woman at the well, and her life and the lives of her neighbors experienced a miraculous change (John 4). Peter preached at Pentecost and three thousand souls came to salvation through faith in Christ (Acts 2). But did you know that our words can start fires? James writes, "Even so the tongue is a little member and boast great things. See how great a forest a little fire kindles" (Jam. 3:5 NKJV)! Solomon says, "Where there is no wood, the fire goes out; and where there is no talebearer, strife ceases. As charcoal is to burning coals, and wood to fire, so is a contentious man to kindle strife" (Prov. 26:20-21 NKJV). In some churches, there are members, deacons, pastors, or teachers who cannot control their tongues, and the result is destruction. Fire burns and hurts, and our words can burn and hurt. Fire spreads, and the more fuel you give it, the faster and farther it will spread. As it spreads, fire destroys; and the words we speak have the power to destroy. Our own words may not have started any wars or wrecked any cities, but our words can break hearts and ruin reputations. This can also destroy souls by turning them to an eternity without Jesus Christ. How important it is to "let your speech always be with grace, seasoned with salt, that you may know how you ought to answer each one" (Col. 4:6 NKJV).

You are a Witness

Now, while God calls some to be teachers or preachers; He calls all His children to be witnesses! When He saved you, He placed His Spirit within you. When the Spirit came in, He gave you gifts, but He also gave you a testimony to share along with a commission to go out and share it (Acts 1:8; Matt 28:18-20). So, while you may never stand in a pulpit and preach a sermon, you can still preach and herald the gospel everywhere you go (Mark 16:15). Jesus still wants His disciples to declare His message and make disciples. But strangely enough, discipleship is not comprehended nor is it practiced in the church like it should today. It seems as though the church does an excellent job on doing evangelism, and sending people out to do evangelism, while discipleship takes a back seat. Most the evangelistic efforts of the church begin with the multitudes under the assumption that the church is qualified to preserve what good is don. The results are that we put major emphasis on number of converts, candidates for baptism, and more member for the church, with little to now genuine concern towards the discipleship of these souls in the love and power of God, let alone the preservation and continuation of the work of Christ.

Surely if the pattern of Jesus at this point means anything at all, it teaches that the first duty of church leadership, which includes pastors, deacons, teachers, etc., is to see that a foundation is laid in the beginning on which we can build an effective and continuing evangelistic ministry to the multitudes. This will require more concentration of time and talents on member of the church while not neglecting the passion for a lost and dying world. It is time for church members to behave, it is time for the church to realistically face the situation. The evangelistic program of the church has become bogged down or is non-existent in some churches due to th fact there is lack of disciples and church members not behaving as church members. In many lands the enfeebled church is not even keeping up with the exploding population. However, in spite of the tragic affairs and condition of the world today, we must not become frantic in trying to reverse the trend overnight. Perhaps that has been our problem, trying to do too much too fast; launching one evangelism program after another to reach the multitudes only to see the program crash.

What is the problem? The real problem is not with the masses, the problem lies with not making sure church members are discipled properly. Discipleship will be slow, tedious, painful, and probably unnoticed by people at first, but the end results will be glorious, even if we do not live to see it. The big question is: "Do we want the momentary applause of popular recognition of the congregation?" Or "Do we want to see the reproduction of Christ as we mirror Him and disciple a few who will carry on the work after we have gone?"

Jesus took twelve ordinary men, saved eleven of them by His grace and made something special out of their lives. He wants to do the same thin in you and me, behave as a church member!

CHAPTER SEVEN

WHAT IS DISCIPLESHIP?

The thief does not come except to steal, and to kill, and to destroy. I have come that they may have life, and that they may have it more abundantly. (John 10:10 NKJV)

The next two spiritual gifts we come to are gift of knowledge and the gift of wisdom. We are going to discuss the gift of knowledge in this chapter and gift of wisdom in the next. The reason I mention both here is because knowledge and wisdom are linked together. In chapter three of my book *Behave as a Follower of Christ*, I said, there was two types of knowledge. "There is the knowledge learned and then there is the knowledge used (or wisdom). These two types of knowledge go hand in hand if a believer is to grow and become like Christ. You cannot have one without the other." (Powers, 2021) A stagnant Christian is one who is not behaving as a church member because he or she is not using that knowledge learned for the edifying of the church. If you have the gift of knowledge then it is very well possible that you have the gift of wisdom. If you have both, then behaving as a church member would imply the strength of your walk in Christ before men. "The amount of know you have is going to aid in the strength of your walk in Christ and the strength of your behavior before men." (Powers, 2021) The gift of knowledge does not imply the amount of education you have, although it helps; and the gift of knowledge does lend help in your "relationship knowledge that comes from those life lessons that stem from following and mimicking Jesus Christ." (Powers, 2021) Furthermore, the gift of knowledge demonstrates itself though teaching, preaching, evangelizing and the training up of disciples. The gift of knowledge is a gift given by the Holy Spirit which provides the church member the ability to continually learn, to have confidence in knowing, and explain to others the great truths found in God's Holy Word.

The Christian believer should have a desire in themselves to want to grow, mature, and know as much as possible there is to know about Jesus Christ and His Word. How are you going to stand against the wiles of the devil (Eph. 6:11), if you are not using your gift of knowledge to behave as a church member. "A Christian should not behave or walk as though he is a question mark, a doubting Christian, nor a Christian without hope. You should behave in your walk with Christ with absolute certainty in the knowledge of Christ, through faith." (Powers, 2021) The writer of Hebrews warns, "do not become sluggish, but imitate those who through faith and patience inherit the promises" (Heb. 6:12 NKKV). We fail to behave as church members, because we have not grown in our knowledge and we behave as though we do not trust God. "We must put forth some effort of making spiritual progress if we want to behave like Christ." (Powers, 2021) That effort should be through the avenue of being discipled, evangelizing and making disciples.

Paul prayed for your discipleship and knowledge in Philippians 1:9-11. He writes, "And this I pray, that your love may abound still more and more in knowledge and all discernment, that you may approve the things that are excellent, that you may be sincere and without offense till the day of Christ, being filled with the fruits of righteousness which are by Jesus Christ, to the glory and praise of God" (Phil. 1:9-11 NKJV). Your effort of growing spiritually in knowledge is a continuous process. You will never be too old to learn, and you are never be too old to start. If you do not grow your gift of knowledge then you may become offensive or have a bad behavior as a church member towards the work of Christ. Our discipleship comes by faith, "So then faith comes by hearing, and hearing by the word of God" (Rom. 10:17 NKJV). Once you allow the Holy Spirit to work in your life and you have grabbed hold of the gift of knowledge that is when you will see that the Holy Spirit has been teaching you all this time. He continues to teach you about the Word of God, and aids in your ability to discern between the truth and lies, plus you are gaining experience that you can apply towards your behavior and to the discipling of others.

But what is discipleship? To answer this let us look to the Old Testament prophet Elisha. Elisha is one of the lesser-known prophets in the Bible, but certainly not one of less importance. When it comes to answering this question about discipleship there is great benefit and blessing in the study of the life and ministry of Elisha. Because he is the prophet of abundant life. What is the abundant life? After all, Jesus told us that He came so that we can have an abundant life (John 10:10). Abundant life is a life where all of your needs are being met, where you are so full of blessings that you have enough to bless others. You see, in the abundant life not only do you receive a blessing, but you become a blessing. The abundant life that Jesus was talking about was not just life out yonder in the future, in the sweet by-and-by; it is the abundant life in the nasty now-and-now. Having an abundant life means joy unspeakable and full of glory (1 Pet. 1:8). Abundant life means Christ's peace (John 14:27), confidence (1 John 2:28), His presence (Heb. 13:5; Matt. 28:20); and the blessed assurance of our salvation (Heb. 10:22-23). We have this abundant life because "You are of God, little children, and have overcome them, because He who is in you is greater than he who is in the world" (1 John 4:4 NKJV). How tragic it is that so many Christian church members around the world are not living the abundant life. The same power that spoke creation into existence, flooded the earth, split the Red Sea, saved the Hebrew children from the fiery furnace, and raised Jesus Christ from the grave is the same power inside of you giving you abundant life! But did you know, that this abundant life begins with a life of discipleship?

DISCIPLESHIP

As you study the life and ministry of Elisha, we can find a graphic and a pointed illustration of what true discipleship is in 1 Kings 19:19-21. There are four elements in the discipleship of Elisha as he followed after Elijah that illustrates our discipleship as we follow after the Lord Jesus Christ. From the life and ministry of Elisha, may we learn what discipleship is.

THERE IS A PERSON TO PLEASE

Before we can define what discipleship is, we need to define what disciple is. A disciple means a person who follows a master (Webster) To be a disciple of someone means that you set your heart, your mind, to please that person. Notice what took place, "So he departed from there, and found Elisha the son of Shaphat, who was plowing with twelve yokes of oxen before him, and he was with the twelfth. Then Elijah passed by him and threw his mantle on him" (1 Kings 19:19 NKJV). Elisha understood the meaning of the mantle. When Elijah came to Elisha, he took off his mantle and he put it on the shoulders of Elisha; to Elisha that meant, "Follow me." Elijah was calling Elisha with mantle. The mantle represented Elijah saying, "I want you to come after me." That is how discipleship works, because our God has called us to be His disciples. A disciple is someone who is dedicated to a person. There is a person to please if you are to become a disciple. Discipleship is not a movement, but a man. Discipleship is not joining a movement, but following Jesus Christ. Jesus does not call you to a plan but to a person, Himself. "Then He said to them, "Follow Me, and I will make you fishers of men" (Matt. 4:19 NKJV). Just as Elisha followed Elijah; James, John, Peter, and the rest of them followed the Lord Jesus Christ. "They immediately left their nets and followed Him" (Matt. 4:20 NKJV). That means they left their nets, boats, and family; they left it all and they followed Jesus. Do you want to be a disciple? Then listen, being a disciple is not just behaving as church member but it is also about behaving as fishers of men, it is about behaving as a follower of Christ. Being a disciple having fellowship with Jesus, knowing Jesus intimately, following Him where ever He leads. When will we ever learn that fellowship with Christ comes before service for Christ? We must minister to Jesus before we can minister and make disciples.

Here is a question: have you ever thought about ministering to Jesus? Over and over and over again in the book of Psalms we are taught to minister unto the Lord. In 2 Kings 3:11, we find out that Elisha "poured water on the hands of Elijah" (NKJV). Elisha ministered to Elijah by being a servant unto Elijah; going and getting a pitcher of water, to pour in a basin to wash Elijah's hands, and taking a towel and dry Elijah's hands. But keep in mind, Elisha was a very successful man. He was the leader, the head, the foreman of a big ranch. He was plowing with twelve yokes of oxen. In the culture of that day, to have one ox meant that you were wealthy. Elisha had twelve, and Elijah just comes by and places his mantle on the shoulders of Elisha as if to say, "Follow me." Elisha left his personal reputation, personal relationships, riches, plows, the oxen; all of it to follow Elijah and minister unto him. And do you know what my job is before I can do anything else, before I can minister to someone else, or make disciples? I have to minister to the Lord. I have to be pleasing to the Lord Jesus Christ. I must follow Jesus. We must minister to Jesus before we can minister to others. Are you willing to be a slave of Jesus? Are you willing to follow Him wherever He goes? Do you want to be His disciple? You cannot behave as church member if you do not first minister to Jesus. You cannot begin to use your gift of knowledge until you have first ministered to Jesus.

The word disciple comes from the Latin word which means, "to learn" (Strong's Concordance, 1984) A is a follower, someone who follows his master. We need to make sure we are teaching this very thought, furthermore, we need to make sure when it comes to discipleship that we ourselves learn this truth. Discipleship is fellowship with Christ, knowing Christ, loving Christ, and abiding in Christ. I am afraid that too many church members have joined a movement rather than having fully surrendered to Jesus Christ. I am afraid that too many believers are trying to do too many things for Christ rather than sitting at the feet of Jesus. There is nothing wrong with service, and we ought to serve, however, when will we learn that we must minister to Jesus, be pleasing to Jesus, before we can minister to others. If you please Jesus, then it does not really matter whom you displease; and if you displease Jesus, then it really does not matter whom you please.

THERE IS A PRICE TO PAY

Eisha "left the oxen and ran after Elijah" (1 Kings 19:20 NKJV). In those days, for one man to own an ox was like owning one of the finest tractors made. Elisha, however, was plowing with twelve yokes of oxen. Which would mean Elisha was the foreman on a big ranch. Here was a man who had a very important position. It may not seem much to you, but it is evident that Elisha came from a place of position and a place of elegance; and he leaves all of this behind to follow Elijah. If you are going to behave as a church member and use your gift of knowledge then it is going to cost you to be a disciple of Christ. If you are looking for an easy way, a cheap way, a lazy way to be a disciple of Christ you are not going to find it. Jesus said, "If anyone comes to Me and does not hate his father and mother, wife and children, brother and sisters, yes, and his own life also, he cannot be My disciple" (Luke 14:25 NKJV). If you are not willing to forsake your position in life, your family, and your possessions; you will never be a disciple of Christ. You must leave whatever position God calls you to leave if He calls you to leave it. The word "hate" in Luke 14:25 is a hyperbole (Strong's Concordance, 1984), and what it means is you are to place Jesus ahead your life and family, because when you love Jesus as you should you will love your family more, not less. What Jesus is implying is, your love for Him must make your love for them, in comparison, be like hate. Remember, you cannot have two masters.

Now notice what Elisha did after running and catching up to Elijah. He said, "Please let me kiss my father and my mother, and then I will follow you" (1 Kings 19:20 NKJV). What price are you willing to pay to behave as a church member with the gift of knowledge, know that you should be following Christ at any cost? Would you pay a price? Think about this: if it an inconvenience for you to be in church, then do you miss church? On a rainy Sunday morning, do you find it difficult to behave as a church member? Do you roll over because it is raining? On Monday morning, if it is raining, you go to work, do you not? But it is okay to miss church if it is raining. This kind of behavior reminds us of the man who told Jesus "Let me first go and bid them farewell who are at my house" (Luke 9:61 NKJV), and Jesus forbade that man; and said "No man, having put his hand to the plow, and looking back, is fit for the kingdom of God" (Luke 9:62 NKJV). But Elijah did not forbid Elisha. Why? Because he knew Elisha's heart. Elisha was not going back to ask permission to leave. He was going back to take leave. There is nothing wrong with being kind and sweet to your father and your mother, but God comes first.

There are things we may not like to do but that should not hold us back. The gift of knowledge is given to you so you will know what is asked of you by God. It may not be what you are accustomed to but you know that God would have you to do it. There was a missionary and his wife that was once asked if they like being missionaries and doing the work. The answer from the missionary shocked the one that asked the question. The missionary said, "No! We do not like the work. My wife and I do not like the dirt, because we have a reasonably refined sensibility. We do not like crawling into revolting huts having to wade through goat excrement. We would rather not associate ourselves with the ignorant, filthy, and ruthless people. However, is a child of God supposed to do nothing for Christ he does not like? Our likes or dislikes has nothing to do with it. We know our orders is to go, and so we go! Love constrains to be a disciple of the Lord Jesus." Have you given your all to Jesus Christ?

So, Elijah was willing to let Elisha go back (1 Kings 19:20). When Elisha turned back, he had himself a barbecue as a going away party. He took those hickory plow handles and he made a little fire, and took an ox, and he killed that ox, and he boiled the flesh there, and they had a little celebration. He was not feeling badly about the fact that he had to leave all of his family and possession behind. As a matter of fact, he was kind of glad to do it, that he might serve. Here was a man who knew that in order to be a disciple there was a price to pay. Do you know what is wrong with the modern church member today? We are looking for a cheap way, an easy way, a lazy way to serve the Lord. I am not saying it is wrong to have a position at a job. I am not saying it is wrong to live with parents. I am not saying it is wrong to have possessions. But I am saying, that these things must first be given to Jesus Christ. If He wants to give them back, He may. If He wants to keep them, He may. But to behave as a church member, know what God would have you to do because the Holy Spirit gave the you the gift of knowledge; there is going to be a price to pay.

THERE IS A PURPOSE TO PURSE

Here is something that is interesting. While Elisha was out there plowing the field, and while he was out there being the foreman of that ranch; God was speaking to Elijah. "Then the Lord said to him: "Go, return on your way to the Wilderness of Damascus; and when you arrive, anoint Hazael as king over Syria. Also, you shall anoint Jehu the son of Nimshi as king over Israel. And Elisha the son of Shaphat of Abel Meholah you shall anoint as prophet in your place" (1 Kings 19:15-16 NKJV). God told Elijah to go and anoint Elisha, because God had chosen him to be His prophet after Elijah. The point is this, God had a plan for Elisha's life even when he did not know it. God has a plan for your life, my life, and for everyone's life. To be followers of Christ means that you seek His plan for your life and get in on it. You may be unaware of God's plan for your life, just as Elisha was at first, but the thing that made Elisha the prophet of miracles and him enjoying the abundant life is the fact that he found the plan of God for his life. This is where the spiritual gift of knowledge comes in and works in your life. The gift of knowledge manifests itself in teaching and training in discipleship. As you learn more about God and commune with Him through prayer, there is sense of desire to be pleasing to Him; we do that through being obedient; and the only way for you to be obedient is for you to know the purpose God has for you. Again, the gift of knowledge is the God-given ability to learn, know, and explain the precious truths of God's Word.

The gift of knowledge is given to aid in knowing what you are supposed to do. As we seek God's will, James encourages us that we "ought to say, 'If the Lord wills, we shall live and do this or that'" (Jam. 4:15 NKJV). When it comes to seeking after God's will, we should have this constant behavior of doing what God asks of us. Jesus said, "My food is to do the will of Him who sent Me, and to finish His work" (John 4:34 NKJV). In a real sense as we behave as church members, we are to have a behavior that God's plans are our plans. When you read Paul's letters, he refers to the will of God, and helps us to understand that God's will for our life is not shackles and chains. Instead, we should see God's plans as the key to what sets us free. Church members will ask me, "Pastor, how do I determine God's will for my life?" What that indicates to me is, they never have really tried to seek nor do God's will. Listen, this spiritual gift of knowledge is given to you, so you can have a starting place of reference. You determine God's will for your life by starting with the things you already know you ought to do. God will then open up the next step and your experience proves what the will of God is.

When we do His will, me must do His will from our hearts. The secret to the abundant life that Jesus said we can have, comes when we delight in our service to Him (John 10:10). When we behave as church members and do the work because we know what to do; that work becomes a delight, those burdens a blessing, those command become praises. When serve as we should, we have "joy inexpressible and full of glory" (1 Pet. 1:8 NKJV). However, if we serve God with a bad behavior or grudgingly or because we have to, we may get the work done, but we are going to miss out on a blessing from God and we could ruin our testimony among our fellow church members.

DO NOT HINDER THE CHILDREN

As mature believers in Christ, we must behave as church members using the gift of knowledge and should not hinder the children. If we are not behaving as we should when we serve God, then we could ruin our testimony to the children of the church. Now when I say children, I am implying both the children and the babes in Christ. This is what Jesus was referring to in Mark 10:13-16. He was referring to the physical children of age and to spiritual children, the babes in Christ.

Here is a little back ground for the scene that took place in Mark 10:13-16 and how it applies to this gift of knowledge and behaving as a church member. Jesus has just finished teaching about the very serious matter of marriage and divorce. As soon as that discussion is finished. Jesus turns His attention to some little children that are being brought to Him by their parents. Back then it was a Jewish tradition to bring small children to a great rabbi so he could bless them and pray for them. It was also common for parents to take their children to the synagogue, where each of the elders would take the child in his hands and pray for the life of the child. This much the same thing we still do today when we dedicate babies and parents to the Lord. These parents are severely rebuked by the Lord's disciples. Apparently, they felt that the Master's time was too valuable to spend on small children. Jesus, in turn, rebuked them for their behavior regarding these children. He told the disciples in no uncertain terms that little children were what the kingdom of heaven was all about.

Now, let us face it; children can be noisy in church. They do require a lot of special attention and special programs. Plus, they cannot contribute to the financial burden of the church. However, children are not a curse to be endured, they are a blessing to be enjoyed! The psalmist writes, "Behold, children are a heritage from the Lord, the fruit of the womb is a reward" (Ps. 127:3). We are blessed by children, even youth, when we have them in church. From the spiritual side of the message. Babes in Christ are a blessing too. However, while we may do a good job at doing outreach programs and children's ministry in the church, we fail to behave as church members by failing to use the gift of knowledge to teach and train up babes in Christ. This passage has something to say about children, and by extension teaches us how we are to serve Jesus and His kingdom.

A LESSON ABOUT SERVICE

Notice what took place, "Then they brought little children to Him, that He might touch them; but the disciples rebuked those who brought them. But when Jesus saw it, He was greatly displeased and said to them, "Let the little children come to Me, and do not forbid them; for of such is the kingdom of God. Assuredly, I say to you, whoever does not receive the kingdom of God as a little child will by no means enter it." And He took them up in His arms, laid His hands on them, and blessed them" (Mark 10:13-16 NKJV). When comes down to serving and teaching our children we do so through evangelizing them. This passage nowhere implies that Jesus was saving these children. He was merely praying for them and pronouncing a blessing on their young lives. This scene teaches us that these parents cared enough about the spiritual condition of their children to bring them to Jesus so they might be blessed through His praying and His touch. The Old Testament challenges believers to share the things of God with their children (Deut. 6:1-2), and the New Testament renews that challenge to parents, "An you, fathers, do not provoke your children to wrath, but bring them up in the training and admonition of the Lord" (Eph. 6:4 NKJV). Parents should do everything in their power to ensure that their children are exposed to the gospel. Which means bringing them to church on a consistent basis, let them see you worship in the worship service, praying in front of them, read your Bible with them, being up front about your faith with them, it means living a consistent life in front of them, and it means that parents have the biggest responsibility of evangelizing their children.

When we serve our children, we are to do so through educating them by bringing them to Jesus. When those parents brought their children to Jesus that day, they were telling them that there was something special in Him. Parents today have the responsibility of modeling their faith in Jesus so the next generation can see He is worth knowing. If my faith does not change my life and cause me to be a better person, my daughter will pick up on that. I can talk about my faith, but if I do not live out my faith, it translates into hypocrisy in the eyes of my daughter. Children are very quick to spot a phony! We are responsible for educating our children about the things of God. In Ephesians 6:4, the word "nurture" refers to "the whole training and education" of a child (Strong's Concordance, 1984) In other words we are to disciple the children. It is not the public school's responsibility to see that your children come to Jesus. It is the parents' duty to bring them face to face with a saving Lord! If we exalt Jesus in front of them, they will be far more likely to come to Him at an early age and remain faithful to Him as they mature.

One last thing, when it comes to serving our children, we do so by encouraging them. When these parents came to Jesus with their children, they were encouraging them to approach Him as well. Christian parents are told to "bring them up in the nurture and admonition of the Lord" (Eph. 6:4 NKJV). The word "admonition" has the idea of "encouragement" (Strong's Concordance, 1984) We ought to encourage our children to seek the things of God. Teach them to pray at an early age. Make the Bible a big part of their daily life. Pray with them not just at the dinner table. Bring them to Sunday School and preaching. Involve them in church activities, outreach programs, decorating for vacation Bibles school, revival services, etc. Expose them to everything that is godly in nature that is available. One of the best things a mature believer can do for a babe in Christ is to show them what it means to be in love with Jesus. When mature adults love Jesus with a sincere devotion, it encourages children, youth, babes in Christ to love Him too! There is not grater blessing than for a child to be saved and for them to live their whole lives for Jesus.

It pays to grow your gift of knowledge, because it benefits the grow your gift of wisdom which is the use of your knowledge. It pays to behave as a church member, because you are doing what God has asked you to do. "Therefore, to him who knows to do good and does not do it, to him it is sin" (Jam. 4:17 NKJV).

CHAPTER EIGHT

WHAT IS WISDOM?

*For wisdom is a defense as money is a defense, but the
excellence of knowledge is that wisdom gives life to
those who have it. (Ecclesiastes 7:12 NKJV)*

If I were to ask you to give me a definition of wisdom, could you give me
a definition? Please understand, wisdom is not necessarily intelligence. As
a matter fact, there are a lot of intelligent people who are not wise. The
Bible even teaches that great men are not wise. You may have a high IQ
and not be wise. Furthermore, let me tell you something else that wisdom
is not; wisdom is not common sense there may be some similarity, but
biblical wisdom and common sense are two separate things. If you have
the gift of knowledge, then it is very well possible that you have the gift
of wisdom as well. If you do not know maybe you should ask for it (Jam.
1:5). Because wisdom will help you behave as a church member in your
everyday life. "Why do we need wisdom? Why not ask for strength to go
through life or deliverance from trial? We need wisdom so we will not

waste the opportunities God is giving us to mature and behave like Christ. Wisdom helps us use the lessons of life for our good and God's glory." (Powers, 2021)

Here is the definition of wisdom: Wisdom is seeing life from God's point of view and to do this you must have the mind of Christ. It is the gift that discerns the work of the Holy Spirit uses it to teach, evangelize and disciple people. "For the Lord does not see as man sees; for man looks at the outward appearance, but the Lord looks at the heart" (1 Sam. 16:7). In other words, man sees one thing and God sees another. Therefore, to have wisdom you must see things from God's point of view.

GOD'S POINT OF VIEW

What is the most significant place in a construction project? Usually when a construction team gets started, they will make a piece of cement with a nail set in it. The nail will be sticking up at a certain height and then they will put a sign on that nail which says, "working point." That point then becomes the point by which everything else in that building is measured by. Anything east, west, north, or south; is east, west, north, or south of that point. Anything high or low, is high or low from that point. So, a foreman was to tell the carpenter to build that up high, he would have to say high according to what? Or if he said low, the worker would say low according to what? Or if he said, east, east of what; west, west of what; north, north of what; south, south of what? Somewhere there must be a starting point if you are going to build a building. Somewhere there needs to be a fixed point or else you are not going to have a building that is worth very much. If you are going to behave as a church member, then you must have a fixed spot; you must have a point of reference; the things of this world, whether good or bad, wise or unwise, are to be measured according to one fixed spot. That one fixed spot is the Lord Jesus Christ and His character. If you do not have a fixed spot, you will not have a point of reference, and you are not going to build an exceptionally godly life; you are not going to be able to use the gift of wisdom and behave as a church member. Wisdom is seeing life from God's perspective, therefore, if you get your perspective right you will have wisdom.

PROBLEMS AND GOD'S POINT OF VIEW

Right now, I want you to do something. As you may know everybody has problems of one kind or another. But I want to ask you to take out a piece of paper and just list your problems. Then, I would like you to take your biggest problem, your king-size problem that is in your life right now, and think about it for just a little bit. Now, I want you to think of the very worst things that can happen to you as a result of that problem, or think about what would happen if that problem takes a turn for the worst it can take. Once you think about the worst your problem can be, let me ask, does your problem seem really big to you? How big is your problem to God? From God's point of view, as God is looking at that problem that seems so big to you, is it a big problem for God? If your problem is too big for God, then your problem is not that your problem is too big, but your god is too small.

Over in Numbers 13, Israel had a king-size problem. God had told them to go into the Promised Land and possess it. However, the Israelites was not real sure about just going in and claiming this land, so they sent out twelve spies to scope things out and bring back a report. "Now they departed and came back to Moses and Aaron and all the congregation of the children of Israel in the Wilderness of Paran, at Kadesh; they brought back word to them and to all the congregation, and showed them the fruit of the land. Then they told him, and said: "We went to the land where you sent us. It truly flows with milk and honey, and this is its fruit. Nevertheless, the people who dwell in the land are strong; the cities are fortified and very large; moreover, we saw the descendants of Anak there. The Amalekites dwell in the land of the south; the Hittites, the Jebusites, and the Amorites dwell in the mountains; and the Canaanites dwell by the sea and along the banks of the Jordan"" (Num. 13:26-29 NKJV). The twelves spies go into the Promised Land and they see the enemy. All the spies, except for Caleb and Joshua, became discouraged at the idea of going into the land and conquering the enemy. Because of those ten spies' lack of faith and discouragement their behavior affected the whole camp. The looked at the enemy, and there were a lot of them, for they were outnumbered. Their doubt turned into unbelief, and eventually that unbelief led to rebellion against God. These are these things we do when we are not behaving as church members and use the gift of wisdom the Holy Spirit has given us. There is something odd about the spies' report. Notice the phrases, "the land where you sent us" (vs. 27 NKJV), and "the land through which we have gone" (vs. 32 NKJV). Why could they have not said, "the land the Lord our God is giving us?" It is because the ten spies did not have the proper perspective, they did not really believe God's promises.

The spies believed that the people of the Promised Land were giants. Verse 28 tells us that there were descendants of Anak (Deut. 1:28; 9:2) and his sons were giants as well. One Anak's sons the children of Israel had already met in Deuteronomy 3; he was king of Bashan whose name was Og. He slept on a bed that was fourteen feet long, and it was six and a half feet wide. But apparently there were a lot of the descendants of Anak in the Promised Land. They also saw that the enemy had a great position, the Canaanite cities were on the mountaintops with great high walls all around them with locked gates. The ten spies look at themselves and thought about army of Israel and saw themselves as grasshoppers. When you were a kid, did you ever play "king of the mountain?" The way you played, was you get somebody on the top of a pile of dirt, and the rest of the kids would come and try to drag that person off. Well, the person on top is going to be awfully hard to drag off, because when you came at him you would have to come up the hill. While the person on top of the hill had the ability to shove you down. When these ten spies went and saw the enemy, they said, "No way, Jose. We cannot do it. There is no way possible." If you say "we are not able" that is a behavior of unbelief, however, if you want to behave as a church member then you need to say, "Our God is able" for that is a behavior of affirmation of faith.

From the human perspective these ten spies were right. But the problem is that they were looking at it from what they could, through their human eyes. As Christians we need to get a grasp on the victory that we have through Jesus Christ if we are going to behave as church members. Here is what we need to hold fast to: victory in the Christian life is not difficult. The reason so many Christians are failing because we think it is going to be too difficult to overcome. We think our Christian walk is impossible. If you do not grab hold of the truth that nothing is impossible with God, then you will never learn to live the Christian life nor will you behave as a church member. There is only one person who has ever lived the Christian life and His name is Jesus. And if the Christian life is going to be lived in your house, it is going to be Jesus who is still doing it through you because it will be Jesus in you. Jesus does the impossible in and through you. If you try to do it on your own, then you are not going to do it. Victory is not by trying; it is by trusting. Listen to what two of the spies said, "But Joshua the son of Nun and Caleb the son of Jephunneh, who were among those who had spied out the land, tore their clothes; and they spoke to all the congregation of the children of Israel, saying: "The land we passed through to spy out is an exceedingly good land. If the Lord delights in us, then He will bring us into the land and give it to us, a land which flows with milk and honey. Only do not rebel against the Lord nor fear the people of the land, for they are our bread; their protection has departed from them, and the Lord is with us. Do not fear them"" (Num. 14:6-9 NKJV). Notice the difference between ten men and two men. The ten men that day saw through human eyes, and two saw through divine eyes. Wisdom is seeing life from God's perspective. The ten looked at those giants and said, "Look how much bigger they are than we are!" The two looked at those giants and said, "Look how much smaller they are than God is! You see, it is a matter of perspective.

TIME FROM GOD'S POINT OF VIEW

Now here is another exercise for you: think about what is the most important thing to you at this moment. Let me ask you, a hundred million years from now, will it be important? One hundred million years from now, that thing that is the most important thing to you will it be important a hundred million years from now? Remember, wisdom is seeing not what it important now but what is important from God's perspective. When it comes to time, God deals in eternity not time. In the book of Hebrews, we are reminded of the time when Moses was offered the opportunity to be king. "By faith Moses, when he became of age, refused to be called the son of Pharaoh's daughter, choosing rather to suffer affliction with the people of God than to enjoy the passing pleasures of sin, esteeming the reproach of Christ greater riches that the treasures in Egypt; for he looked to the reward. By faith he forsook Egypt, not fearing the wrath of the king; for endured as seeing Him who is invisible" (Heb. 11:24-27 NKJV). Moses had it all laid out before him to be the next pharaoh of Egypt, but Moses refused to be named as a son of Pharaoh's daughter. At Moses' fingertips was something that was immediately his, he could lay his hands on it and have it right now if he wanted it. He could have had a great position in the kingdom (vs. 24). He could have been the grandson of Pharaoh and been an heir to the throne. He could have great influence and unlimited power, and many possessions as heir to the throne. But he refused (vs. 26).

The reason why he refused is because Moses sat down and did some figuring and looked at things from God's perspective not his. He said, "Well, would I rather be a child of God, or a grandchild of Pharaoh? Had I rather have favor with the king, or favor with the King of kings? What is more important to me, material things or spiritual things? What is more important: now or tomorrow?" You see, folly calculates on beginnings, but wisdom always reckons on endings. If you want to teach your children or be about making disciples, then behave as a church member and use the gift of knowledge and the gift of wisdom to teach them to look past today and prepare for tomorrow. Teach them about how everything works together for our good (Rom. 5:8), that the testing of faith produces patience (Jam. 1:3), and that patience when it is allowed to work in your life you are going to be complete and lack nothing (Jam. 1:4). Wisdom sees time from God's point of view. Wisdom does not get antsy about now; wisdom looks into the future.

POSSESSIONS AND GOD'S POINT OF VIEW

With the gift of wisdom, you begin to learn how to evaluate what we call riches and possessions from God's perspective. If you want to know what you really, really own, then add up everything that you have which money cannot buy and death cannot take away. We have clothes, furniture, cars, camping trailers, roof over our heads, but those things are not ours. They belong to God. Therefore, if something was to happen to these material things, if He cannot take care of them, then that is His prerogative. They are His, if He wants to mess them up, He has the right to go ahead and do that because they belong to God. If you want to grow and have wisdom, then you are going to have to look at your problems, your time, and your wealth from God's perspective.

Over Revelation 2, there is a church in Smyrna that John wrote a letter to, here is what it said, "And unto the angel of the church in Smyrna write; These things saith the first and the last, which was dead, and is alive; I know thy works, and tribulation, and poverty but thou are rich" (Rev. 2:8-9 NKJV). The church in Smyrna was going through some suffering, and world said they were poverty-stricken, but He said, "You are rich!" Then John writes a letter to a church at Laodicea, and He said, "Because you say, I am rich, and increased with goods, and have need of nothing; and know not that thou are wretched, and poor, and blind, and naked" (Rev. 3:17 NKJV). They were living in a prison house of prosperity and did not know it. Are you wealthy? Have you seen what really counts in life? A wise man does, because it is all a matter of perspective on what real wealth is.

Take the early church for example, they were behaving as church members because "the church was compassionate, and Christians were demonstrating the love of Christ by taking care of one another." (Powers D. C., 2021) Because the early church was behaving as church members, many of them had received the gift of wisdom and had God's point view concerning their possessions. Therefore, they began to share their wealth and as a result "the multitude of those who believed were of one heart and one soul; neither did anyone say that any of the things he possesses was his own, but they had all things in common" (Acts 4:32 NKJV).

PEOPLE AND GOD'S POINT OF VIEW

"But the Lord said to Samuel, "Do not look at his appearance or at his physical stature, because I have refused him. For the Lord does not see as man sees; for man looks at the outward appearance, but the Lord looks at the heart"" (1 Sam. 16:7 NKJV). When behaving as a church member the gift of wisdom gives us the reminder that the unwise man cannot see people from God's point of view. Samuel is looking for the next king of Israel. He wants to anoint a king, and Jesse is bringing his sons to Samuel.

He brings out Eliab, and Samuel thought this is the man that God wants to anoint as king (vs. 6). That is when God spoke to Samuel in verse seven, and reminds us that it is a matter of perspective. Let me ask you this: think of the person that you admire the most. Think of the person you would most like to be. If you could trade places with this person, who would it be? Now I am afraid that we have a generation that does not have wisdom, because it has the wrong heroes. Therefore, we do not see as God sees, we do not see what is important. Some people are celebrated and made celebrities. What right do they have to be a celebrity? Well, they born with a certain set of genes and chromosomes that allows them to throw a football with accuracy; or they vocal cords that all them to make a sweet note; or they have some sort of quirk about their personality that makes them interesting. Real wisdom sees as God sees them and sees who the important people are.

WISDOM CAN MAKE LIFE BETTER

Let me restate our definition of wisdom: Wisdom is the capacity to see things from God's perspective and to respond to them according to scriptural principles. Simply, wisdom is seeking heavenly opinions on earthly circumstances. We are called to be wise in every decision of our lives. We need wisdom in our business dealings, our health, our relationships, our parenting, our finances, and our behavior. However, the wisest man that ever lived, Solomon, argues in Ecclesiastes 1:12-18 that wisdom did not make life worth living. "For in much wisdom is much grief, and he who increases knowledge increases sorrow" (Eccl. 1:18 NKJV). But after giving wisdom a second thought Solomon revised his views towards his question, he purposed in Ecclesiastes 6:12 which says, "For who knows what is good for man in life, all the days of his vain life which he passes like a shadow? Who can tell a man what will happen after him under the sun" (Eccl. 6:12 NKJV)?

So, let me ask you, are you wiser than God, who made your body, when it comes to knowing how to live healthy? Are you wiser than God, who caused you to be born in a specific time and place, to a specific set of parents, in a specific set of circumstances, when it comes to developing a plan and purpose for your life? Are you wiser than God, who created all natural resources and everything of real value on this earth, when it comes to knowing how to manage your finances and material resources? Solomon concluded that earthly wisdom cannot explain all of life's mysteries, but godly wisdom can make life better. Solomon explains in Ecclesiastes 7:1-10 that better things come to those who seek to grow the Holy Spirit's gift of wisdom.

IS SORROW BETTER THAN LAUGHTER?

Which would you rather go to: a birthday party or a funeral? If you were Solomon, you would rather go to a funeral. Why? "Sorrow is better than laughter, for by a sad countenance the heart is made better" (Eccl. 7:3 NKJV). If you study the life of Solomon then you would understand that he was not a sad miserable man. Listen to what King Solomon wrote, "A merry heart makes a cheerful countenance, but by sorrow of the heart the spirit is broken" (Prov. 15:13 NKJV). "A merry heart does good, like medicine, but a broken spirit dries the bones" (Prov. 17:22 NKJV). If you want to heal a broken heart, then laughter is the best medicine. However, if you want to strengthen your soul, then sorrow is food for the soul. When it comes to behaving as a church member you need to be a balanced believer and that is going to take both sorrow and laughter.

Solomon makes this statement, "A good name is better than precious ointment, and the day of death that the day of one's birth" (Eccl. 7:1 NKJV). What Solomon is getting at is; when you are born is the moment you start to die. Human beings have been given two important dates in their life time; when they are born and when they die. But what is the most important date that shows up on a tombstone? That would be the dash. The dash represents the life lived between those two significant days. The name that is associated with that dash tells whether or not that person left a beautiful fragrance or a stinky name. Reputations are built by the life that is live during the dash, therefore, when you die your reputation is sealed. So, in a sense, your death is better than your birth. Solomon writes "The memory of the righteous is blessed, but the name of the wicked will rot" (Prov. 10:7 NKJV).

The gift of wisdom helps us look at death and learn from it. That does not mean that we should be obsessed with it, nor should we try to avoid death because to behave as a church member you need to take life seriously. The psalmist writes, "So teach us to number our days, that we may apply our hearts unto wisdom" (Ps. 90:12 NKJV). Solomon is encouraging us to keep a balance life, because there is a time to laugh (Eccl. 3:4).

TODAY IS BETTER THAN YESTERDAY

My grandparents used to talk about them "good old days", and I can see why now that I am older. Because when life get tough and we get impatient to the new things that are coming out, it is easy to long for them days. Take for example, the building of the temple in Ezra 3:12-13. As the foundation is being laid for the second temple wept. "But many of the priest and Levites and heads of the fathers' house, old men who had seen the first temple, wept with a loud voice when the foundation of this temple was laid before their eyes. Yet many shouted for joy" (Ezra 3:12 NKJV). The old men wept and longed for the good old days, while the young generation shouted for joy and the "people could not discern the noise of the shout of joy from the noise of the weeping of the people, for the people shouted with a loud shout, and the sound was heard afar off" (vs. 13 NKJV). When you get down to them good old days have been balanced by sorrow and laughter (Eccl. 7:1-4), rebuke and praise (Eccl. 7:5-6), and patience and shortcuts (Eccl. 7:7-9). Yesterday is gone, it is history you cannot change it; you are not promised tomorrow because it may never come; and so, what Solomon says in Ecclesiastes 7:10 is "Do not say, "Why were the former days better than these?" for you do not inquire wisely concerning this" (NKJV). The Latin phrase that means "seize the day!" is "Carpe diem" (Dictionary, 1828) A behaving church member uses the gift of wisdom to live today in the will of God and not worried about what tomorrow will or will not bring. A behaving church member is not bothered by their past.

WISDOM VERSES MONEY

"Wisdom is good with an inheritance, and profitable to those who see the sun. For wisdom is a defense as money is a defense, but the excellence of knowledge is that wisdom gives life to those who have it" (Eccl. 7:11-12

NKJV). There is not a competition when you are comparing wisdom to money. In all actuality, money is worthless when it is compared to wisdom. Money can be stolen, burned, lost, lose its value, however, godly wisdom keeps its value and can never be lost. Godly wisdom preserves our lives from human pitfalls. Solomon gives us the example of an inheritance. With inheritance comes the pitfall of pride and wisdom keeps from that. Godly wisdom also can preserve us from affliction that can cause us to have doubt and discouragement. Therefore, wisdom is a defense, it is a shelter to those who obey it, and gives greater protection than money; God's wisdom has the ability to give life.

Here is how wisdom helps preserve us: the person who is seeking to walk in wisdom is going to reflect about his or her own relationship with the Lord Jesus Christ and how Jesus desires to work in the believer's life. The church member is going to a great desire to be pleasing unto the Lord, to grow in his relationship with Jesus, and to experience the presence of the Lord at all times. As we walk in wisdom, we see God's hand at every turn and know He is with us. We become more and more familiar with His voice, His prompting, His leading, His tug at our hearts. The more we come to know God, the more we are going to learn the way God works, the things God desires to do in our lives and in the lives of others, and the plans God has made for mankind's eternal good. We are going to feel God's heartbeat. What disappoints God is going to disappoint us; what brings joy to heaven is going to bring joy to us. What brings concern to the Lord is going to concern us. We are going to see thing from God's perspective, and we are going to grow in our desire to love others as God loves them. As we grow in our knowledge of God and His ways, the more we are going to know how much God loves us, how much He desires to bless us, and how much He desires to use us to bless others. That is what it means to behave as church member.

WISDOM AND GOD'S PLAN

"Consider the work of God; for who can make straight what He has made crooked" (Eccl. 7:13 NKJV)? Just think of the mighty power statement this verse makes. If God has made something crooked, then He has the power to make it straight. Now, we might not understand God's plan for our lives, however, we do know this, "He has made everything beautiful in its time" (Eccl. 3:11). Those who walk in wisdom receive God's clear direction for their lives. That means they are spared the many mistakes and false starts. They are kept from making wrong decisions or entering into hurtful relationships. They take few detours in life and experience fewer obstacles in their path. Never lose sight of the fact that God sees the big picture of your life. He knows you inside and out; your thoughts, feelings, physical makeup; your past, present, and future. God see the whole you; what you are called to do, and what you are facing right now. The more you see your life from God's perspective, the stronger your ability to discern the right way to go.

"Hear, my son, and receive my sayings, and the years of your life will be many. I have taught you in the way of wisdom; I have led you in right paths. When you walk, your steps will not be hindered, and when you run, you will not stumble" (Prov. 4:10-12 NKJV). Oh, how heart felt this verse is, and to think that it is pure joy to walk in the will of God and know that you do not have to be tripped up, held back, or hindered in any way. What a joy to run towards the fulfillment of God's plans for your life and not stumble. God's desire is to guard us and guide us with every step of every day. Jesus said, "The thief does not come except to steal, and to kill, and to destroy. I have come that they may have life and that they may have it more abundantly" (John 10:10 NKJV).

We live in the so-called information age and we have more information today that we know how to process and use. Even when we are trying to relax, we have information forced upon us; pagers beep, phone rings, television commercials, and computer apps signaling that you have a new message waiting for your response. For all of our information that we have are we increasing in wisdom? Certainly not! When we look at the recent political history, we gain an understanding that knowledge and wisdom are different. Many highly knowledgeable people work for our government. Each makes it his or her life's work to become informed about certain issues, as well as about history, economics, and the Law. But do they always live wisely? Do they pass laws that are in line with God's Word? Do they always live moral lives that are yielded to God's will?

Earthly wisdom is limited by man's ability to perceive, to sense, to learn, to understand, to create, and to control. Earthly wisdom is doing what comes naturally; and what comes naturally to unredeemed people is that which satisfies the senses, feeds human pride, and fosters greed. Earthly wisdom can never rise above man's fallen nature. Godly wisdom is marked by God's ability to work through mankind. Paul proclaimed, "I can do all things through Christ who strengthens me" (Phil. 4:13 NKJV). When we behave as church members and allow God to work in us and through us, our abilities to perceive, to sense, to learn, to understand, to create, and to manage life's resources are powerfully extended; thanks to the gift of wisdom. Godly wisdom is doing what the Holy Spirit compels us to do and as a result it is pleasing to God and ultimately beneficial to man. God's wisdom is not forced upon us, after all it is a gift. We must choose to seek wisdom; we must invite God to lead us to His way and His plan. We must ask God to give us His wisdom. Are you behaving as a church member with godly wisdom? If so, is godly wisdom making life better for you? If not, then you need to seek out His wisdom.

SEEK THE HOLY SPIRIT'S GIFT OF WISDOM

It is very easy for us to talk about the teachings of Jesus, but to put then into practice; well…that is another story. Because that is easier said than done. The behavior of the church member is much more than a valiant effort to put a victorious Christian life together on principles taught by Jesus. The Holy Spirit is described as "the Spirit of Wisdom" in Isaiah 11:2 and in Ephesians 1:17 (NKJV). When you receive Jesus as your Lord and Savior, He will give you power of the Holy Spirit to move you in the direction of wisdom. For instance, Timothy had been given significant responsibility for an important church early in life, and he was beginning to feel overwhelmed. He tended to listen too much to his feelings and his moods, which began to make him nervous and cautious. So, Paul wrote to encourage him, "For God has not given us a spirit of fear, but of power and of love and of a sound mound" (2 Tim. 1:7 NKJV). In other words, "Timothy, you do not need to be driven by impulse, the Spirit of God lives within you!"

Over in Job, he asked this question, "But where can wisdom be found? And where is the place of understanding" (Job 28:12 NKJV)? Then he asked it again, "From where then does wisdom come? And where is the place of understanding" (vs. 20 NKJV)? The reason Job is asking the questions is because he is getting tired of the clichés and platitudes that his three friends were giving him in the name of wisdom. His friends were sure that their words were pure as gold, but Job concluded that they were glittery and trash. The three men had knowledge, but they lacked wisdom. The same could be said of church members today or anybody for that matter. They know a great deal, and are the great fools for it. There is no fool so great a fool as the knowing of a fool. But to know how to use the gift of knowledge is to have the gift of wisdom. Job did provide us with some insight as to where wisdom can be found.

YOU CANNOT MIND WISDOM

When you read Job 28:1-11, Job takes us deep in the earth where brave men are mining gold, iron, copper, and precious stones. Precious metals and precious stones are often used in Scripture as symbols of wisdom. Once you have it, you must refine it in the furnace and then mint it for practical uses. Paul said that the opposite of God's wisdom is man's wisdom which consists of wood, hay, and stubble; material that are not beautiful, durable, or valuable (1 Cor. 3:12). You can find wood, hay, and stubble on the surface of the earth, but if you want real treasures, you must dig deep.

Job describes how men work hard and face great dangers to find material wealth. They tunnel through hard rock and risk their lives to get rich. To behave as a church member then you are going to have to work at seeking to grow your gift of wisdom. The Word of God is like a deep mine filled with precious treasures; but the believer must put forth effort to discover it riches. It takes careful reading and study, prayer, meditation, and obedience to mine the treasures of the Word of God; and the Holy Spirit is willing to assist you.

WISDOM IS FROM GOD

If you were to go as high as the birds can fly, then you would find out that wisdom was not there. If you go as deep as destruction and death, then you will not fine wisdom there. Only God knows where wisdom is to be found, for God sees everything (Job 28: 20-28). God has the wisdom to adjust the pressure of the wind and the measure of the amount of water in the atmosphere. If these proportions were changed, what a disturbance in nature it might cause! God knows how to control the rain and guide the storms as it moves across the earth. Flashes of lighting and peels of thunder may seem random to us, but God even controls them.

The answer to Job's where is wisdom question is answered by Job in verse 28. He says, "And to man He said, "Behold, the fear of the Lord, that is wisdom, and to depart from evil is understanding"" (Job 28:28 NKJV). But what is the fear of the Lord? Fear of the Lord is a loving reverence for God, who He is, what He says, and what He does. It is not a fear that paralyzes, but one that energizes. When you fear the Lord, you obey His commandments, walk in the His ways, and serves Him. You are loyal to Him and give Him your wholehearted service. Like Job when you fear the Lord, you depart from evil.

The first step towards growing you gift of wisdom is a reverent and respectful attitude toward God, which also involves a humble attitude towards ourselves. Personal pride is the greatest barrier to spiritual wisdom. The next step is to ask God for wisdom (Jam. 1:5); and make diligent use of His gift of wisdom that He gives through the Holy Spirit. Study the Word of God, then obey what God tells you through the Word of God; and as you behave as a church member by faith, we discover that the gift of wisdom is needed in the everyday life and in the life of the church.

CHAPTER NINE

THE IMPORTANCE OF PROPHECY

So, then faith comes by hearing, and hearing by the
word of God. (Romans 10:17 NKJV)

Blessed is he who reads and those who hear the words of
this prophecy, and keep those things which are written in
it; for the time is near. (Revelation 1:3 NKJV)

The next spiritual gift that is given to the believing church member is the gift of prophecy. What is prophecy? I hear some people say, "I have the gift of prophecy" and they behave as though they have been anointed by God to tell people off. Now that is not what the gift of prophecy is. As a matter of fact, quite to the contrary, "But he who prophesies speaks edification, and exhortation and comfort to men" (1 Cor. 14:3 NKJV). That means you do not have the right to tell people off if you have the gift of prophecy. To behave as a church member with the gift of prophecy, you should edify which is to build up; exhort which is to fire up; and comfort which is to shore or hold up your fellow believers in Christ in the church. That is what a prophet does.

There is a lot of misunderstanding when it comes to this word prophecy. The word "prophecy" means "to predict" or "to speak or write by divine inspiration" (Concise Oxford English Dictionary Eleventh Edition, 2004) A "prophet" then is "an inspired teacher or preacher or proclaimer of the will of God" or "a person who predicts the future" (Concise Oxford English Dictionary Eleventh Edition, 2004) This word prophecy is used in both a limited and a general sense. In the limited sense the word prophecy is about foretelling, or predicting the future. There are some people who think that we should not study prophecy. They think that we are riding a hobbyhorse, or that we are oddballs or fanatics if we study prophecy. They believe prophecy is unnecessary and unrelated to our everyday lives. Please understand in the limited sense when we use the word prophecy we are studying and talking about things to come, the Second Coming of Christ, and Heavenly things. Furthermore, twenty-five percent of the Bible is given to prophecy, and if twenty-five percent of the Bible is given to prophecy, then did the Holy Spirit make a mistake when we have the prophecy of God's Word? Of course not! There is an incredible, wonderful blessing in the study of prophecy.

Now, in the general sense, the word prophecy is used to mean preaching God's message; therefore, preaching is prophesying, and the preacher is a prophet in that he proclaims the message of God. Prophecy is the ability to speak for God through His Holy Word, it is not merely foretelling, which some of it could be included, it is more of forthtelling the message of God. Some church members have the gift of prophecy which according to Paul this is the gift that should be desired among the church (1 Cor. 14:5). The gift of prophecy is the proclaiming of the Word of God with boldness. Which builds up the church and brings about convictions of sin. But how do we profit from prophecy? And how do we behave as a church member if we have the gift of prophecy? John writes, "Blessed is he who reads and those who hear the words of this prophecy, and keep those things which are written in it; for the time is near" (Rev. 1:3 NKJV). In other words, we are to read about prophecy, we are to head it, and we are to be blessed by it. In this chapter, it is my prayer that we gain understanding what we can do with prophecy. It is not going to be a study of prophecy but a study about prophecy.

THE IMPORTANCE OF PROPHECY

What is the importance of biblical prophecy? What do we need to know about Bible prophecy to aid with growing the gift of prophecy. Let me give you six basic things we need to know about Bible prophecy.

First, we need to know that God knows the future. "Known to God from eternity are all His works" (Acts 15:18 NKJV). Since God is the eternal, all-knowing, omnipresent God, and lives where time does not exist, then that means God knows what will happen before it happens. Therefore, God gave us His revelation of things we need to know concerning the future and future events. God through His living Word, the Bible, reveals His truths gradually to His people. His plan for the church, the cross was not a plan B, they were settled from the beginning (Acts 2:23; 4:27-28). The second thing we need to know is, since God does reveal His truths gradually to us through His Word, He also reveals the future before it happens. "Remember the former things of old, for I am God, and there is no other; I am God, and there is none like Me, declaring the end from the beginning, and from ancient times things that are not yet done, saying, 'My counsel shall stand, and I will do all My pleasure'" (Isa. 46:9-10).

Another basic thing we need to know is the Bible is full of prophecy. As I have already mention that twenty-five percent of the Bible is given to prophecy, however, let me break this down a little more. God put eighteen books of prophecy in the Bible. He put five books which we call the Major Prophets in the Bible; twelve books of the Bible we call the Minor Prophets; and then He put the book of Revelation in the Bible. Plus, He put whole chapters of prophecy in the Bible found in Matthew 24-25. The Bible is full of prophecy. Another thing we need to know is Bible prophecy is reliable. "But the prophet who presumes to speak a word in My name, which I have not commanded him to speak, or who speaks in the name of other gods, that prophet shall die" (Deut. 18:20 NKJV). God's prophet had to be right 100% of the time. If it was not from God, then it is from Satan.

The fifth basic thing we need to know is, there is proof of the accuracy of prophecy. The Old Testament records more than three hundred prophecies about the first coming of Jesus. Some prophecies are repeated two or three times. After the repetitions are removed, the Old Testament still records 108 specifically different prophecies about the first coming. Someone took the time to calculate the probability of one person fulfilling just forty-eight prophecies to be 1 in 10 to the 127 power (that is 1 with 127 zeros; and by the way, one trillion has just twelve zeros). With the odds being so great for one person to fulfill just forty-eight prophecies, one must wonder what the odds would be for one person to fulfill all 108 prophecies. Understand, fulfilling prophecy is indisputable proof, that Jesus is the Messiah and God knows end from the beginning. God is in control and the Bible is the Word of God and is infallible. The last basic thing we need to know is what Peter said about Bible prophecy. "And so, we have the prophetic word confirmed, which you do well to heed as a light that shines in a dark place, until the day dawns and the morning star rises in your hearts; know this first, that no prophecy of Scriptures is of any private interpretation, for prophecy never came by the will of man, but holy men of God spoke as they were moved by the Holy Spirit" (2 Pet. 1:19-21 NKJV). Peter said the Bible is sure or accurate; and we would do well, (or be wise), to pay attention to Bible prophecy; for the Bible is like a light because the Bible is full of prophecy given by the Holy Spirit. If we are going to behave as a church member, then we need to know these basic things, especially as we seek to grow the gift of prophecy.

So, why would it be wise to study prophecy? First, we would be wise to study Bible prophecy because it teaches accountability. "And as it appointed for men to die once, but after this the judgment" (Heb. 9:27 NKJV). Bible prophecy teaches accountability to prepare us for what comes after death. We would be wise to study Bible prophecy because it changes lives. "Beloved, now we are children of God; and it has not yet been revealed what we shall be, but we know that when He is revealed, we shall be like Him, for we shall see Him as He is. And everyone who has this hope in Him purifies himself, just as He is pure" (1 John 3:2-3 NKJV). Bible prophecy cause people to give up their sins, as they grow in their walk with Christ. Another reason it is wise to study Bible prophecy is because loving the Second Coming of Jesus will be rewarded. "Finally, there is laid up for me the crown of righteousness, which the Lord, the righteous Judge, will give to me on that Day, and not to me only but also to all who have loved His appearing" (2 Tim. 4:8 NKJV). This is the only doctrine mentioned in the Bible that will be rewarded with a crown.

Jesus gives us a reason it would be wise to study bible prophecy in His parable of the wheat and tares. "Therefore, as the tares are gathered and burned in the fire, so it will be at the end of this age. The Son of Man will send out His angels, and they will gather out of His kingdom all things that offend, and those who practice lawlessness, and will cast them into the furnace of fire. There will be wailing and gnashing of teeth" (Matt. 13:40-42 NKJV). From prophecy we understand that the lost will be removed from the earth at the end of this age. Jesus presents this same truth in His parable of the dragnet (Matt. 13:47-50). Therefore, we need to behave as church members and start telling the world what Jesus said would happen to the lost.

Another reason it is wise to study Bible prophecy is because some followers of Christ are interested in prophecy, and it would be wise to have some understanding what the Bible has to say. "Now as He sat on the Mount of Olives, the disciples came to Him privately, saying, "Tell us, when will these things be? And what will be the sign of Your coming, and of the end of the age?"" (Matt. 24:3 NKJV). There is nothing wrong with being interested in Bible prophecy, the disciples were interested in it, just make sure that you are allowing the Holy Spirit to teach you and not man's opinion. Jesus even wants us to be patient and not be deceived by certain things. "And Jesus answered and said to them: "Take heed that no one deceives you. For many will come in My name, saying, 'I am the Christ,' and will deceive many. And you will hear of wars and rumors of wars. See that you are not troubled; for all these things must come to pass, but the end is not yet."" (vs. 4-6 NKJV). It would be wise to understand that there are still many things that must happen before the end of the age arrives.

We would be wise to study Bible prophecy because according to the Bible the end will come. Jesus said, "And this gospel of the kingdom will be preached in all the world as a witness to all the nations, and the end will come" (Matt. 24:14 NKJV). End will definitely come there is no "if's" or "but's" about it. Then because we know the end is coming, we should behave as a church member showing love and mercy to human beings. Love and mercy are reasons why He has waited; Jesus does not want to judge the world, but He will eventually do just that. Since Jesus gave us the command, which we call the Great Commission, it would be wise to study prophecy (Matt. 28:18-20). The end of the age will come, in the meantime we should be actively telling them about Jesus. Not to mention, it is wise to study Bible prophecy because it pleases God (1 Chron. 12:32). God is pleased with those who understand the signs and tells His people what they need to do. He reveals these things for the good of all mankind. If God did not want us to study these Scriptures, all He had to do was leave them out of the Bible. But God put them in the Bible. He told us to study them (2 Tim. 2:15; 3:16-17). He told us we would be wise to study them, and He told us He would reward us if we study them.

PROPHECY IS ABOUT JESUS

The last part of Revelation 19:10 says, "For the testimony of Jesus is the spirit of prophecy" (NKJV). So, from this verse we can conclude that prophecy is about Jesus Christ our Lord and Savior. When you go back to the first chapter of the book of Revelation and in the very first verse it tells us who the whole book is about. It says, "The Revelation of Jesus Christ, which God gave Him to show His servants things which must shortly take place. And He sent and signified it by His angel to His servant John" (Rev. 1:1 NKJV). Do you know who the Bible is about? It is about Jesus Christ. Jesus is the hero of the Bible. If you read the Bible and you do not find Jesus, I suggest you go back and read it. So many people want to study prophecy, and yet they get so hung up on, more concerned about things which are happening than they are about who the One is going to come.

The word "revelation" is actually the word "apocalypse" which literally means "an unveiling (Strong's Concordance, 1984) An example of how this word revelation is used is to think of a statue in the park. The sculptor has finished it, and the mayor, the city council, and everybody is there; and they are going to unveil the statue, revelation. The statue is covered with a canvas, and then the artist pulls the string, and the canvas falls away; and there is the statue. What has been veiled is now unveiled. The book of the Revelation is the unveiling of Jesus Christ. Prophecy is about Jesus Christ. When Jesus came the first time, born into this world through the portals of a virgin's womb, laid in a feeding trough in a stable with flies buzzing; cow manure on the floor, the step-son of a carpenter according to the flesh; the Son of God; His mother, a Jewish peasant; and all that glory was veiled. But, in the Book of Revelation, the veil is drawn back. The first time, He came to redeem; when He comes again, He is coming to reign. He came to a crucifixion the first time; He is coming to a coronation the second time. The first time He came, He stood before Pilate; when He comes again, Pilate is going to stand before the Lord Jesus Christ. He came the first time as a servant. The Book of the Revelation shows Him coming as the Sovereign, as the Kings of kings and the Lord of lords. It is the revelation of Jesus Christ. He is the central person of the book. Prophecy is about proclaiming Jesus to a lost and dying world. Prophecy is about the testimony of Jesus.

THE REVELATION OF JESUS CHRIST

The clear purpose of the book the Revelation of Jesus Christ is to give His servants an understanding of this book. The word servant in Revelation 1:1 means bond slave (Strong's Concordance, 1984) A bond slave was somebody who had been a slave, who had been set free, who willingly went back to his master and said, "I do not want to be free. I want to be your slave. I want to stay with you. I love you master." A bond slave is a follower of Jesus Christ, a believer. Therefore, to behave as a church member, then you need to behave as a bond slave. Are you a slave to Jesus Christ? Be careful how you answer that, because if you say "No, I am not a slave to Jesus Christ," then you will not be able to understand the book of the Revelation of Jesus Christ or anything about prophecy.

John does give us a comforting promise, he writes, "Blessed is he who reads and those who hear the words of this prophecy, and keep those things which are written in it, for the time is near" (Rev. 1:3 NKJV). The comforting promise is that you are going to be blessed if you read prophecy and heed prophecy. Why are you going to be blessed? Because you are going to understand the mystery of history. This world does not make sense apart from the book of the Revelation and what God reveals here. In the book of the revelation, we learn what God is doing. God is moving all things to a purpose, "The kingdoms of this world have become the kingdoms of our Lord and of His Christ, and He shall reign forever and ever" (Rev. 11:15 NKJV)! One of these days this old world which has been battered with war, saturated with sin, and crumbling society is going see Jesus high and lifted up, sitting upon the throne; and the kingdoms of this world will become the kingdoms of our Lord and Savior Jesus Christ. That is a blessing which should cause us to behave as church members.

Let this wonderful thought sink in: in the first two chapters of the Bible, you will not find the devil there, and in the last two chapter of the Biles you will not find the devil there. That is such a wonderful blessing. "For the earth will be filled with the knowledge of the glory of the Lord as the waters cover the sea" (Hab. 2:14 NKJV). Now, think about this church member. The reason that everything is in such mess today is because things our not in their right place. The church is the Bride, but the Bride belongs with the Groom. Therefore, we are not with Him yet. Jesus is the King and the King belongs on the throne, and He is not ruling yet. The devil is a criminal, he belongs in prison and he is not there yet. Oh, praise the name of the Lord our God, one of these days, the King is going to be on the throne; the devil is going to be in prison, and we will be with the Lord forevermore! You see, prophecy is a blessing and behaving church member behave as though they are blessed.

Since we are blessed through an understanding of the mystery of history through the study of prophecy, then we will be blessed where we can make sense of our suffering. We live in a world which is cursed with sin, suffering, pain, death, tears, and destruction; and because of all this tribulation in the world, all of creation moans and groans (Rom. 8:22). What do you say to a husband who is standing beside the grave of his young wife? What do you say to a young couple that has experienced their second miscarriage? What do you say to a child of God, a believer in Christ who is not behaving as a church member? What do you say to a child of God who is always in unbearable pain. What do you say? Here is what to say, "It is not over yet, this is not God's final plan. The best is yet to come". There was an elderly lady on her death bed and she knew it was getting close. She had her family call her pastor in, because she wanted to make plans for the funeral. The pastor came in and sat down beside her bed. She began to discuss the things she wanted the pastor to know. One of the things she wanted was to be buried with a fork in her hand. The pastor was taken back by this request. He asked her, "Why a fork in your hand?" She replied, "When I was a small girl, and we were finishing up our meals around the family table, my parents would always say to us children, "Keep your fork, the best is yet to come." Pastor, I want to be buried with a fork in my hand and as the people come to view my body, they will see the fork and ask just as you did, "Why the fork?" And I want you to tell them, "The best is yet to come."'" That is the reason to it is such a blessing to read the book of the Revelation and to study prophecy you have stability in tough times. If you have the gift of prophecy then you have stability and as you behave as a church member you bring stability to the church.

PRAYER BRINGS ABOUT PRAYER

Did you know that once you start understanding prophecy that it will cause you to want to, desire to pray? Prophecy leads us to intercession. We know from prophecy that the Kingdom of God is coming. Therefore, since the Kingdom of God is coming and the kingdoms of this world will become the kingdoms of Jesus, that does not give a right to stop praying about it. What did Jesus teach us to pray? "Your kingdom come your will be done on earth as it is in heaven" (Matt. 6:10 NKJV). Well, the Bible teaches that it is going to happen, and yet, Jesus told us to pray that it would happen.

Over in 1 Kings 17:1, Elijah had received word from God that He was going to bring about a drought upon the land. "Then Elijah said to Ahab, "Go up eat and drink; for there is the sound of abundance of rain" (1 Kings 18:41 NKJV). Understand, from chapter 17 until chapter 18 and verse 41, there had not been any dew nor rain for three and a half years. So, why did Elijah say there was "a sound of abundance of rain?" Well, in 1 Kings 18:1, God spoke to Elijah again with a prophecy. "And it came to pass after many days that the word of the Lord came to Elijah, in the third year, saying, "Go, present yourself to Ahab, and I will send rain on the earth"'" (1 Kings 18:1 NKJV). After Elijah goes to Ahab and tells him the Word of the Lord, he goes up on top of Mount Carmel to pray, and he bows his face to the ground, his face between his needs and prays with authority (vs. 42). The reason he could pray with such fervency is because he had the Word of God behind him. God had promised to send rain. Elijah knew that God had promised to send rain. He announced beforehand that God would send rain. For most of us, we would behave as though, God said it and that settles it. We would then proceed to not pray at all or not prayed very much. The promise did not cause Elijah not to pray; the promise is what cause him to pray. The promise given is not where prayer ends, the promise given is where prayer begins.

We still need to learn that even though God has promised, He still does not act until His people pray. It is hard for us to learn that God does not do anything, even when He has spoken His Word and made clear His will, until His people pray. However, we do need to remember that prayer does not bend God's will to fit our will. Prayer finds the will of God and gets in on it. "Confess your trespasses to one another, and pray for one another, that you may be healed. The effective, fervent prayer of a righteous man avails much" (Jam. 5:16 NKJV). Do you have consistency? Elijah prayed and continued to pray. The Bible teaches us about persistency in prayer, so we might have a constant prayer life. Seven times Elijah sent his servant to go and look towards the sea for any sign of rain. Six times there was no answer (1 Kings 18:43-44). To behave as a church member, we need to learn to wait on God even with a fervent prayer life (Col. 4:2; Isa. 30:18).

The prophesies that Jerusalem will be the capital city of the whole earth and there will be peace in Jerusalem. Yet, the Bible tells us to "pray for the peace of Jerusalem" (Ps. 122:6 NKJV). Why? Because when God prophesies something that is going to happen, however, God uses the prayers of His people to bring it about. Listen to Ezekiel, "Then the nations which are left all around you shall know that I, the Lord, have rebuilt the ruined places and planted what was desolate. I, the Lord, have spoke it, and I will do it" (Ezek. 36:36 NKJV). And so, we know that Jesus is coming. Nothing can stop His coming. But we are to pray for His coming. Do you know the last prayer in the Bible? The prayer goes like this, "Amen. Even so, come, Lord Jesus (Rev. 22:20 NKJV)! There is something about prophecy that turn prophecy into prayer.

PROPHECY BRINGS FORTH PROCLAMATION

In Revelation 19:10, an angel is talking to John and gives him this revelation. You see, John wanted to fall at the feet of the angel and worship this angel, however, the angel says to John, "See that you do not do that! I am your fellow servant, and of your brethren who have the testimony of Jesus. Worship God! For the testimony of Jesus is the spirit of prophecy" (Rev. 19:10 NKJV). Notice that phrase: Jesus is the spirit of prophecy. What does that mean? Because it seems that everybody these days are interested in prophecy. The astrologers, the mystics, and the fortunetellers are all interested in prophecy and not necessarily Bible prophecy, but everybody wants to know the future. There are some in churches who want to study prophecy, but they miss the message of prophecy. I mean there are those who want to know the meaning of the third toe on the left foo of some beast in the book of the Revelation. Therefore, they get all involved in it, and there is nothing wrong with seeking the information out; however, because they get so involved, they fall into the temptation, and this is where their study starts going south, of trying to set dates and figure out programs and all of the other things.

But let me tell you what prophecy is all about: real prophecy is the testimony of Jesus Christ. Prophecy is not looking for something to happen, it is looking for someone to come! The testimony of Jesus is the spirit of prophecy. Do you know the real mark whether or not you believe Bible prophecy? It is not whether you have your head in the clouds of prophecy, but whether you have your feet on the sidewalk of soul winning. Let me ask you, what are you doing to warn people to flee from the wrath to come. Paul knew, through prophecy, that the great tribulation was coming. He knew, through the study of prophecy and divine revelation, that there was an everlasting hell. Therefore, he writes, "Knowing, therefore, the terror of the Lord, we persuade men; but we are well known to God, and I also trust are well known in your consciences" (2 Cor. 5:11 NKJV). If you believe that soon the rapture is coming, that soon the great tribulation is going to descend upon this earth, soon the Antichrist is coming, soon there will be the mark of the beast, soon there will be hell on earth, and soon all of these terrible things are going to happen after the church is taken out; what should you do? Yes, it is great that you are taking great links to study prophecy, so you can understand every jot and tittle, but are you behaving as a church member by getting involved in the ministry of church and going out to try and wind your neighbor to Jesus Christ? The spirit of prophecy is the testimony of Jesus. It is not enough to unpack all the divine mysteries. We need to bring people to Jesus Christ. If studying prophecy and the things to come does not cause you to get ready for the One who is coming and then help others to get ready, then you are not using your gift of prophecy and you are not behaving as a church member.

CHAPTER TEN

DEFEND MY SHEEP

Be sober, be vigilant; because your adversary the devil walks about like a roaring lion, seeking whom he may devour. (1 Peter 5:8)

If there was ever a time for the children of God to behave as a church member, the time is now. There is plethora of different ideologies of theology in this world today. And when it comes to the church, there has to be something in place to defend His sheep, protect His sheep, feed His sheep, and lead His sheep. Thankfully there is, along with the gift of wisdom there is the gift called the gift of discernment. Plus, with wisdom comes the ability to discern. The gift of discernment is the antivirus gift that protects the body. It is the gift that aids the church by being able to recognize the true intentions of those within the church and those outside the church. A church member with the gift of discernment will also have the ability to test the message and actions of others which aids in the defending of the sheep. This gift comes alongside the gift of prophecy and the gift of teaching to discern if there is a false prophet who may be prophesying something that contrary to the Word of God; or a false teacher who teaching a false doctrine. It also comes along side of the gift of shepherding to aid in defending the sheep.

DISCERNMENT AND FORGIVENESS

The gift of discernment also aids the sheep in the area of forgiveness. One theologian said he believe the sin that is causing Christians more difficulty than any other is the sin of unforgiving spirit, and that one sin was holding back the power of God in prayer in the hearts of church members. Forgiveness is a problem that keeps church members from behaving properly, because they have not dealt with it. There are some church members that are chained by their guilt, and there are others who are chained by their bitterness. Those who are chained by their guilt were chained up because they have wronged someone and have not been forgiven. Those who have been chained by bitterness are chained up because someone has wronged them and they have not forgiven that individual. I believe that bitterness in the heart of a person is the leading cause of so many health issues. Bitterness can cause murders, wars, divide churches, divorces. And we need to learn how to deal with bitterness, as well as learn how to forgive one another. Thankfully the gift of discernment helps us to forgive and heal.

The gift of discernment helps us determine whether a person is living or what a person is saying is honest and truthful, plus whether that person is showing humility or pride. When we behave as a church member and start living in an atmosphere of humility and honesty, there is going to be some risks and we can expect some dangers. Now, one way to determine if a person is being humble and honest towards repairing and building the relationships is that there is going to be forgiveness. In Matthew 18:21, Peter recognized the risks involved and asked Jesus how he should handle them in the future. However, we remember that Peter, made some serious mistakes. Peter lacked humility because he was certain that his brother would sin against him, but not him against his brother. Plus, Peter thought there should be a limit to forgiving a person, but according to Ephesians 3:17-19 there can be no limits. Peter assumed just because he forgave a person seven times showed that he had great faith and love. Then Jesus replies to Peter's question by saying, "I do not say to you, up to seven times, but up to seventy times seven" (Matt. 18:22 NKJV). Peter did the math, four hundred and ninety times that number must have shocked him, because after all who could keep count of that many offenses? That was what Jesus was trying to teach him, love does not keep a record (1 Cor. 13:4-8). Therefore, by the time you have forgiven that many times, now you are in the habit of forgiving.

Please understand, Jesus is not giving us permission to just carelessly forgive. Because, thanks to the Holy Spirit and the gift of discernment Christian love is not blind. "And this I pray, that your love may abound still more and more in knowledge and all discernment, that you may approve the things that are excellent, that you may be sincere and without offense till the day of Christ" (Phil 1:9-10 NKJV). Jesus gave us instruction on how to discern and offer forgiveness in Matthew 18:15-20. That is the reason Peter asked his question based on those instructions. Jesus gives Peter the answer to his questions then proceeds to tell a parable about forgiveness (Matt. 18:23-35). But the question is why do we need to forgive? What reason is there for forgiveness? First of all, we should forgive because Jesus has forgiven us, that is what the parable Jesus is sharing with Peter and others is all about. If God has forgiven us, then it is only logical that we ought to forgive one another. "And be kind to one another; tenderhearted, forgiving one another; even as God in Christ forgave you" (Eph. 4:32 NKJV).

The second reason to forgive is, if you do not forgive, then you are blocking out the forgiveness of God. Jesus said, "But if you do not forgive men their trespasses, neither will your Father forgive your trespasses" (Matt. 6:15 NKJV). To behave as church member and have an unforgiven spirit is unforgivable, as long as you have that kind of spirit in your heart, you cannot be forgiven of God. The third reason why we should forgive is because if we do not forgive, the unforgiving spirit will cause us great emotional and health damage. The Bible calls it bitterness and bitterness is an acid that destroys the vessel. There are so many Christians who do not want to forgive because they would rather seek out revenge upon the person that has wronged them. That is the wrong behavior to have as a church member. The final reason we are to forgive is because forgiveness restores a broken fellowship. If there is a person that you are holding a grudge towards, then you have a broken fellowship. That is the reason Jesus said, "Moreover if your brother sins against you, go and tell him his fault between you and him alone. If he hears you, you have gained your brother" (Matt. 18:15 NKJV).

The reasons to forgive are all Bible reasons. But now let me give tell you how you should forgive. First you are to forgive freely. That means that you are to forgive before you seek your revenge. You are to forgive before the wound gets infected. Cleanse the wound quickly, just like Jesus did when He was on the cross, while they were crucifying Him; Jesus prayed a prayer of forgiveness. We should be anxious to forgive people, not only do we forgive them if they come to us and ask forgiveness, but we should literally seek them out to forgive them. We should never have the attitude where we want to go tell them off; go to get them back, but we should go to gain your brother (Matt. 18:15). Secondly, we should forgive fully. Do not forgive half-heartedly. Do behave as a pretender. If a person says you, "Would you forgive me?" and you say, "Well, that is no big deal. Do not worry about", listen, that is not forgiveness. The reason we say that it is not a big deal and not to worry about it is our pride. We do not want to admit how deeply we have been hurt. Do not ever let a person say that if you come to that individual for forgiveness and they say, "Never mind, just forget it." Listen it cannot be forgotten until it has been cleansed. If somebody asks you to forgive them, do not just act all big and high-minded. Truly forgive them, make sure it is forgiveness that you get. Do not merely apologize if you have done wrong. Ask an individual, in the name of Jesus to forgive you. Finally, when you forgive, forgive fully. Once you forgive, bury it in the grave of God's forgetfulness and do not bring it up again. It cost to forgive. You have to taste a little bit of Calvary when you forgive, and the way to do that is to let the Spirit of the Lord Jesus be in you. It is not in us by nature to forgive, we want to get even, strike back. But it is only when the nature of Jesus Christ has free reign in my heart that I can truly forgive. The gift of discernment moves us towards the nature of Jesus Christ and aids in the ability to forgive.

A DAY ON THE BEACH

This is one of the many things that Jesus was alluding to when He recommissioned Peter to service. "So, when they had eaten breakfast, Jesus said to Simon Peter, "Simon, son of Jonah, do you love Me more than these?" He said to Him, "Yes, Lord; You know that I love You." He said to Him, "Feed My lambs." He said to him again a second time, "Simon, son of Jonah, do you love Me?" He said to Him, "Yes, Lord; You know that I love You." He said to Him, "Tend My sheep." He said to him the third time, "Simon, son of Jonah, do you love Me?" Peter was grieved because He said to him the third time, "Do you love Me?" And he said to Him, "Lord, You know all things; You know that I love You." Jesus said to him, "Feed my sheep"" (John 21: 15-17 NKJV). Peter had already met with Jesus privately and sought forgiveness of his sin (Luke 24:34; 1 Cor. 15:5), however, Peter's sin of denying Jesus three times was done in public, so it would be important for Jesus to restore Peter publicly. Since Peter denied Jesus three times, Jesus asked Peter three personal questions and then gave him three commissions that restored Peter to his ministry. It is from these threefold commissions that we see the need to behave as a church member using the spiritual gifts that the Holy Spirit gives us. The gift of discernment is a gift that aids in helping the church, or protecting the church from our adversary, the devil (1 Pet. 5:8).

What can a church member gain from the interaction between Jesus and Peter in John 21:15-17? "The lesson is obvious that no matter what we have done in our Christian walk with Jesus, we are to still keep His commandments. Because if you are out of fellowship with God, chances are you will be out of fellowship with people. If you are out of fellowship with people, then you are out of fellowship with God." (Powers, 2021) Peter was asked "Do you love Me?" which is a reference back to his boasting that he loved Jesus and even made the statement, "Lord, why can I not follow you now? I will lay down my life for Your sake" (John 13:37 NKJV). Matthew records his statement like this, "Even if all are made to stumble because of You, I will never be made to stumble" (Matt. 26:33 NKJV). From these two statements of Peter, we get the idea that he believed that he loved Jesus more than the other disciples. There has been plenty said about Peter's confession and the word play between Jesus and Peter. In His questions in John 21:15-16, Jesus used, both times, the word *agape* for the word love, and Peter answered, both times, with the word *phileo* word for love. Then in verse 17, both Jesus and Peter use the word *phileo*. *Agape* is the Greek word for the highest form of love, while *phileo* is love of a friend, fondness for another (Strong's Concordance, 1984) To behave as a church member we need to go beyond the *phileo* love that says, "I am fond of you, like a brother" and we need to come to the place where we love the Lord with a genuine *agape* love. When we come to agape kind of love, then the second greatest commandment will not be a problem for us (Matt. 22:39). Furthermore, the world will see us behaving as church members and know that we are His disciples (John 13:25).

What is our duty as church members and especially if we have the gift of discernment? In what way can we demonstrate genuine love for Jesus? Well, is it enough to say, "I love the Lord!"? It is enough for our church to say, "We really love Jesus here!"? No! True love for Jesus always presents itself, manifest itself, in obedience to His commands, "If you love Me, keep My commandments" (John 14:15 NKJV). According to John 21:15-17, there are two duties of the church member given by Jesus. First, we are to supply the saints. Peter is given three commands: "feed My lambs," "Tend My sheep," and "Feed My sheep." Both lambs and more mature sheep need to be feed properly and tended to on a regular basis. The point is clear, Jesus expected Peter to communicate the mind of God to all ages. Here is the problem, we have men in churches who communicate their opinions, their politics, and the influence of society. Men who communicate the mind of the Convention or denomination. There are those who communicate their favorite preacher. However, if we are going to feed the lambs and the sheep, then we must open the Word of God and communicate the mind of God to His people. When they receive a steady diet of God's Word, they are going to grow!

Of course, there are those who are going to say, "That is the preacher's job to feed the sheep, discern the spirits, and protect us from wolves in sheep's clothing." Yes, it is an awesome responsibility to be a pastor/ shepherd of God's flock! However, the duty of every child of God in this matter cannot be over stated, you need to know how to behave as a church member when someone is teaching or preaching if it lines up with the Word of God. If you have the gift of discernment, you will know. While it is true the Holy Spirit equips people to serve as shepherds, and gives these people to the church (Eph. 4:11), it is also true that each individual Christian must help to care for the flock. There are many who stand up and teach or preach in the church. And if you are one of them, then you have a word from God. For the rest, behave by holding up the hands of those who are standing teaching or preaching as they communicate God's truths to the flock of God. Pray for God's men and for those who teach in the church. It takes every member behaving as church member in their appointed place to get the job done. Each of us has a gift or gifts from the Holy Spirit, and we should use what we have been given to help protect and grow the flock.

The second duty given to church members by Jesus is to support the saints. There in John 21:16, the word "feed" literally means "to tend, or to keep sheep." (Concise Oxford English Dictionary Eleventh Edition, 2004) Peter is told that the sheep need more than food. They are to be looked after and all their needs are to be supplied. Again, there is a message to pastors, yes, but also to every church member. Paul writes, "Bear one another's burdens, and so fulfill the law of Christ" (Gal. 6:2 NKJV). The needs of church members need to be discerned and if they are real needs then they must become a reality in the modern-day church. When people enter the church, they should know that they are part of a group that cares for them and that they are loved. That may mean putting aside petty differences and pointless squabbles, but when we genuinely love one another, the world will notice and God Himself will manifest His power and presence among His people. There are going to be times of persecution that will demand that God's people have adequate leadership. And if judgment begins at the house of God (1 Pet. 4:17), then God's house needs to be in order, or it split.

WHAT PETER LEARNED

What did Peter learn from Jesus that day on the beach? There are a great number of things that Peter learned while on the beach that day with Jesus and the other disciples. In his conversation with Jesus, in front of everyone, in John 21:15-17; he learned about the church. Maybe, that day Peter connected the dots between this conversation and the conversation where Jesus said, "and I say that you are Peter, and on this rock, I will build My church, and the gates of Hades shall not prevail against it" (Matt. 16:18 NKJV). Remember that Jesus is not building His church on Peter but upon Peter's statement, "You are the Christ, the Son of the living

God" (Matt. 16:16 NKJV). Jesus is the Rock, the Chief Cornerstone upon the church is built and the sheep make up the church. This is possibly the conclusion Peter came to out there on that beach that day. We see this though as he addresses the church in 1 Peter 5:1-4. The church was living in tough times and dangerous times, and he reminds them of their behavior and what the church should truly be like. Peter uses an analogy about raising sheep, which the people would understand and could relate to, as he talked about the church.

He tells them that the church, the body of Christ, genuine believers of Christ are like sheep. The psalmist writes, "We are His people and the sheep of His pasture" (Ps. 100:3 NKJV). Symbolically, if God's people are like sheep, then that would make the church His flock. Jesus said, "Do not fear, little flock, for it is you Father's good pleasure to give you the kingdom" (Luke 12:32 NKJV). Since we are talking about the gift of discernment; if the people are like sheep, the church is like a flock, then that would make the pastor like a shepherd. Basically, that is the duty of the pastor; to shepherd the flock. And one of his duties is to defend the flock, and in order to do this he needs the ability to discern between truth and error. Since, the pastor is like a shepherd his correct position is that of an under-shepherd, because Jesus is the Chief Shepherd to who the under-shepherd is going to have to give an account one day of how he took care of the flock.

HIS SHEEP

Jesus calls us His sheep, and if you think about that, it is not all that complimentary. I mean, He could have called us strong as an ox, or stout as a horse, or graceful as a gazelle, or busy as a bee, or proud as a peacock, or as brave as a lion; but He did not, He said we are sheep. The reason He called us sheep is because sheep are wayward animals. As a matter of fact, sheep are just plain silly animals, and it is really hard to train imprudent sheep. You can train dogs, cats, horses but sheep are just thoughtless. They are so imprudent that sheep get lost and do not know how to get back. Peter says, "For you were like sheep going astray" (1 Pet. 2:25 NKJV). Isaiah says the same thing, "All we like sheep have gone astray; we have turned ever one, to his own way, and the Lord has laid on Him the iniquity of us all" (Isa. 53:6 NKJV). A sheep will feed just about anywhere. They will graze over here, and then go over there and browse and graze; they just never look back or look where they are going. Pretty soon they are away from the flock and do not know how to get back, unless the shepherd goes and gets them. Sheep are just some kind of silly, unwise animals. This is the way Jesus characterizes His children. That is why the gift of discernment is so vital to the body of Christ. We are His sheep and because we tend to stray from the truth, from time to time, we need someone who is gifted with discernment to bring us back in.

But not only does His sheep stray from the truth and have a waywardness about them, sheep are also weak. How do sheep protect themselves? "As a sheep before its shearers is silent" (Isa. 53:7 NKJV), sheep are just silent, they are led as lambs to the slaughter. Horses can run to defend themselves, the mule kicks, the cat scratches, the dog bites, the skunk sprays, and the sheep are just silent. That is the way most church members behave when trials and tribulations come, when someone opposes them, someone brings up a false doctrine and begins to teach worldly truths contrary to the bible; they are just silent. Praise God for the gift of discernment that will speak up when all these errors raise up within the body of Christ.

In spite of a sheep's waywardness and weakness, sheep are very valuable. In that day, a man would count his wealth by the number of sheep he had, because sheep gave wool, milk, meat, and lambs. In spite of our waywardness, weakness, wretchedness, God consider us to be valuable enough to love us (John 3:16), and even die for us (Rom. 5:8), we are His children (1 John 3:1). Therefore, we need to behave as such.

THE UNDER-SHEPHERD

The Lord so loves these sheep, and the Lord know that they are so weak, and they tend to wander but He values them so much He puts His sheep together in a church, making the church His flock. The Bible does not teach that a sheep should go off on his own, but the Bible teaches that every sheep is to be a part of the flock. And because the church is a flock, God gives each flock a shepherd, because it is very important that the sheep congregate themselves together for their protection. There are some Christians that way, "Well, I am a Christian, I love the Chief Shepherd, but I just do not want to be a part of the church." That is a dangerous behavior for a church member to have. As a matter of fact, it is a good way for the sheep to get devoured by the enemies of God, and there are lot of enemies of God around devouring His sheep today (1 Pet. 5:8). God wants to protect His flock; therefore, the Holy Spirit gives the gift of discernment and God gives the sheep a shepherd to lead them.

The pastor is the shepherd and he is to set the example of using the gift of discernment so we can know how to use our gift of discernment and behave as a church member. Peter writes, "Nor as being lords over those entrusted to you, but being examples to the flock" (1 Pet. 5:3 NKJV). This verse has as much to say to you as it does about the pastor. The things that apply to the pastor, the pastor in turn should be an example to the flock. Which means in a way, those things said about the pastor is going to apply to you or to anybody who hopes to be in church leadership, spiritual leadership, or has the gift of discernment. Now let's face it, we all have some kind of flock that we have to be shepherd's over. Your flock may be your family, Sunday School class, friends at school, or co-workers and we all have the potential to be a spiritual influence. We all should be pointing men, women, boys, and girls to Jesus Christ.

When comes to the gift of discernment what is the role of the pastor? Peter says, "The elders who are among you I exhort, I who am a fellow elder and a witness of the sufferings of Christ, and also a partaker of the glory that will be revealed: Shepherd the flock of God which is among you, serving as overseers, not by compulsion but willingly, not for dishonest gain but eagerly" (1 Peter 5:1-2 NKJV). I want you to notice three words: elder, feed, and oversight. Remember we are looking at what Peter learned from that day on the beach with Jesus. Jesus gave Peter three commands from which we see the words: feed, tend, and feed. The words that Jesus told Peter, told him what he was supposed to do as a shepherd.

The words Peter used shows that he learned what he was to do and is now sharing with us the role of the pastor. First, Peter used the word "elder" the pastor is an elder (Strong's Concordance, 1984) That does not necessarily mean he is to be of old age, it does mean "one of maturity, one of wisdom." The second word Peter uses is the word "feed," and we know that word is a verb, but did you know that in the noun form of the word it means pastor or shepherd (Concise Oxford English Dictionary Eleventh Edition, 2004) The last word that Peter uses is the word "oversight," it also is a verb, in the noun form it means bishop (Strong's Concordance, 1984) So, for example I am Elder Powers, Pastor Powers, and Bishop Powers and from these three words we can understand the role of the pastor. In other places of the Bible, these words are used interchangeably. People often ask me, "What should I call you? Rev. Powers, Dr. Powers, Brother Powers?" All of those will work, because the words that Peter used are interchangeable in the Bible. A good example of how interchangeable these words are, can be found in Acts 20. In that chapter you will discover how those three terms all speak of the same office and the same person. But let's look at the role of the pastor.

The pastor is to be about feeding the flock or shepherding the flock which would include: first, guarding the flock. Paul warned, "For I know this, that after my departure savage wolves will come in among you, not sparing the flock" (Acts 20:9 NKJV). Peter also warned, "Your adversary the devil walks about like a roaring lion, seeking who he may devour" (1 Pet. 5:8 NKJV). The pastor knows that the devil is going to try to harm the flock. Satan will try to divide the flock, discourage the flock, and devour the flock. There are those out there that would steel the sheep, and lead the sheep astray. The pastor or church member who has the gift of discernment must be vigilant about those who would come in and try to harm the flock, therefore they should behave as church members.

Second, the pastor is to guide the flock. The word "shepherd" means a "leader" (Strong's Concordance, 1984) In the Bible it is the shepherd that leads. Jesus said, "My sheep hear My voice, and I know them, and they follow Me" (John 10:27 NKJV). The pastor is to guide or lead the flock. You know as well as I know that sometimes people have the idea that a church is a democracy. But the problem is, they did not get that idea from the Bible. A church is not a democracy, it is a theocracy. A church is a living organism that is led by God who call his shepherds. The Chief Shepherd is Jesus Christ and He calls His under-shepherds. The under-shepherd is to lead. What is sad is the fact that there are some churches where the shepherd is not the leader. The church members are telling the pastor what to preach, what to say, what to wear, and how to act; needless to say, they are not behaving like church members.

One more thing that a pastor is to do, he is to grow the sheep. You see, that is the idea behind feeding the flock. Let me be clear, "It is not the pastor's job to reproduce sheep!" The church may not be growing and the people will say, "We are not growing and what we need is to find a pastor who is a great soul-winning pastor, then we begin to see the people come in and we will be growing again." That is not what you need. Yes, it is true that a pastor should be out there along with all the church members soul winning, remember the pastor is to be the example (1 Pet. 5:3). Here is how you grow a church. There should be a man of God that stands in the pulpit of God. He is to open the Word of God, and in the Spirit of God, preach Jesus Christ. He is to build up the saints in the power of the Holy Spirit and Word of God will nurture the church members, which will result in healthy church members who are behaving as church members. When the church members are feed, they will begin to understand their spiritual gifts and begin to use them as they are growing since they are being feed by the pastor. And there should be unity and harmony in the church, a church that is vibrant and on fire for the Lord doing the ministry of the church by follow the great commission of Jesus Christ (Matt. 28:18-20).

THE TEST OF A PROPHET

Knowing how to use the gif of the discernment can be clearly seen in 1 John 4. John writes, "Beloved, do not believe every spirit, but test the spirits, whether they are of God; because many false prophets have gone out in the world" (1 John 4:1 NKJV). As you ponder on those first three words of verse 1, think about the wonderful things we need to believe, and in the Christian life we have what we call faith. "But without faith it is impossible to please Him" (Heb. 11:6 NKJV). Please understand, we are not told to be believer anything, because faith is no better that its origin or its object. Somehow, we get it in our heads the we are supposed to believe anything and everything because not only are we called sheep we are called believers. Faith is not deciding on what you want to believe and then believing it. Faith is getting a word from God and acting on His Word. John says that without faith it is impossible to please God and that mean it is very dangerous for a church member to live without faith. But did you know that it is also dangerous to believe and put your faith in the wrong thing (1 John 4:1)?

You see, John is warning us about false prophet that can come in to the church, and as we know from Paul, they can come in looking like sheep but are actually wolves (Acts 20:29). John also warned us, that everything spiritual is not of God. He said, "test the spirits, whether they are of God" (1 John 4:1 NKJV). The devil had rather get you to believe a wrong thing than do a wrong thing. Why? Because if he can get the wrong thoughts into your mind, then he does not have to worry about the deeds. Proverbs 23:7 says, "For as he thinks in his heart, so is he" (NKJV). If you sow a thought, then you are going to reap a deed. If you sow a deed, then you are going to reap a habit. If you sow a habit, then you are going reap a behavior. If you sow a behavior, then you are going to reap a destiny and this began with a thought. A false belief system, a false doctrine, or a false ritual is what the devil is trying to set up around you, through you, in the church, or where ever he can. Just as the Bible teaches us what to believe, it also teaches that we are not to believe every spirit (1 John 4:1). We are to test our faith. Why? Because, the faith that cannot be tested cannot be trusted. Paul writes, "Test all things; hold fast what is good" (1 Thess. 5:21 NKJV). Testing all things is so important in the day and age in which we live. We are constantly being bombarded with all kinds of ideologies. So, how do you test a prophet using the gift of the discernment? Let me give you some ways to test a prophet and whether or not he is of God and these shows us how to use the gift of discernment.

Let me first say that these tests do not have to be done in order, nor do they all have to be done, when testing the prophets and spirits. The first test we come to is, test prophets by their motive. Peter writes, "And many will follow their destructive ways, because of who the way of truth will be blasphemed. By covetousness they will exploit you with deceptive words; for a long time, their judgment has not been idle, and their destruction does not slumber" (2 Pet. 2:2-3 NKJV). False prophets tend to be those people who are covetous. Meaning they want to be the center of attention, want all the pats on the back, and all the accolades. The are capable of being a smooth talker, and make merchandise of gullible people. So, their motive to exploit people through finances, political issues, or your personality. Now they may not really care for the money or political power, but they want to show people that they are somebody.

The second test of a prophet is to test prophets by their method. In Jude's letter, he talks about false prophets and says, "For certain men have crept in unnoticed, who long ago were marked out for this condemnation, ungodly men, who turn the grace of our God into lewdness and deny the only Lord God and our Lord Jesus Christ" (Jude 1:4 NKJV). Jude points out that the method of false prophets is to creep in unnoticed. That is the thing with the teaching of a false prophet, it brings with it unbelief and false doctrine that can be very subtle and come in through the side door that no one sees it coming. It just creeps in. The method of the false prophet is very subtle, which mimics that of Satan in the garden of Eden. He is "more cunning that any beast of the field" (Gen. 3:1 NKJV). According to Jesus, the devil is a liar and the father of it (John 8:44). And the best lie sounds the most like the truth.

The third test of a prophet is to test prophets by their morals. Again, in Jude, we notice that phrase "who turn the grace of our God into lewdness" (Jude 1:4 NKJV). The word "lewdness" means "immoral" (Strong's Concordance, 1984) I had one Southern Baptist person, who had the audacity, to tell me that the reason they were Southern Baptist was because they were saved by grace and they could go out and live however they want to. That type of person is a person who has turned the grace of our God into lewdness. You cannot trust a false prophet by their morals.

The next test is to test prophets by their ministry. Jesus said, "Beware of false prophets, who come to you in sheep's clothing, but inwardly they are ravenous wolves. You will know them by their fruits. Do men gather grapes form thorn bushes or figs from thistles?" (Matt. 7:15-16 NKJV). From this test is the reason I can say that not all of these tests have to be performed to discern whether someone or some teaching is false. Because when you look at the fruit of a false prophet it will reveal what kind of doctrine they are teaching. Measure those who are following him they will behave and believe like the false prophet. False prophets who teach a false doctrine will only produce a false righteousness (Acts 20:29). Their fruit is the result of their ministry and it is a fruit that will not last. Their immoral lives and destructive teachings betray them. They magnify themselves not Jesus Christ.

Another test is test prophets by their message. This test it the best way to test them. "By this you know the Spirit of God: every spirit that confesses that Jesus Christ has come in the flesh is of God, and every spirit that does not confess that Jesus Christ has come in the flesh is not of God. And this is the spirit of the Antichrist, which you have heard was coming, and is not already in the world" (1 John 4:2-3 NKJV). When you look up that prefix "anti" it has a double meaning "against" and "instead of." (Concise Oxford English Dictionary Eleventh Edition, 2004) That is the way Satan operates, he works against Christ by bringing a substitute instead of Christ. We tend to think that Satan does like religion, but to the contrary religion is his chief tool or method of operation through which he offers misrepresentation. If you were to ask a false prophet, "Do you believe in Jesus?" and he says, "Of course I believe in Jesus." Paul warns us about being foolish when we start listening to someone tell you about another Jesus (2 Cor. 11:4). The gift of discernment will help in discovering the false prophet by their message.

We are to test prophets by the Word of God. John, one of the apostles, says, "We are of God. He who knows God hears us; he who is not of God does not hear us. By this we know the spirit of truth and the spirit of error" (1 John 4:6 NKJV). It was the apostles who were the ones that brought us the Word of God. John opens his letter up with this, "That which was from the beginning, which we have heard, which we have seen with our eyes, which we have looked upon, and our hands have handled, concerning the Word of life; the life manifested, and we have seen, and bear witness, and declare to you that eternal life which was with the Father and was manifested to us; that which we have seen and heard we declare to you, that you also may have fellowship with us; and truly our fellowship is with the Father and with His Son Jesus Christ" (1 John 1:1-3 NKJV). The apostles were the ones who saw and heard Jesus. They were anointed by Him to bring the Word of God. Paul says, that the church is squarely "built on the foundation of the apostles and prophets, Jesus Christ being the chief cornerstone" (Eph. 2:20 NKJV). The prophets wrote the Old Testament and the apostles wrote the New Testament. So, when you have a prophet or a spirit that comes along and starts teaching and moving in the church, how do you discern if they are teaching the truth? You discern by checking them out by the Word of God. How did Jesus deal with the devil? By using the Word of God. If you are to behave as church member and whether you have the gift of discernment or not, you need to get a firm handle on the Word of God. Because if you do not, then you are a sheep that has gone astray and you will be easy pickings for the false prophets, and you will not be able to test the spirits.

Test a false prophet by the Son of God. "By this you know the Spirit of God: every spirit that confesses that Jesus Christ has come in the flesh is of God, and every spirit that does not confess that Jesus Christ has come in the flesh is not of God. And this is the spirit of the Antichrist, which you have heard was coming, and is now already in the world" (1 John 4:2-3 NKJV). John is talking about Christmas, the Incarnation of Jesus; when He was born in Bethlehem. When God became a man, it was done in heaven. When Jesus put on humanity, it was not done here on earth, it was done in heaven. When He ascended into heaven, He took his humanity back with Him and now for all eternity He will be a man. Let that sink in, because as you study the book of Revelation you have to keep in mind that John was on the Island of Patmos when he wrote the book of the Revelation of Jesus Christ. John walked and talked with the Lord Jesus Christ. John has a vision while there and writes down what he saw. "Then I turned to see the voice that spoke with me. And having turned I saw seven golden lampstands, One like the Son of Man, clothed with a garment down to the feet and girded about the chest with a golden band" (Rev. 1:12-13 NKJV). John sees Jesus who became the Son of man that you and I might become sons and daughters of God. Jesus was born of a virgin that we might be born again. That is what Christmas is all about and if you do not understand that, then you are not going to understand Christmas. Therefore, if you do not accept the meaning of Christmas, John tells us that you are not of Christ, which would mean you are the spirit of the Antichrist. John says, "Beloved, do not believe every spirit, but test the spirits whether they are of God" (1 John 4:1 NKJV).

Finally, you test a false prophet by the Spirit of God. "You are of God, little children, and have overcome them, because He who is in you is greater than he who is in the world. They are of the world. Therefore, they speak as of the world, and the world hears them. We are of God. He who knows God hears us; he who is not of God does not hear us. By this we know the spirit of truth and the spirit of error" (1 John 4:4-6 NKJV). Solomon says, "a threefold cord is not quickly broken" (Eccl. 4:12 NKJV) and the threefold cord which we have is the Word of God, the Son of God, and the Spirit of God. When you put these together you can take the Bible along with the gift of discernment and understand the subtleties of the false prophet. However, let me say that you are never going to understand the Bible unless you read it, pray on it, and meditate on the Bible. Just FYI, the word "meditate" means to "mutter" (Strong's Concordance, 1984) and if the Bible is not speaking to you, it is because you are not letting the Holy Spirit teach you. Jesus warned, "For false christs and false prophets will rise and show great signs and wonders to deceive, if possible, even the elect. See, I have told you beforehand" (Matt. 24:24-25 NKJV).

These are the test that we need to perform to test the spirts and the prophets. The gift of discernment aids in know the truth. Once we learn the truth, we are to help our fellow brothers and sisters in Christ see the truth. Because, if it were possible the devil would be able to deceive even the children of God. We are to behave as church members.

CHAPTER ELEVEN

STIRRING UP GOD'S PEOPLE

When he came and had seen the grace of God, he was glad,
and encouraged them all that with purpose of heart they
should continue with the Lord. (Acts 11:23 NKJV)

One of the great tragedies of our time is the fact there are so few enthusiastic people around. Take for example the women that heard that Jesus is not here, His risen! In Matthew 28:8 notice their reaction, "So they went quickly from the tomb with fear and great joy, and ran to bring His disciples word" (NKJV). These women were "receivers" and "transmitters" of the resurrection message. Each Church member should behave as a church member by receiving and transmitting God's word. Remember, we have been commissioned by God to go and make disciples and do evangelism. It is a great responsibility and privilege of each church member to share the message of salvation with a lost and dying world. God has chosen the body of Christ to be His heralds, His messengers in these perilous times. The fact that we are God's children does not excuse us from the work of sounding forth the Gospel message. We need more enthusiastic church members to share the message and make disciples. "Did you know that a bee's stinger is 1/16th of an inch long? The rest of what you feel is enthusiasm!" (2019) Are you a church member with enthusiasm? The gift of exhortation encourages believers to be involved and enthusiastic about the ministry of the church. Those who have this gift are typically good at being counselors and motivators.

Now you do not have to be enthusiastic to be an encourager, but it helps. If there was ever a day in which we were to behave as a church member it would be in our day where there seems to be so many mean-spirited, hateful people. I believe that every church member ought to be more kind to one another. "And be kind to one another, tenderhearted, forgiving one another, even as God in Christ forgave you" (Eph. 4:32 NKJV). In our society, there are many people who are opinionated, self-centered, rude, and just plain mean. Our Lord and Savior Jesus Christ would want us to behave by practicing the ministry of encouragement, especially in these perilous last days we live in.

In Acts 4:36 we are introduced to a man by the name Joses. We know him better by the name Barnabas. When this man appeared on the scene in the early days of the church, he stepped out of obscurity doing good, and when he stepped off the stage a few years later; he exited doing good. The Bible's record of this man's life and ministry reveals for us as a man who had a heart to do good to all with whom he came in contact. Barnabas is someone who can be seen as an encourager as a matter of fact in the King James Version the verse reads, "And Joses, who by the apostles was surnamed Barnabas, (which is, being interpreted, The son of consolation,) a Levite and of the country of Cyprus" (Acts 4:36 KJV). In the New King James Version it reads, "(which is translated Son of Encouragement)" (Acts 4:36 NKJV). Not the word "consolation" comes from the same word that is translated "Comforter", (Strong's Concordance, 1984) and refers to the Holy Spirit (John 14:26). A comforter is someone who comes alongside of another person to offer help and encouragement. This is the reputation Barnabas had gained among the disciples, as he helped and encouraged other believers. So, how do you become an encourager? How do you stir up church members? In this chapter we are going to look at two individuals; Barnabas has already been introduced, the second one is the prophet Haggai.

Let me give you a little background on Haggai. When the foundation of the temple was laid in Jerusalem in the year 536 B.C., the young men shouted for joy while the old men wept (Ezra 3:8-13). Although Haggai probably seen Solomon's temple in its glory days (Hag. 2:3), he was undoubtedly among those who expressed joy for the Lord was at work among His people. However, it did not take long for the zeal to cool off and God's people to grow apathetic, especially when opposition begins to growl and then turn into a roar. Those shouts of joy awakened the enemies of the Jews, it aroused the officials of the opposition, and it caused the work to stop (Ezra 4:1-6). The temple then remained unfinished from 536 B.C. to 520 B.C., when Haggai and Zechariah brought God's message to Zerubbabel and Joshua. In chapter one of the book of Haggai, he gave four admonitions (encouragement messages) to the leaders and to the people to get them back working on finishing the temple.

These two show us how to stir up church members by using the gift of encouragement. You know we need some admonitions from God time to time. We need someone to encourage us to behave as church members. We need someone who will stir us up to get about the work that Jesus has commissioned us to do. Have you ever mixed water and oil together? What happens after it sits there for a while? Maybe a better example you can relate to is Italian dressing. What do you have to do to it before you can use it? Well, just like water and oil, the bottle of Italian dressing has to be stirred up. This is what these two men did. So here is how to stir up church members.

YOU MUST LEARN TO REACH OUT

Barnabas show us that we need to reach out to others by encouraging someone who was desperate. After Saul was converted, he tried to unite himself with the other disciples who were in Jerusalem, but out of fear and prejudice about his past, they were afraid to allow him into their group. However, Barnabas came to Saul's side and stood up for him and told the others about Saul's conversion (Acts 9:26-27). Today in the church there is still a need for this kind of ministry. We need to make the effort and take the time to reach out to those around us who seem to be lonely or who have been rejected by others. We need to behave as church member by doing our best to make everyone who comes to our church feel as if they belong and are accepted just as they are. We need to love them and welcome them and accept them into the flock.

Barnabas even encouraged the new converts (Acts 11:22-23). When the church in Jerusalem heard that there was a new group of believers in Antioch, they sent Barnabas to them to help them along. "When he came and has seen the grace of God, he was glad, and encouraged them all that with purpose of heart they should continue with the Lord" (Acts 11:23 NKJV). Barnabas was excited about what God was doing and how these new church members were serving the Lord and he did his best to encourage them to carry on the work of God. We ought to do everything in our power to encourage other believers in their walk with the Lord. We need to praise others when they labor for Jesus and gently rebuke our brothers when they stray. Our duty to our fellow believers is to help them to grow in the Lord and be an encouragement to them. "Therefore, let us pursue the things which make for peace and the things by which one may edify another" (Rom. 14:19 NKJV). That word "edify" means "to lift up" (Strong's Concordance, 1984) When you lift someone up, you are encouraging them or motivating them. The gift of encouragement helps the church member to behave by coming along side someone and lifting them up.

Barnabas also reached out by encouraging those who were discouraged. Paul, Barnabas, and John Mark were together on a missionary journey, and for some reason John Mark left them and returned to Jerusalem (Acts 13:13). When Paul and Barnabas get ready to go out again, Barnabas wants to take John Mark to give him a second chance. However, Paul disagrees with Barnabas, and the two of them part way (Acts 15:36-40). Paul takes Silas and goes out with him, while Barnabas take John Mark and disappears from the biblical account. While Barnabas is never heard from again, his ministry to John Mark had far reaching results. Because Barnabas gave the discouraged John Mark a second chance, his life as a servant of God was salvaged. In fact, before Paul died in Rome, he requested that Mark be sent to him (2 Tim. 4:11). Even more important is the fact that because Barnabas took the time to encourage a discouraged brother, Mark was used of the Lord to pen the Gospel of Mark which give us an exciting account of the life and ministry of the Lord Jesus Christ. We need to behave as church members by displaying the grace of the good Samaritan.

You must Learn to Reach Up

The encourager uses his spiritual gifts and love for the Lord and the Lord's people to see that the work of the Lord is carried out in this world. Barnabas was an encourager who promoted the work of God by giving of himself freely. He gave of his goods to see that the church and its work went on (Acts 4:37). He used the things at his disposal to enhance the work of the Lord. This describes how we out to behave as church members as well. We ought to all strive to give our time, our tithes, and our talents so the church can prosper and the burden of ministry does not rest upon the shoulders of one or two. When we give of ourselves and our stuff as we should, others are then encouraged to do the same.

Barnabas was in awe of God's work that was being done, he gave great praise to the work of God (Acts 11:23). When Barnabas had seen all the Lord was doing in Antioch, he set out to find Paul and to share the news with him. Barnabas refused to keep the good blessings of God quiet! There is a need for this kind of behavior in the church. There are far too many who want to bad mouth the church and the church members. There are church members who will, when things do not go their way, they will get mad and go around town running down the church. There are some church members who will behave badly enough to even threaten to withhold their tithes. They are behaving like a little child trying to hold his breath; which by the way, we all know that if they hold it long enough, they will pass out. Listen, threatening to withhold your tithes will not hurt the church. God does not need your money to keep the church open. No one person can close a church. Jesus said to Peter, "And I also say to you that you are Peter, and on this rock, I will build My church, and the gates of Hades shall not prevail against it" (Matt. 16:18 NKJV). Jesus called it

His church. We need to praise God that He is still the one in control of His church and the work of the church. We need to go out into the world and brag on what Jesus is doing! We need to encourage one another with testimony services, good prayer meetings. We need tell of people getting saved, tell others about backsliders getting thing right with God. Listen, there are enough whiners and bellyachers; we need some who will exalt the work of God.

Barnabas was chosen by the Holy Spirit to be actively involved in the Lord's work because Barnabas made himself available to Jesus. God's call upon his life was something that changed his life forever. From that moment on, everywhere Barnabas went, he was a servant of the Lord. The lesson for us is obvious! No matter where we go in this world, we are the servants of the Lord. We are to make ourselves available to do whatever he asks us to do. He called me to preach, and I surrendered to the call. He leads me to pastor this church, just as He leads me to leave and go to another church. I have never been disappointed in what God has instore for me. However, in school I did not like writing at all, down right hated it. But through the years of being as faithful as I could and God blessing, I would have never dreamed that God would call me to write books. Therefore, whether we are at home, at work, in town, on vacation, etc., we are God's servants and we are to make ourselves available to God and live and behave accordingly. When we do, we serve as an encouragement to other to do the same. When we serve the Lord with enthusiasm and zeal, we stand as an encouragement to others. Therefore, when it comes time to go to church and do our part for God, arrive on time, arrive alert, arrive prepared, and arrive excited and ready to worship and serve Jesus our Lord and Savior. Wherever you go, especially at church show people how much you enjoy what you are doing and if you do not enjoy it, as the Lord to restore your joy, or simply find another job through which you can serve Him!

FINISH THE WORK OF GOD

Let me encourage with this, as an encourager you are to finishes the work that God calls you to do. Do not just start something, say you will do that job, or serve here and not finish the work that needs to be done. Listen to Acts 12:25, "And Barnabas and Saul returned from Jerusalem when they had fulfilled their ministry, and they also took with them John whose surname was Mark" (NKJV). Paul and Barnabas both finished their ministry. They stayed with the ministry work until it was finished. As a result, they stood as an encouragement to those around them! If you want your life to be an encouragement to those who watch you serving the Lord, then never leave a job unfinished. Be faithful, diligent to the task God has called you to and stick by God, walk with God, trust in God, until He calls you to a new job, or until He calls you home! There is no room for quitting in the work of the Lord. It is an encouragement to me to see people sticking with the Lord through all the times of their life. It is a blessing and gives me a deeper desire to press on towards the prize (Phil. 3:14).

YOU MUST LEARN TO REACH IN

If you are going to behave as a church member using the gift of encouragement then you need to demonstrate Christ by your life you live. "So, when they heard that, they raised their voice to God with one accord and said: "Lord, You are God, who made heaven and earth and the sea, and all that is in them…" (Acts 4:24 NKJV). This verse indicates that Barnabas was a genuine man of God. He possessed all the characteristics that marked him as being surrendered, sold out, and on fire for the Lord Jesus Christ. His life served as an encouragement to holiness by being holy and blameless. Our lives should stand as an encouragement to lead others deeper into their walk with Jesus. We do this by getting ourselves as close to God as we can. When others see the Lord working in and through our lives, they will be challenged and encouraged to seek the Lord for themselves and to become more like Him.

Also, an encourager is going to display contentment in his life. Barnabas, along with Paul, was preaching the Word of God. "And the word of the Lord was being spread throughout all the region" (Acts 13:49 NKJV). As a result, persecution arose against them and they were forced to leave town. Instead of being discouraged and quitting as many others would have done, they shook the dust from their feet and went on their way rejoicing (Acts 13:50-51). That is what is going to bring encouragement to fellow church members who are going through great battles in life. We show true depth of our faith, when we behave as church members when we are in the valley. We show how real our faith in God is by how we react to difficulty and hardship. We should seek to react to adversity by expressing joy and faith in the Lord (Job 1:20-21). When we do, we will behave as church members and be an encouragement to those around us. Our faith and joy will help them when they face their dark day.

PUT GOD FIRST IN YOUR LIVES

Haggai, just like Barnabas, was an encourager. While the similarities between the two closely resemble each other, each one had their own approach. Remember Haggai is trying to encourage the people of Israel to get back to work rebuilding the temple. "Thus speaks the Lord of hosts, saying: 'This people says, "The time has not come, the time that the Lord's house should be built"'" (Hag. 1:2 NKJV). When Haggai spoke his first message to the people, he begins by speaking right to the heart of the problem and exposes their hypocrisy and their unbelief. He points out three problematic areas of the people.

EXCUSES

The first problem the children of Israel had was their excuses. From verse 2, we notice that they said that it was not time to rebuild the house of the Lord. This is nothing more than an excuse to explain why they had not been working on building the house of God. Do you know what an excuse is? An excuse is the skin of reason stuffed with a lie. Let me just say, to behave as church member you need to quit making excuse for the reason you are not fulfilling the Great Commission, serving in the church, going to church, worshiping, singing, praying, reading your Bible, tithing.

In one of those times when my dad was in between pastoring churches and I was a teenager, we were members of Third Baptist Church in Murfreesboro, TN. The church was busting at the seams. They already had two Sunday morning services and was toying with the idea of a third.

One Wednesday night at a business meeting, the subject was brought up of starting a building campaign called "Together We Build". The floor was open for discussion on the subject building a new sanctuary. You should have heard some of the excuses the people offered for not wanting to build. "The economy is not good at this time." "If we build, we might lose some of our members because they do not want to deal with the construction." One person said, "What if the pastor leaves us in the middle of the building program? It would be tragic if there is a building program without a leader." They put the matter to a secret ballot vote. I voted no, because even I had my excuse. I was a teenager and did not really care for change at that time. Nevertheless, the building project passed with over whelming majority. God led us through and that church has a beautiful sanctuary and God saw them through. We need to quit making excuses and start putting more faith, more trust, and more dependency on God. This is what Haggai was trying to encourage the people about as the temple lay unfinished.

EVIDENCE

God had moved upon the heart of King Cyrus of Persia to let the children of Israel, who were captives of the Babylonian empire, go back to their land. He also commissioned them to rebuild the temple and then gave them the money and all the materials they need for the rebuilding project. That should have been evidence enough to know what they should have been doing. However, God provided more evidence for the children of Israel. He protected them as they carried all that King Cyrus had given them as they went back to Judah. God had told them to go build the temple. He even had the prophet Isaiah record information about Cyrus. "Who says of Cyrus, 'He is My shepherd, and he shall perform all My pleasure, saying to Jerusalem, "You shall be built," and to the temple, "Your foundation shall be laid"'" (Isa. 44:28 NKJV). Isaiah later said this about Cyrus, "I have raised him up in righteousness, and I will direct all his ways; he shall build My city and let My exiles go free, not for price nor reward" (Isa. 45:13 NKJV). What evidence! What more did they need to prove that it was time to build God's house and restore worship in Jerusalem?

Because actions speaks louder than words, their behavior to stop building the temple proved they did not have any faith in God, His word, nor His ability to see them through.

What more evidence does the children of God need to behave as a church member today? We have God's Word that was divinely inspired. We have His promises, that will never fail. We have the blessed assurance, the blessed hope, His salvation. We have His Holy Spirit living inside us, guiding us, protecting us, giving us spiritual gifts. Yet we behave as though we do trust God nor want to obey God. Yes, it is true that there are prophecies that we do not fully understand yet nor have they occurred. The same could be said of the children of Israel as to why they refused to obey God and build the temple. They had the prophecy from Jeremiah and Isaiah that one day the nation of Israel would be restored and would amaze the other nations. They could not understand those promises would be fulfilled in the end times, because they were only looking at their present situation. Their situation caused them to even question the dependability of God's Word. We behave the same way. Therefore, Haggai was in encouraging them to look at the correct evidence.

EVASION

So, the people would use the excuse that it was not time to build God's house, however, there was some discrepancies in their excuses because it seems they had enough time to build their own houses. They did not build just any ordinary house or dwellings, but "paneled houses" (Hag.1:3). Now in those days, when some built panel houses it usually meant that they were wealthy. They would build these houses to impress the king or keep up appearance or stay in good social standing with the upper crust of society. The children of Israel had their priorities all wrong. Jesus said, "But seek first the kingdom of God and His righteousness, and all these things shall be added to you" (Matt. 6:33 NKJV). "These things" implies food, clothing, shelter the necessities of life. Haggai's congregation never heard Jesus speak those words, but it is possible that he could have used the law to encourage them to get to work (Lev. 26:3-13; Deut. 16:17; 28:1-14; 30:3-9).

Now it is obvious that the people of Israel were not all that discouraged, they just had misplaced their priorities. The same is thing is happening to church members, they misbehave because they do not have their priorities in order. Local churches cannot expand their budgets and set aside money for evangelism because the people are not giving like they should. The reason could be that the members are behaving like they just do not believe what Jesus said in Matthew 6:33, therefore they do not place God first when comes to tithing. If we were to measure the Christians in the western world by third world standards, then Christians in the western world would be living a life of luxury. However, Christians in the western world have low giving and high debt, because they are giving their money to things that do not matter.

But is it not funny how we always come up with reasons as to why we cannot serve God, but find the time and the money to serve ourselves? Someone put it this way: "Isn't it strange how twenty dollars seems like such a large amount when you donate it to the church, but such a small amount when you go shopping? Isn't it strange how two hours seems so long when you are at church, and how short they seem when you are watching a good movie. Isn't it strange you cannot find a word to say when you are praying, but you have no trouble thinking what to talk about with a friend? Isn't it strange how difficult and boring it is to read one chapter of the Bible, but how easy it is to read one hundred pages of your favorite book? Isn't it strange how everyone wants front-row-tickets to concerts or games, but they do whatever possible to sit at the back row in church? Isn't it strange how we need to know about a church event three weeks in advance so we can include it in our agenda, but we adjust it for other events in the last minute? Isn't it strange how difficult it is to learn to share a truth about God with others, but how easy it is to learn, understand, extend, and repeat gossip? Isn't it strange how we believe everything the magazines and newspaper say, but we question the words in the Bible?" (Unknown, 2015) As an encourage you are to behave as a church member by putting God first. The children of Israel had failed to do so, but perhaps that is why God inspired Haggai to write the phrase "Consider your ways" (Hag. 1:5 NKJV)!

BELIEVE GOD'S PROMISES

The second encouragement that Haggai gave the people was to invite them to examine how they were living and examine their behavior towards God's covenant with Israel as they entered the Promised Land (Lev. 26; Deut. 27-28). "Now therefore, thus says the Lord of hosts: "Consider your ways" (Hag. 1:5 NKJV). The word "consider" means "to give careful thought to" (Strong's Concordance, 1984) Haggai was encouraging the people to do so serious self-examination before the Lord. If you study the covenant between God and Israel it clearly states: if Israel obeyed the Lord, then He would bless them; if they disobey, then He would discipline them (Lev. 26:18-20). Certainly, this covenant promise would be encouragement to obey the Lord, however, from the Bible we know they did not always obey. While in the Promised Land, they would sow their fields but would only bring a skimpy harvest. When they would go to eat and drink in their homes, they found themselves never satisfied. Their clothes would never keep them warm; they could never bring in enough income to pay their bills. And it seemed as though they were keeping their money in wallets with holes as inflation of the economy got worse. This is the opposite of what happen as they depended upon the Lord in their wilderness wonderings.

How many times has the church put on evangelism events and seen meager results? How many times has the church put on Vacation Bible School and seen meager results? How many times has the church been knocking on doors and seen meager results? How many times have you given your tithes and offering and seen nothing in return?

Haggai had to be an encourager because he was dealing with people who was returning back to their land in obedience to the Lord and they began to think that He would give them special treatment because of their sacrifices. Boy, were they behaving badly. What happened is God brought a drought upon the land, which means there was no rain and there was no dew. Because they disobeyed Him, He took His blessings away from those who worked really hard in the fields, vineyards, and orchards. He even went as far as to stop blessing their water, grain, wine, and oil (Hag. 1:11). The reason for all the people's problems, Haggai again pointed it out, "You looked for much, but indeed it came to little; and when you brought it home, I blew it away. Why? Says the Lord of hosts. Because of My house that is in ruins, while every one of you runs to his own house" (vs. 9 NKJV). They did not believe in the promises of God, because if they had then they would have enjoyed His blessings (Matt. 6:33). Our obedience to God should be based on faith and love. The giving our tithe and offerings should never be treated as though it is some kind of business arrangement. If the reason you give is because you believe it pays to give, then guess what it will not. Listen, nowhere in the Bible will you find that God made a "prosperity covenant" with the people. As a matter of fact, Jesus said, "Blessed are the poor in spirit, for theirs is the kingdom of heaven" (Matt. 5:3 NKJV). You can behave as a church member by being an encourager and meeting the needs of others, because you believe God's promises that He will meet your needs (Phil. 4:10-20).

HONOR GOD'S NAME

"Thus says the Lord of hosts: "Consider your ways! Go up to the mountains and bring wood and build the temple, that I may take pleasure in it and be glorified," says the Lord" (Hag. 1:7-8 NKJV). As an encourager you want to do everything you can to bring honor to God's Holy name. One way you do this is by being encourager, God gifts you the things you need in life (Phil. 4:19). You, in turn, encourage others when you use His gifts for His glory. Over in Ezra 3:7, he tells us that the Jews would go to Tyre and Sidon to purchase the wood to build the temple. Later, Solomon would do the same thing when he built the temple (1 Kings 5:6-12). However, here we see Haggai having to encourage the people to go to the mountains, into the forests to cut down trees to rebuild the temple. This should make you scratch your head, because what happened to the supply of wood? Is it possible that the people used it for building their houses? Or perhaps some businessman sold it off and pocketed the money? Because we do not know what happened to the wood, it does however, make you begin to speculate where the people got the material to build their fancy houses; while God's house lay in shambles.

Did you know that there are some professing Christians that buy the best for themselves and give to the Lord whatever is left over? Worn-out furniture is given to the church and worn-out clothing is sent to the missionaries. Just like the priest in Malachi's day, we bring the Lord gifts we would be embarrassed to give to our family and friends (Mal. 1:6-8). But when we do this, we actually commit two sins: we displease the Lord and we disgrace His name. The Lord encouraged the people through Haggai by saying, "that I may take pleasure in it and be glorified,' says the Lord" (Hag. 1:8 NKJV). God delights in the obedient service of His people, and His name is glorified when we sacrifice for Him and serve Him.

Haggai gave his encouraging word to the people on August 29, 520 B.C. but it was not until September 21 that the people actually got started on the rebuilding the temple. That means it took three weeks before the work started. Why? As an encourager you need to get a grasp on this reason, or you can quickly become discouraged. For one thing, Haggai's message was given during the time of harvesting figs and grapes. Therefore, the people did not want to lose their crop. Furthermore, they did not start right away rebuilding the temple because they would have to remove all the debris from the temple site. They needed to take inventory of their supplies. They would have to schedule work crews. Plus, in order for the work and the workers to be pleasing to the Lord they probably took the time to confess their sins and purify themselves. Listen, it takes time before a ministry can get off the ground. And as an encourage do not become discouraged in the early stages of the work. Instead behave as a church member and be an encourager like Barnabas and Haggai.

CHAPTER TWELVE

BE STRONG AND COURAGEOUS

Only be strong and very courageous, that you may observe to do according to all the law which Moses My servant commanded you; do not turn from it to the right hand or to the left, that you may prosper wherever you go. (Joshua 1:7 NKJV)

Our next spiritual gift that we come to is the gift of shepherding. This gift is displayed in Christians who watch out for the spiritual welfare of others. Yes, typically pastors, who is like a shepherd, do care for the members of the church, however, this gift is not limited to a pastor or staff member. When Jesus described His people, He called them sheep. If you remember from chapter ten of this book, sheep are not the brightest animals to ever appear on the earth. In fact, they have a reputation for being quite silly! They are unwise and they are defenseless! They require a shepherd to care for them. They require a shepherd to protect them. They require someone who will look after their smallest needs and who will lead them to where they need to be. When Jesus calls us sheep, it may not be flattering, but it is right on target!

Since sheep are so needy, they end up forming a special bond with their shepherd. He is required to get to know them intimately. He knows the ones who are prone to wander. He knows the weaker ones. He knows the loyal ones too. He even knows them all by name. The sheep, despite their unintelligence, becomes familiar with the voice of the shepherd. They know his sound and his smell. There is a bond between sheep and the shepherd that just is not found anywhere else in the world of agriculture. If church members would ever come to understand this, then being called sheep isn't such a bad thing. If church members could ever understand this bond, then we could begin to behave as church members.

In chapter four, we discovered that Joshua had great leadership skills because he was the image of a shepherd. Joshua was shepherd because he had to look out for the welfare of the children of Israel and get them ready to cross over the Jordan River (Josh. 1:1-18). The crossing of the Jordan River has been equated to that of the believer dying and going to heaven. However, when we get to heaven, there will be no more wars, no more enemies, no more suffering or death, and no more sin. All of these things are present in the book of Joshua and dealt with in its pages. No, Canaan Land is not Heaven. The land of Canaan is brilliant picture of the victorious Christian life that is available to every child of God, every church member. It is a picture of victory in the midst of struggle. The events recorded in the book of Joshua have to do with the life of God's people and not their death!

In our day and age, there are many misunderstandings surrounding the Christian life. A trip to the local Christian bookstore, or searching an online bookstore shows us there are books which claim to be able to teach us how to make the Christian life easier for the believer and the church more acceptable to the world. The truth of the matter is, there is nothing easy or acceptable about the Christian life. It is not always easy to behave for Jesus. The Gospel of Jesus Christ will never be acceptable to the world. The church member, the genuine saved child of God, life is not a walk in the park. We do not live and work on a playground; we are on a battleground! As church members we are engaged in warfare with a spiritual enemy who is far more powerful than we are. "For we do not wrestle against flesh and blood, but against the rulers of the darkness of this age, against spiritual hosts of wickedness in the heavenly places" (Eph. 6:12 NKJV). In our own strength, we cannot defeat our enemies! The good news is the fact that our enemies are nowhere near as powerful as our God! "You are of God, little children, and have overcome them, because He who is in you is greater than he who is in the world" (1 John 4:4 NKJV). Therefore, even in the midst of our battles, there is always hope for victory (Rom. 8:31, 37). In fact, the Bible tells us, we are the recipients of victory through the Lord Jesus Christ (1 Cor. 15:57). While we are engaged in the battle with evil, there is the expectation that we can and will walk in victory in our lives and it is all because we have the Shepherd. We can behave as church members because of Jesus is the good Shepherd (John 10:14). The good Shepherd gives us the Holy Spirit, who gives us those who have the gift of shepherding. We can see this gift in Joshua.

God made a promise to Moses in Exodus 33:14, "And He said, My Presence will go with you, and I will give you rest." (NKJV) The Jews certainly had no rest in Egypt or during their wilderness wanderings, but in the Promise Land God would give them rest. Moses later reminds the Israelites of God's promise in his farewell address by saying, "For as yet you have not come to the rest and the inheritance which the Lord your God is giving you" (Deut. 12:9 NKJV). After forty years of wandering in the wilderness, Israel is about to take possession of the land God promised Abraham many centuries earlier (Gen. 12:7). The Canaan rest is a picture of the rest that Christian believers, church members experience when they yield their all to the good Shepherd and claim their inheritance by faith. The gift of shepherding helps those who are struggling spiritual. The person who has this gift watches out for spiritual welfare of other sheep. As we take a look at Joshua as an example of this spiritual gift may it help us to behave as church members by being strong and courageous.

GOD'S CALL

After the death of Moses, God calls upon Joshua to get up and go into the land that God has given them (Josh. 1:1-4). Again, let me remind you, Canaan represents the Christian life as it should be; which includes conflict and victory, faith and obedience, spiritual riches and rest. It is a life of faith, always trusting in Jesus who leads us from victory to victory through conflict. Because you cannot have victory over something is there was no conflict in the first place. Here Joshua 1, Moses, the man of God is dead, but the work of God goes on. This is a reason we need to behave as church member being faithful to the service of God. God can use you as you make yourself available to Him. Joshua made himself available to God and God commanded him to lead the people into Canaan to claim the land which was promised and given by the Lord. The land was theirs there was no need for them to continue wandering around in the wilderness. They have a land and all they need to do is go in and claim it!

We are seeing today, church members who are behaving as though they are defeated. Church members who are struggling with sins and allowing them to keep them in bondage. There are church members who for all intent and purposes are wandering around in a spiritual wilderness. It does not have to be that way! God has a place of victory and He as promised us that we can live in that place of peace and blessing. I believe with all my heart that God did not save me to see me to behave and live a defeated life. He came that I might have life and have it more abundantly (John 10:10)! However, most of the time, the reason we behave as though we are defeated is because we refuse to walk in victory. I believe there is a place of conquest for every child of God, but I also believe there a place of victory for every child of God to go in and grab hold of promises that God has given you.

Joshua is reminded of some very precious promises. "No man shall be able to stand before you all the days of your life; as I was with Moses, so I will be with you. I will not leave you nor forsake you. Be strong and of good courage, for to this people you shall divide as an inheritance the land which I swore to their fathers to give them" (Josh. 1:5-6 NKJV). So, Joshua was promised victory over every enemy, the presence and power of God, the faithfulness of God, absolute victory, and that God would keep His promises. What did Joshua have to do to make things happen? Just one thing: Trust in God! God was going to give Israel the victory. Joshua was merely the instrument that God had chosen to use to do it. These things were going to happen! For Joshua to be a part of it, all he had to do was have faith in God! As shepherd this would be important because not only is he setting an example before the people, but he is also watching out for the spiritual welfare of the people. Furthermore, you and I have the same promises from God which He made to Joshua. You can count on the Lord to do everything He promised Joshua. What do we have to do to see these promises come to pass in our lives? Just one thing: trust God! When we can learn to place our faith in God at all times in every situation, and then we will walk in victory in our lives. When everything else fails, faith will ever stand the test (Heb. 11:1).

As someone who has the gift of shepherding, Joshua was called upon to lead the people to the place of rest that God was giving them in Canaan. However, God tells Joshua that when they go, they must take the Law of God with them (Josh. 1:7-8). If you are going to be strong and courageous and behave as a church member, then your strength and courage is going to come from meditation on the Word of God, believing its promises, and obeying its precepts. This was the counsel Moses had given to all the people, and now God was applying it specifically to Joshua, His under-shepherd. But notice what the Lord told Joshua about the Law and how this applies to our lives today. First, he was to keep the law by doing everything the law said to do, not turning from it the least little bit. Next, he was to meditate on the law, day and night. His mind was to be occupied with the law. He was to love it and let it fill his heart and mind. The reason, so his life might be centered in the law and therefore in the will of God. Another thing that Joshua was to do, he was to prosper by honoring the law. God's promised to Joshua was that if he lived his life around the law of God, then God would prosper him in everything he did and that God would make him very successful. Here is the lesson for us today: we are no longer under the law thanks to Jesus's death upon the cross we are now under grace. There are those who say that since we are no longer under the law, then the child of God is free to do anything he or she pleases. That kind of behavior is dangerous and is a guarantee to bring about ruin. If you want to behave as a church member today, then you must develop a love for the Word of God. Just as Joshua, a picture of a shepherd, was commanded to honor the law, we are commanded to honor the Word of God. Be strong and courageous as a church member to set aside each day to study, read, and meditate on the Word of God.

The gift of shepherding is manifested in pastors or leaders in the church, this was certainly true in the life of Joshua. He was called to be courageous in leadership. Three times Joshua was given the phrase "be strong and courageous" by God (Josh. 1:6-7, 9). These words carry the idea of "standing firm and strong in the face of opposition." (Strong's Concordance, 1984) Joshua would need great courage to face the enemies of Israel and to lead the people to victory in the Promised Land. God's challenge to Joshua is for him to stand! There is just as great a need for people today to stand for the Lord as there was in the days of Joshua! All around us, Christian, church members, children of God, are falling by the wayside. What we need is for God's children to be moved in the depths of their souls to stand up, renew their commitments to the Lord and say, "By God's help, I will stand and not fall all the days of my life!" We need people today who will take the lead, who have been gifted by the Holy Spirit with spiritual gifts, to make their stand for the Lord. It is high time that the church member stop serving as doormats for the world and the devil. It is time we behave as church members and stand together, work together, serve together with the spiritual gifts that God has given each church member. And those with the gift of shepherding is time you stand up for the things of God and encourage the spiritual walks of the church members to be right with Jesus Christ. We need men and women of courage, conviction, and integrity. Are you standing of the Lord? Or, have you fallen out along the way?

JOSHUA'S CHALLENGE

After shepherd Joshua receives his command from the Lord, without hesitation, he goes to the people and tells them that the time has come to take their land. "Then Joshua commanded the officers of the people, saying, "Pass through the camp and command the people saying, 'Prepare provisions for yourselves, for within three days you will cross over this Jordan, to go inn to possess the land which the Lord your God is giving you to possess'"" (Josh. 1:10-11 NKJV). These were the words they have been waiting to hear for forty years. However, before they could go in, they had to get ready. God told them to prepare some food for the journey, because the manna was about to stop. God told them that He would give the manna while they were in the desert, but it would cease when they entered the Promised Land (Ex. 16:35). The manna was desert diet, now they were about to move up to something a whole lot better. The person with the gift of shepherding is watching out for the spiritual welfare of others as well as their growth in their walk with Christ. The children of Israel were about to go into a land that flowed with milk and honey. What had worked in the wilderness would not suffice in the land of blessing. Before we can enter our Canaan, we have to make the proper preparations. The way we live must be changed. The things we feed on must change. Our priorities and passions must be brought in line with the will of God. The entire scope of our lives must be altered to adjust to living differently than the world around us. This is why so many never enjoy the victorious Christian life. They simply refuse to make the necessary changes to adjust to living and behaving in spiritual victory. The fact is, if you expect to walk in victory, then you have to learn to walk by an entirely new set of rules. "Therefore, we were buried with Him through baptism into death, that just as Christ was raised from the dead by the glory of the Father, even so we also should walk in the newness of life" (Rom. 6:4 NKJV).

Shepherd Joshua also challenges Israel to fulfill their responsibility (Josh. 1:12-15). In these verses, Joshua addresses the tribes of Rueben, Gad, and the half tribe of Manasseh. These tribes had sought, and gotten, permission from Moses to remain east of the Jordan, just outside of the Promised Land. Why did they make this request? Because the land east of the Jordan River was a land that was good for raising cattle (Num. 32:1, 4, 16). Still, Joshua reminds them that they had promised to fight alongside their brethren until the land was conquered (Deut. 3:12-20). These people are challenged to remember their promise and to aid the nation until victory was secured. While these people settled in a land of prosperity, they were also in a land of danger. Later, these tribes would be the first to go away into captivity, when the Assyrian army attacked Israel from the east.

There is a powerful lesson for those who have the gift of shepherding. You need to keep watch over those church members who are just like these two and a half tribes of Israel. Those church members are more concerned about making a living than they are about behaving as a follower of Christ. The primary thing that motivates them is getting ahead in life. In other words, they are materially minded, not spiritually minded. They are those church members who sit on the fringe, on the fence and those with the shepherding gift need to watch out for their spiritual welfare. These church members are people who have trusted Jesus for salvation, but that is as far as they are willing to go. They attend church when they want to or when it is convenient. They give and tithe when the feel like they can afford to. They may even fight a battle now and then, but for the most part they just play around the edges of their Christian walk, refusing to put God first in their lives. They need to be watched over because they are usually the first to fall in times of attack, temptation, and strife.

People who live like this can say anything they want to, but the truth is obvious; they have other gods in their lives to whom they worship. A shepherd will help them to see, that if we really love God, we need make up our minds to cross over, come off the fence, into the place of victory which the Lord has prepared for us. Those with the gift of shepherding can set the example of behaving as a church member by making the decision to leave behind anything that is holding you back from serving God like you should. And helping others see, that if you refuse to line up with the will of God for your life, then you can be assured of the fact you will fall. We cannot play around the edges if we are going to behave as church members.

HOW THE SHEPHERD ENCOURAGES HIS SHEEP

The 23rd psalm is a well-beloved psalm that allows us a glimpse into the unique relationship between the Heavenly Shepherd and his human sheep. We are reminded in this Psalm 23 that we too can enjoy a special bond with our Shepherd. We also can see how someone with the gift of shepherding is to behave as they watch out for the spiritual welfare of others.

David indicates that his relationship with the Heavenly Shepherd is very close and personal. He writes, "The Lord is my shepherd; I shall not want" (Ps. 23:1 NKJV). David knew from personal experience how close the Shepherd to sheep relationship was. He knew that the shepherd was intimately involved with every are of each sheep's life. The shepherd lived with the sheep. He knew them by name. They were accustomed to his voice and his presence. They willingly followed him wherever he led them and they trusted him to supply every need they had. He took this relationship and applied to what he enjoyed with the Lord. This is the same relationship that every redeemed child of God enjoys with the Lord Jesus Christ today. We are in an intimate, personal relationship with Him.

David then goes on to describe for us how the shepherd has a responsibility to the sheep, by telling us how the Lord ministers to His sheep. "He makes me to lie down in green pastures; He leads me beside the still waters. He restores my soul; He leads me in the path of righteousness for His name's sake" (Ps. 23:2-3 NKJV). David tells us what the Lord has taken upon Himself to do for all those who belong to Him. First, He provides for their needs. David reminds us that the Good Shepherd takes His sheep into place where they can feed on the best grasses, rest from their travels and find refreshment and peace beside placid pools. In other words, David is saying that those who belong to the Lord are well tended to and have all their needs met by the Shepherd of their souls. Second, the Good Shepherd leads us down the good paths. The Good Shepherds knows the way we go down and always leads us the right way. Now please understand, whether His path leads us through the glen (vs. 2), or into the gorge (vs. 4); He always leads us in the best path of all, His path! Now how can those with shepherding gift know the right path to take? Well, as long as you have your eyes on the Good Shepherd's leading then you are going down the right path. But still, no one is always going to like where the path leads them, but if you are following the Good Shepherd, and they are following the Good Shepherd; then they can be assured that He will always lead them in the right path (Ps. 37:23).

Third, the Good Shepherd has promised He will always be with them. The presence of the Good Shepherd with His sheep is a theme that permeates the very fabric of this psalm. From the idea of His leadership (vs. 2-3) to His presence in the darkest of times in verse 4, to His intimate activity in verse 5, the Lord is seen in close proximity to His sheep. He is always there to lead them, feed them, and protect them and to watch over them at all times. This is the blessed truth God's children should rejoice in today (Heb. 13:5; Matt. 28:20). Fourth, the Good Shepherd protects His sheep. David mentions the implements of the shepherd's protection: the rod and staff (Ps. 23:4). Each of these tools had a very specific purpose in the life of the sheep. The staff was a long pole with a crook near the end. With this implement, the shepherd would correct the sheep, draw them close when they began to wander and lift out of the crevices into which they might fall. The rod was much shorter than the staff and was used by the shepherd to protect the sheep from anything that might try to attack the flock. If you are a genuine child of God, then the Good Shepherd is going to protect you both night and day. We enjoy a place of absolute protection with Him (Col. 3:3). Our enemy may walk about as a roaring loin looking for victims to devour (1 Pet. 5:8), but he has been chained and our heavenly Father holds the leash!

David also describes how the Good Shepherd restores His sheep. Just as a weary sheep is refreshed by feasting in the green pasture and drinking from the still waters and lying in a place of safety and peace, so are the saints of God refreshed by their divine Shepherd. Think of the drought that was in your soul when you were yet in sin. Remember how the Lord came and brought life to you in that terrible condition? Remember the times since you neglected His house, His Word, and His fellowship and you became weary and worn and once again the cruel tentacles of the deadness and coldness began to entwine themselves around your soul? As a person with the shepherding gift, you are to behave as a church member, by showing the same kindness and grace the Good Shepherd shows you towards others who are in the same condition you were in. Think of how He came to you in your lost condition or in your backslidden condition and how He forgave you all your sins and trespasses. How he breathed new life into your soul. How he brought back the blush of youth into the cheeks of your spiritual life. Remember when He lifted you out of the pit of apathy and complacency and let you look into the promised land of spiritual victory. That is what He does for His sheep. He replaces their deadness with His life He melts the coldness of their hearts with the warmness of His embrace. He transforms the spirit and revives the cold heart. If you cannot show this same behavior that the Good Shepherd showed you when you at odd with the Shepherd, then you are not behaving as a church member. You are behaving as the man in the parable of unforgiving servant (Luke 18:22-35).

Dr. Christopher Powers

How the Shepherd Entertains His Sheep

In Psalm 23:5, the scene changes from a Shepherd and His sheep to a Host and His guests. David writes, "You prepare a table before me in the presence of my enemies; You anoint my head with oil; my cup runs over" (Ps. 23:5 NKJV). David tells us that even while moving through the territory of the enemy, the Lord takes the time to treat him like an honored guest. This is seen in a couple of ways in this verse. First, the Host does this through His arrangements. Usually, a soldier in enemy territory would be forced to gulp down a hasty meal as best he could while he cowered in fear of being discovered, captured, or killed. However, the Lord spreads the table for His children right in the middle of the enemy's territory and all the enemy can do is watch us as we feast on the blessings of the Lord. I do not think we will ever fully grasp this, but there are times in life that seem almost unbearable to us humans. It is those times when the enemy comes to us and mocks us and to question our determination to follow the Lord. But, through the ministry of the Good Shepherd, He is able to turn the worst of times into the greatest of blessings. He leaves us feasting on His grace while the enemy sulk, unable to hinder us, harm us, or even touch us! That is how the Lord arranges life for His glory and our good (Rom. 8:28; 2 Cor. 4:17). With the gift of shepherding, we are to go to those who are struggling or being persecuted and hold their hand; we are to weep when they weep, laugh when they laugh, and rejoice when they rejoice (Rom. 12:14-16).

Second, the Host does this through His anointing. When guest visited in a home, they were often anointed with oil to show them how much they meant to their host. It was considered an insult not to wash the feet and anoint the head of your guests. As we move through this life, the Lord takes many opportunities to anoint us with the oil of His grace. His goodness and blessings are all reminders that we are precious in His sight. I do not care what the devil may have told you, you are precious to the Lord! So precious, in fact, that He sent His Son to die for you on the cross (John 3:16; Rom. 5:8). So precious that He gave His all so that you might be saved! If you are saved, then you are His child! Adopted in His family and His heir! This means that you have brothers and sisters to worship with you. And if you have the gift of shepherding that means that you are to watch out for your brothers and sisters. You are precious in His sight and they are precious in His sight.

Third, the Host does this through His abundance. David tells us that the Lord's blessings in his life are so great, he has more than he can handle! His cup has passed full and has run over into the saucer! That is exactly how the Lord treats His precious children. If you are in a place where He blesses you, then you had better look out because He certainly will! Has there been a time in your life where the Good Shepherd has given you more blessings than you can handle and your cup is running over, then do not try to gather it up for yourself; share it with others. This is a testimony to tell someone who is lost, it is a testimony to tell to the wayward one, tell it to others who are hurting. That is what someone who has the gift of shepherding does. That is how we are to behave as a church member. However, most importantly, if He has blessed you and your cup is overflowing, then thank the Lord for the times when He has overflowed your cup! Yes, it sad that there are some who will not bring their cup to the table and as a result they are never filled with all of His blessings. Others have their cups filled with too much other stuff and there is no room for Him to put anything into their lives. Others believe that it is not for them. God want to bless your life beyond your wildest dreams. The very best thing you could do today is to bring yourself to Him and ask, "Lord. Fill my cup!" If you do, and do it with an honest, hungry heart, He will fill your life to where it overflows and beyond. He is looking for people who are willing and who want all that He had to give them. Is that person you?

HOW THE SHEPHERD EXCITES HIS SHEEP

"Surely goodness and mercy shall follow me all the days of my life; and I will dwell in the house of the Lord forever" (Ps. 23:6 NKJV). The scene changes again and now David pictures himself as a pilgrim headed to a city. This verse tells us what He will do for us along the way home. First, He provides them with His grace. The pilgrim is assured that goodness and mercy will be his constant companions along the way home. These are the components of grace and reminds us that as we travel, we will always be blessed with grace sufficient to the need (2 Cor. 9:12). We need to know that that there is nothing in life that we can face that will be greater than His ability to see us through. We are following the One that plans and knows the way we take (Ps. 37:23; Job 23:10). He also goes with us along the way to ensure us a safe passage through this violent and harsh land. With Him near, there is nothing to fear!

Second, He promises them His glory. David concludes this psalm with a precious reminder that this life down here will end someday, but that those who know the Lord will move to a new realm to live for eternity. Some people believe that David is referring to the Tabernacle in this verse. I like to think that he is looking a little farther away than that! I think he is looking forward to a time when he will be in the presence of the Lord in heaven. That is the destination of every child of God. If the thought of His grace here and His glory there does not light your fire, then your wood must be wet! There is something about knowing that He is going to see me through this life and usher me into that glorious, eternal, sinless life in heaven that just stir my heart. Thank God for our Shepherd know how to thrill His Sheep and make them strong and courageous.

The Heavenly Father has given us a place of victory. We do not have to be defeated by sin, by life, by spiritual depression, or by devices of the devil. We can walk in victory today. If we are going to do that, then we must make the necessary changes that will allow us to achieve that goal. Those who have this gift of shepherding are to be watching out for others and lift them up.

CHAPTER THIRTEEN

THE POWER OF BIBLICAL FAITH

So, Jesus answered and said to them, "Have faith in God." (Mark 11:22 NKJV)

Genuine biblical faith is a miracle! Faith in God is something we do not possess naturally. According to Ephesians 2:8 (NKJV), it tells us the faith you used to place in Jesus for your salvation is "the of God." God give you the faith which enables you to believe in Him for salvation, and then after you ask Jesus in your heart the Holy Spirit gives, as a gift, to every believer some "measure of faith" (Rom. 12:3 NKJV). The next spiritual gift we are going to talk about is the gift of faith. The gift of faith trust God to work beyond human capabilities. Church members with this gift are using it to encourage others to put their trust in God, even in times when it seems that everything is falling apart, like you are suffocating, or the cards are stacked against you. The gift of faith empowers His children to believe Him, serve

Him, to glorify Him through the power of "the faith" in Him that He gave us. This outworking of faith in God's people has allowed them to see demonstrations of God's power that boggles the mind. It has allowed them to receive answers to prayers for things that appeared impossible.

Consider the following: Joshua commanded the sun to stand still so Israel could defeat the Amorites (Josh. 10:12-14); King Hezekiah was told that he would die, so he prayed to the Lord and God added fifteen years to his life (Isa. 38:1-6); Abraham was told to sacrifice his son Isaac, who was the son of promise. He obeyed by faith and God spared Isaac, providing a ram in his place (Gen. 22:1-14); at the age of 85, Caleb believed God for the power to defeat a mountain infested with giants and God gave him the mountain (Josh. 14:6-16); as a teenage boy named David believed God for the power to defeat a giant named Goliath and God gave him the victory (1 Sam. 17:1-54); Shadrach, Meshach, and Abednego believed God to keep them for the power of a pagan king and a fiery furnace and God met them in the furnace and protected them there (Dan. 3:1-30). Many, many more examples could be listed, but these are enough to teach about the power of biblical faith in God. In our economy, the dollar is the medium of exchange but in the kingdom of heaven, faith is the medium of exchange. "Then He touched their eyes, saying, "According to your faith let it be to you"" (Matt. 9:29 NKJV). Whatever we receive from God is according to our faith; not according to our friends, our family, our fortune, our feelings, or our fate, but according to our faith. Not only do we need to possess this gift of faith, but what we need is for faith to possess us. We need a mighty faith because we have a mighty God. Mark 11:20-26 is a passage of Scripture that magnifies the power of biblical faith.

On the Monday morning of what we call the Lord's Passion Week, as Jesus and his disciples walked towards Jerusalem, Jesus cursed a fig tree (Mark 11:12-14). When they passed by the next day, the fig tree was dried up. Jesus uses this experience to teach His disciples a lesson about the power of biblical faith. When we exercise biblical faith in God and His promises, we can expect amazing results. There are a lot of people who think that faith is a blank check. They believe they can ask for anything they desire and that God is obligated to do all they ask Him to. This is not exactly what the Bible teaches. True biblical faith must be based upon a command or a promise of God. Expecting to perform some spectacular stunt in order to gratify a personal whim is not faith but a presumption. But if God guides a believer in a certain direction or issues a command, then the Christian can have confidence that the mountain of difficulty will be miraculously removed. Noting is impossible to those who believe. Nothing is impossible when God's children behave as church members.

THE OBJECT OF BIBLICAL FAITH

"So, Jesus answered and said to them, "Have faith in God"" (Matt. 11:22 NKJV). The disciples are amazed at the fig tree which has withered, and all Jesus says is for them to have faith in God. The emphasis of that command is that church members should behave with a deep-settled consistent, ongoing confidence in Who God is, in what God has said, and in obedience to God. This phrase, "Have faith in God" is given to encourage your faith and my faith in several aspects of God's character. First, we should have faith in the fact that God is indeed a person. If you are saved, then God is your Father. As your Father, He cares about every need in your life, "casting all your care upon Him, for He care for you" (1 Pet. 5:17 NKJV). As your Father, He invites you to bring your needs, burdens, and concerns to Him (Phil. 4:6-7; Heb. 4:16). As your Father, He desires to open the resources of His kingdom and give them to you. "Do not fear, little flock, for it is your Father's good pleasure to give you the kingdom" (Luke 12:32 NKJV). We are not dealing with some person who is aloof, some disconnected deity that does not have any compassion nor care for his people. Our Father loves His children and He wants them to come to Him on the basis of simple, childlike faith. Just as a child trust its parents for every need, the child of God can trust the heavenly Father.

Second, we should have faith in the promises of God. When it comes to the matter of faith and approaching God in prayer, the people of God have some very precious promises at their disposal. Here are some of those promises: God invites us to pray to Him (Phil. 4:6; Matt. 11:28; 1 Pet. 5:7); God promises to hear us when we pray (Jer. 33:3, Ps. 10:17; 65:2); and God promises to answer our prayers (Matt. 7:7-11; Isa. 58:9). When it comes to the promises of God, we have the Lord's guarantee that He will keep every one of them (Rom. 4:21; Heb. 6:18; Num. 23:19). God will not back away from a single promise He has give His people.

Third, we should have faith in the power of God. It is one thing to make a promise, however, it is another thing to have the power to keep those promises. The children of God can have absolute confidence in God's power to do everything He has promised to do. He has the power to do anything we ask Him to do. He has the ability to do anything He pleases to do. We serve an awesome God who possess all power in heaven and on earth (Matt. 28:18; Eph. 3:20; Jer. 32:17; Job 42:2; Luke 1:37; Isa. 40:12). Our heavenly Father can do anything!

Finally, we should have faith in the purposes of God. When it comes to faith in God, we must always remember that He has an eternal plan that He is working to accomplish. He has a purpose, and everything in the universe, even our request, are subject to His will. He will do nothing that is outside the bounds of His eternal purpose. He will do nothing that is not part of His plan. He will not do everything we ask, just because we ask it. He will do those things that He wills to do, and He will accomplish all things that He has willed to do. A lot of people believe that they can ask for anything they want, and that God has to do what they want Him to do. Nothing could be farther from the truth. Prayer is never about getting what we want from heaven. Prayer is always about aligning our will with God's will so that His will is done on earth.

THE OPPORTUNITIES OF BIBLICAL FAITH

Jesus goes on to say, "For assuredly, I say to you, whoever says to this mountain, 'Be removed and be cast into the sea,' and does not doubt in his heart, but believes that those things he says will be done, he will have whatever he says. Therefore, I say to you, whatever things you ask when you pray, believe that you receive them, and you will have them" (Mark 11:23-24 NKJV). When you are presented with an opportunity to exercise your faith, it allows us to believe the impossible. From where Jesus and His men were standing, they would have been able to see the Mount of Olives and the Dead Sea. Jesus was giving them a vivid illustration, while using a familiar Jewish proverb, to teach them a deeply spiritual truth.

The Jews commonly spoke of moving a mountain to refer to something that was absolutely impossible, or to something that would be a long task. There are so many situations in life that appear hopeless. There are people that seem so lost that will never be saved. There are needs so great that it appears they will never be met. There are problems so big it appears they will never be overcome. Faith in God and in the promises found in His Word, allows us to believe God even in the most impossible situations of life. I can believe God for the salvation of that lost soul because of what He said in His Word (2 Pet. 3:9; 1 Tim. 2:4). I can have faith that God will meet the need which seems so impossible to meet, because of His promises (Matt. 6:25-34; Phil. 4:19). I can have faith that I am saved (Rom. 10:9-10, 13). I can have faith that I am secure in Jesus, because of His promise (John 6:37; 10:28). I can have faith in a place called heaven because of His promise (John 14:1-3). I can have faith that He will never leave me alone (Matt. 28:20; Heb. 13:5). The list could go on and on, that being said, faith in God and His promises allow us to believe Him for those things appear impossible to us!

Something else, when you are presented with an opportunity to exercise your faith it allows us to receive the impossible. Jesus said, if we could believe Him, we would have what we ask for. Faith has the remarkable ability to enable us to hold in our hands things that have yet to be seen. "Now faith is the substance of things hoped for, the evidence of things not seen" (Heb. 11:1 NKJV). The word "substance" in that verse means "foundation, or that which stands under something." (Strong's Concordance, 1984) Faith is the guarantee, the assurance that we will have the things God has promised to us. The word "evidence" means "conviction." (Concise Oxford English Dictionary Eleventh Edition, 2004) In modern language it refers to "the smoking gun." Faith allows us to hold in our hearts things that have yet to appear; for example: the Second Coming of Christ. The faith described in Hebrews 11:1 is the absolute, God-given, present confidence in a future reality. It is the conviction that what we believed by faith, is already ours, even though we cannot yet see it. This kind of faith is not based on what the eye can see, but it is based on what God has promised! Just think that the Holy Spirit gives us this gift of faith to believe in His promises! Therefore, we should behave as church members.

THE OBSTACLES OF BIBLICAL FAITH

While faith in God is powerful and allows us to experience the incredible and receive the impossible, faith can be hindered. Over in John 4:46-54, we meet a man who came to Jesus with a weak faith; to be precise he had a superficial faith and what makes it worst is the fact that he had a superstitious faith. But after spending time with Jesus, he went from having superstitious faith to have a strong faith to having a saving faith. The man that came to Jesus that day was a nobleman and had many resources at his hand; and yet he had a problem. His son was sick and he wanted Jesus to heal his son. Now, understand before this man came to Jesus with his problem, his faith was almost nonexistent. "Then Jesus said to him, "Unless you people see signs and wonders, you will by no means believe"" (John 4:48 NKJV). This man had faith that was based on signs and wonders. Evidently, his motto was, "Seeing is believing." There are people who will pray, "God, if you will just give me a sign, if you will just give me a wonder, then I can believe." Let give you some food for thought to this kind of think, believing, and behavior: this belief is not based on dependence of the Word of God. No doubt this man had heard about Jesus turning the water into wine (vs. 46), and because of what he has heard about Jesus he is taken in, amazed by this miracle. He so blown away with the thought; here is Jesus and if he can turn water into wine then surely, he can heal my son. But Jesus knew that miracles, (signs and wonders), do little good when you are trying to grow your faith.

Please understand the response that Jesus had to this man's request is not harsh (vs. 48). In fact, it is the same way He responded when He turned the water into wine. "Now when He was in Jerusalem at the Passover, during the feast, many believed in His name when they saw the signs which He did. But Jesus did not commit Himself to them, because He knew all men, and had no need that anyone should testify of man, for He knew what was in man" (John 2:23-25 NKJV). The word "commit" and the word "believe" in these verses is the Greek and they are the same words in the Greek (Strong's Concordance, 1984) Here is how those words are used, they believed in Jesus, but He did not believe in them. They had a superficial faith and Jesus knew that those at the wedding and this nobleman were following Him, believing on Him, because of the miracles. They did not have strong faith, they had superficial faith that was rapidly becoming a superstitious faith.

You would be amazed at how many people today want signs and wonders and as the closer we get to the end times that will become more prevalent. People today want visions, emotions, and dreams. They want liver shivers, chills crawling up their spines, and angels tickling their ribs. They want something where they can say "Hey! I know this is real now I've seen it with the lust of my eyes! I have touched it with my fingers! I have smelt it, and heard it, therefore with pride I know it is real! The world is full of people just like that, and sadly many of them sit in our churches today. They are not behaving as church members.

It is true, Jesus did in fact perform miracles, there is not any question about that. But why did Jesus perform miracles? Why did Jesus give signs and wonders? Jesus gave signs and wonders to authenticate His ministry. "Men of Israel, here these words: Jesus of Nazareth, a Man attested by God to you by miracles, wonders, and signs which God did through Him in your midst, as you yourselves also know" (Acts 2:22 NKJV). But the miracles which Jesus performed was not for the sake of doing miracles. The miracles were done in order for you to believe on Jesus and have eternal life. Did you know that the disciples did signs and wonders as well? Some people think we ought to do signs and wonders because the apostles did them. "Truly the signs of an apostle were accomplished among you with all perseverance, in signs and wonders and mighty deeds" (2 Cor. 12:2 NKJV). Paul had power to do miracles because God authenticated the ministry of the apostles with signs and wonders. "God also bearing witness both with signs and wonders, with various miracles, and gifts of the Holy Spirit, according to His own will" (Heb. 2:4 NKJV). Understand, they did not have the power to do signs and wonders according to their own will, but God took the apostles, and because they were apostles, they were setting the foundation of our faith, therefore God authenticated their ministry with signs and wonders.

WHAT IS WRONG WITH DEMANDING A SIGN

What Jesus said to the nobleman (John 4:48), closely resembles what He said in Matthew 12:39, "But He answered and said to them, "an evil and adulterous generation seeks after a sign, and no sign will be given to it except the sign of the prophet Jonah"" (NKJV). So, is asking for a sign really bad? Well, asking for a sign does two things. First, it brings dishonor to God. We have His Word which says, "He who believes in the Son of God has the witness in himself; he who does not believe God has made Him a liar, because he has not believed the testimony that God has given His Son" (1 John 5:10 NKJV). When you cannot take God at his word by faith, you are not behaving as a church member because you are lacking faith. The second reason why it is bad to ask for a miracle is because it deceives man. If you think about it signs and wonders can be easily deceiving. When the Antichrist, Satan's superman, appears during the tribulation he will be doing signs and wonders to try to authenticate his ministry. Jesus tells us that this Satan powered superman could, if possible, deceive the children of God (Matt. 24:24). Paul writes, "The coming of the lawless one is according to the working of Satan, with all power, signs, and lying wonders" (2 Thess. 2:9 NKJV). The Antichrist will be able to make you think black is white, good is bad, and cause you to cut your mother's throat with a smile on your face because of his ability to deceive you with signs and wonders. People will often come to me, after hearing these things, and say, "What about Gideon? Did he not ask for a sign and God honored his requests?"

GIDEON

Yes, it true that the phrase "putting out the fleece" is familiar in religious circles. What that phrase means is someone is asking God to guide their decision by fulfilling some condition that they have laid down. In my pastoral ministry, I have met people who have gotten themselves into trouble by "putting out the fleece." If they received a phone call at a certain hour from a person, God was telling them to do this, or if the weather changed at a certain time, God was telling them to do something else. "Putting out the fleece" is not behaving as a church member, nor is it a good behavior for someone who has the gift of faith. Rather, it is an approach used by people like Gideon who lack faith, who have a superficial faith, who want to see signs and wonders that do not trust God to do what He said He would do.

Twice Gideon reminded God of what He had said, and twice Gideon asked God to reaffirm His promises with a miracle. The fact that God stooped to Gideon's weakness only proves that God is a gracious God who understands how we are made. Who are we to tell God what conditions He must meet, especially when he has already spoken to us in His Word? But here is what we need to understand: God is in the process of training Gideon to be the next deliver of Israel. As part of his training, God commanded Gideon to destroy an altar to Baal an to build an altar to Jehovah in its place. Gideon passes the test with flying colors. The people in his village were not pleased with Gideon's actions, because they wanted to kill him for what he had done. Gideon's father stepped in and defended his son's actions (Judg. 6). After that very public test came a time of private testing. This second test was not instigated by God, but by Gideon. He had demonstrated great bravery in his public testing, but he shows a clear lack of faith in the private testing. Someone has said, "who you are in private is who you really are." Sometimes it is easier to put on a public face and appear to be one person when we are someone totally different in private. In Judges 6:33-40, we see Gideon waver between faith and fear, however, notice a few observations about Gideon.

As the scene in Judges 6:33-40 opens, we see a young Gideon energized and excited from his recent victory, calling Israel to prepare for war. This is the Gideon the Lord saw when He first commissioned Gideon for the task of delivering Israel (vs. 12). However, Gideon and Israel had some enemies that would come in at harvest time (vs. 11). As the crops were being gathered in, every year for the past seven years (vs. 1), the Midianites and their allies would use Israel as their own private grocery store. They would come in and take the harvest for themselves, leaving the people of Israel with absolutely nothing (vs. 3-7). This is what taking place in verse 33 which says, "Then all the Midianites and Amalekites, the people of the East, gathered together; and they crossed over and encamped in the Valley of Jezreel" (NKJV). This valley was the largest and most fertile valley in all of Israel. Many of the crops that sustained the nation were produced here. Therefore, having an enemy that would come in and steal the harvest would have been a serious blow to Israel. (Just as a side note, the Valley of Jezreel is also known as the Valley of Megiddo and many great battles have been fought on that piece of ground. It is here that the final battle will be waged, for the Lord Jesus Christ will defeat the Antichrist and his armies at the end of the Tribulation Period).

When the enemy comes, Gideon has the courage to do what no man has done in over seven years. "But the Spirit of the Lord came upon Gideon; then he blew the trumpet, and the Abiezrites gathered behind him" (Judg. 6:34 NKJV). No one in the land had possessed the courage to pick up the trumpet and call the people to war. Gideon appears ready for the task he has been assigned. He places his hand on the trumpet, licks his lips, and calls Israel for battle. Where did Gideon get this kind of courage? We are told the Spirit of the Lord came upon Gideon. In other words, God took control of Gideon and caused him to sound the war call. This man blowing the trumpet, calling Israel to war is not the same man back in Judges 6:11-24). That man was defeated, disillusioned, discouraged, and filled with doubt. The man in Judges 6:34, is decisive, daring, defiant, and determined. Something has happened to Gideon and that something is the power of the Spirit of God. Gideon had a personal encounter with God in verses 11-24. He made a decisive commitment by faith to obey the Lord in verses 25-32. Now, he has come under the control of the Spirit of God (vs. 34). When those things take place in a person's life, they will not be the same.

The same principle holds true in our lives today. If you want to behave as a church member and want the power to serve the Lord, then that power can only come through faith which is a gift, a ministry of the Holy Spirit in our lives. We are His temple (1 Cor. 6:19), and we are to yield, surrender our lives to His will (Eph. 5:18). While the Spirit of God still empowers people to service in these days, the way He operates is different now than the way He operated then. In the Old Testament the Spirit of God did not indwell in every believer. The Holy Spirit anointed people for special task. The Holy Spirit did not come upon people permanently in those days. We are told that the Spirit departed from Saul (1 Sam. 16:14) and from Samson (Judg. 16:20). When the Spirit did move on a person in those days, they were given great strength and courage to accomplish God-size feats through the power of the Holy Spirit. In our day, every believer is indwelt by the Holy Spirit (Rom. 8:9; 2 Cor. 12:13). He does not merely anoint us for specific tasks; He gives us help, gifts, power, strength to behave as church members (Gal. 5:16-25; Rom. 8:14). The Holy Spirit does not depart from God's children, but He takes up permanent residence in our hearts forever (John 14:16-17). His presence guarantees our eternal security in Jesus (Eph. 1:13). When the Spirit of God is in control of our lives, we are changed inwardly first. As we are changed on the inside it begins to make its way to the outside demonstrated by godly living and good works (2 Cor. 5:17; Eph. 2:10; Jam. 2:18).

Gideon has displayed great courage in calling the people to war and gathering together his army. That was the public Gideon. In private, Gideon is still filled with doubts concerning what the Lord is calling him to do. "So, Gideon said to God, "If You will save Israel by my hand as You have said"" (Judg. 6:36 NKJV). The key word in this verse is the word "if." God had already told Gideon repeatedly what He wanted Him to do (vs. 12, 14, 16), and Gideon is not content to simply trust the Lord and take Him at His Word. Gideon wants some kind of tangible proof that he can see with his eyes, feel with his hands that this is God's will. In other words, Gideon is not willing to walk by faith, he wants to walk by sight too. In a sense we tend to want the same thing that Gideon wants. To behave as a church member means, as Paul said, "For we walk by faith, not by sight" (2 Cor. 5:7 NKJV).

Because of Gideon's behavior, he gives a demand to God. "Look, I shall put a fleece of wool on the threshing floor; if there is dew on the fleece only, and it is dry on all the ground, then shall I know that You will save Israel by my hand, as You have said" (Judg. 6:37 NKJV). Gideon comes up with a test to determine God's will. God does exactly what Gideon ask him to do (vs. 38). However, this does not satisfy the mind of Gideon (vs. 39), because he knows that a piece of sheepskin is like a sponge and it will soak up all the available moisture in the air around it. So, even though he was able to wring a bowl full water from the fleece, he is still not convinced. The next night he asks God to reverse the conditions of the test. So, God makes the ground wet and the fleece dry. This apparently satisfies Gideon (vs. 40), because he did not question God's call again. Of course, he could have just taken God at His Word instead of wasting two precious days playing the fleece game with the Lord.

It is possible that we all have done what Gideon did, once or twice in our lives. You have set up a test to prove the Lord. You have dictated your terms to Him and you have expected Him to do exactly what you have told Him to do. So, let me just show you how our practice of "putting out the fleece" is something that will not please the Lord and keeps us from behaving as a church member. Gideon faced the same problems we all face in life. As previously stated, Gideon simply lacked the faith to take God at His Word. God told Gideon what to do, but Gideon did not want to trust God by faith. God expects His people to walk with Him in humble faith in His Word and His promises (Rom. 1:17). When we seek a tangible sign to determine God's will, instead of taking Him at His Word, it displeases God (Heb. 11:6), and it causes us to fall into sin (Rom. 14:23). We can trust His Word because He has promised to lead us (Ps. 32:8; 37:23-24). Another problem I see in Gideon's fleece is that Gideon is dictating the terms to God. Gideon's responsibility was not to tell the Lord how thing would be, it was to simply obey the will of God for His life. Our duty is the same, we are not called to tell the Lord how He should answer our prayers. We are commanded to obey His Word and His will fro our lives without question (Rom. 12:1-2).

Gideon learned that seeking a sign does not solve the problem. He got a wet fleece the first time, but he was not sure it was the Lord's work. Did God cause the fleece to be wet, or did the fleece simply draw moisture from the air? Gideon was not better off after the first fleece than he was before, he still had the same promises from the Lord he just still had doubt in his life. When we throw out our fleece before the Lord, and we set conditions, we are setting ourselves up for doubt. For instance, you are trying to find God's will in a matter so you pray something like this: "Lord, if this is your will let snow three inches today." Well, what if it snows three inches tomorrow? Does that mean God is telling you "No"? What if it only snows two inches today? What would that mean? Could it mean the devil is trying to make you have doubt? Do you see the problem? "If the next car I see is like the one I want, then I will know it is your will to trade." Even when things go almost like we ask for them to go, we are still prone to doubt. If you cannot take God at His Word, then you are not going be able to trust a fleece either.

The real problem with "putting out a fleece" is that a fleece is always placed out of doubt and not faith. "Putting out a fleece" is not the biblical method for determining the will of God. It is a method used by people like Gideon who lack the faith to simply trust the Word of God. So, how does God guide His people so we can behave as church members using the gift of faith? The Bible tells us exactly how God leads us to know His will for our lives. First, God guides us through the Holy Spirit (John 16:13). Second, God guides through His Word (Ps. 119:105). Third, God guides through His peace (Col. 3:15). Next, God guides through the desires He gives us (Ps. 34:3-4). Then finally, God guides through the godly counsel of His people (Prov. 11:14). Take note, all of these will be in agreement. For example, I have known preacher s who have left a church or taken a church saying, "I have peace about my decision." Then I have watched as God shelved them or allowed them to endure a time of terrible testing at the church they took. That peace did not come from God. When God guides, the leadership of the Holy Spirit will line up with the Word of God. These assurances will produce peace in your heart. The Spirit of God, the Word of God, and the peace of God will combine to give you a desire to do what the Lord is leading you to do. Others around you will see the hand of God in your decision.

You do not need a fleece to determine God's will for your life. You merely need to listen to the Lord. He will speak to you through His Word, by the His Spirit, giving you a desire for His will and He will provide peace about doing it. Forget the fleece and just walk by faith. Have you ever stopped to think about what could be accomplished for the glory of God in this world if every believer simply did what God wanted him or her to do and behaved as a church member by faith? There would be more power and glory in the church. There would be more souls being saved. There would be more of the miraculous manifestations of God's presence and power in the world. Far more would be accomplished that we could ever imagine, if we would just behave as church members and take Him at His Word and step out on faith! Biblical faith is a powerful weapon in the hands of church member. Mountains yield to its power. Sin, Satan, and sorrow all must bow before its authority. Faith is among the greatest of God's spiritual gifts that He gives through His Holy Spirit to His children.

CHAPTER FOURTEEN

CAN THEY SEE JESUS IN ME

The Lord is not slack concerning His promise, as some count
slackness, but is longsuffering toward us, not willing that any
should perish but that all should come to repentance.
(2 Peter 3:9 NKJV)

In my book *Behave as a Fisher of Men*, I go into detail about how every child of God is to go out and share the Gospel of Jesus Christ. The book takes a look at some the teaching that Jesus taught His disciples about becoming fishers of men. This brings us to our next spiritual gift, the gift of evangelism. Every church member should at the very least be able to talk about their salvation experience, which is called giving a testimony. God gives His church, people who have the ability to just lead people to the Lord effectively and enthusiastically. I often hear church members say, "O, how I wish our church would just grow." Well, the gift of evangelism is just that gift for the purpose of adding to new members to the church. However, I purposed this question in my book *Behave as a Fisher of Men*,

"Is a person a fisherman if, year after year, he never catches a fish? Is one behaving as a follower of Christ if they are not fishing?" (Powers, 2021) The same could be said about the church member are you really behaving as a church member if you do not do your part in evangelism?

There are many legends that surround the building of the Taj Mahal. One of those legends involves Emperor Shah Jahan. The emperor's wife passed away and he became distraught, however, in order bring healing to his sorrow, he decided to build a temple as her tomb to honor her. As the construction began, the emperor had his wife's casket brought out to the middle of the site. The temple began to take shape around the casket, fortunately, weeks became months and the emperor seeing all the elaborate and expensive build being built did eventually forget about his wife's death. One day a construction worker discovered this wooden box; which the emperor ordered the worker git rid of it because it was just in the way. Little did the emperor know that he just ordered the disposal of his wife's casket, which had been hidden beneath layers of dust and time. It seems that the very reason the temple was erected in the first place and for whose honor it was to remember is now long forgotten. You are probably thinking, "Oh, how sad." Yes, it is tragic, however, that is what can happen to us when we are not behaving as church members and not using the gift of evangelism. Chruch members today have forgotten why we evangelize in the first place.

When you do behave as church members and evangelize as you should, you never know the lives that you touch because you are behaving. For instance, one day as a woman was crossing a street in London, an old man stopped her. He said to her, "Excuse me, ma'am, but I want to thank you." She looked up and exclaimed, "Thank me?" He replied, "Yes, ma'am, I used to be a ticket collector, and whenever you went by, you would always give me a cheerful smile and a good morning. I knew that smile must come from inside somewhere. Then one morning I saw a little Bible in your hand. So, I bought one too, and I found out about Jesus from that Bible. Now I too am saved!" That man saw something in that woman that touched his heart. What did he see? He saw Jesus living in and through her life. Every church member should live and behave in such a way that the world can see Jesus in our lives.

On the night that Jesus was arrested and taken to the home of the high priest, Peter and the other disciples were not behaving as followers of Christ according to Matthew 26:56-75. All the disciples ran away (vs. 56) leaving Jesus alone with the multitude that came with swords and clubs (vs. 47). They lead Jesus away to the home of Caiaphas the high priest, and Peter did follow them from a safe distance (vs. 57-58) and sat down outside by a fire. That night, by the fire, Peter has his greatest failure and was not behaving as he should have been. Peter was given a great opportunity to do some evangelism and shine brightly for the Lord, however, he decided to remain invisible. No one was able to see Jesus that night. Peter was saved, he was born again, he was living a new life, but on that night, no one could tell it! So, let's purpose this question to ourselves; can they see Jesus in me? Everyone who is a church member is to behave as a church. Why? Because everyone who is saved is living the new life. We have been born again and we are new creatures in Christ Jesus. We are to be different that the world around us. We are to be the light for Jesus in a dark and dying world. We are to be a living, walking testimony to the life changing power of the Lord Jesus Christ. Can they see Jesus in me?

THE WONDER OF THE NEW LIFE

On this night Peter is nothing like the man he used to be. Peter had been radically transformed by the power of Christ, but on that night, he was behaving totally different. I wonder what happen? We know that Peter was a fisherman; and fisherman in those days were notorious for their vulgar ways and wicked lifestyles. By Peter's own admission, he was a sinful man (Luke 5:1-8), however, he started following Jesus and Jesus cleaned him up and saved Him. Where were you when Jesus found you? How long has it been since you looked to "the hole of the pit from which you were dug" (Isa. 51:1 NKJV). Do you remember what you were before He saved your soul? Let me remind you, "There is none righteous, no, not one; there is none who understands; there is none who seeks after God. They have all turned aside; they have together become unprofitable; there is none who does good, no, not one. Their throat is an open tomb; with their tongues they have practiced deceit; the poison of asps is under their lips, whose mouth is full of cursing and bitterness. Their feet are swift to shed blood; destruction and misery are in their ways; and the way of peace they have not known. There is no fear of God before their eyes" (Rom. 3:10-18 NKJV).

Peter bowed before Jesus and called Jesus, "Lord" (Luke 5:8 NKJV). Later we see Peter's confession of who Jesus is has grown as he becomes more mature in his walk with Christ. "Simon Peter answered and said, "You are the Christ, the Son of the living God."" (Matt. 16:16 NKJV). There were times when Peter excelled in his walk with the Lord, while in other times he was silent. In Matthew 26:50-54, Peter had sought to defend Jesus by using a sword. Peter had real fruit in his life, just as every branch in the vine should be baring fruit (John 15:1-8). In spite of all that Peter had in his plus column, he still fell into sin. He denied Jesus three times with one of the times using cursing (Matt. 26:72). Regardless of the changes we have experienced through Jesus, it is always possible for us to fall back into sin. Why? Because we still wear this old, fallen, wicked flesh! It never gets better, but if progressively gets worse (Eph. 4:22). You are just as capable of sin as you have ever been. Nothing but the good grace of God stands between you and the most terrible of sins.

THE WITNESS OF THE NEW LIFE

Every life of every redeemed person is a living, walking sermon about the Lord Jesus Christ (2 Cor. 3:1-3; 1 Thess. 1:8). Your life either says, "Jesus saved me and radically changed my life." Or your life says, "Yeah, I am a believer, but Jesus has not changed my life at all." Peter, when he denied Christ, demonstrated a very poor testimony. Several factors contributed to this tragic display on Peter's part. First, he was in the wrong place. Peter followed Jesus, but he did not go all the way with Jesus. He stays outside warming himself around the enemy's fire. He would have been better off hiding with the other disciples, or in custody with Jesus than where he was. There are just some places in this life that a believer has no business being. Before you go anywhere, you ought to ask yourself, "If Jesus were to accompany me there, would He be comfortable?" If the answer is "No!", then you have no business going either. Why? Well, if you are saved, then the Holy Spirit is living in your heart, and Jesus goes everywhere you go. Be careful where you go, because people are always watching you.

Dr. Christopher Powers

Second, Peter was with the wrong people. That night Peter associated with the wrong crowd and it was not long until he was acting just like them. You need to exercise great caution when it comes to the people you associate with. Why? Because the Bible tells us that the wrong kind of influence on our lives can have tragic results (1 Cor. 15:33). Do not think you can hang around with the wrong element and change them, you will find that your old, fleshy nature will always take the path of least resistance. Instead of you lifting them up to your level, they will drag you down to theirs. Finally, Peter shows the wrong behavior. The Bible tells us that Peter began to swear (Matt. 26:72; Mark 14:71). He certainly did not behave like a preacher at that moment in time. What does your life have to say about Jesus? If a person follows you everywhere you go and watches all that you do for twenty-four hours, would they conclude that you were a pagan or a Christian church member? You need to give serious thought about that, because many church members are having an identity crisis of sorts. They have forgotten Who they belong to and they are sending the wrong message to a lost world. We are supposed to make Jesus look good and not bad (Phil. 1:27). We are supposed to help weaker believers grow and lead them into error (Matt. 18:6). What kind of message does your behavior send to a lost and dying world?

The Way of Evangelism

"But Peter said, "Man, I do not know what you are saying!" Immediately, while he was still speaking, the rooster crowed. And the Lord turned and looked at Peter. Then Peter remembered the word of the Lord, how He had said to him, "Before the rooster crows, you will deny Me three times." So, peter went our and wept bitterly" (Luke 22:60-62 NKJV). When that rooster crowed, Jesus turned and looked directly into the eyes of Peter. I wonder if Peter could feel Jesus' eyes of flaming fire (Rev. 1:14), just piercing to his heart. In that brief, moment Peter remembered what Jesus had predicted early. (Matt. 26:33-35). No matter how far you may wander off into sin; no matter how cold your old heart gets towards the things of God; no matter how low the ember may burn in your soul, you will never be able to get away from what Jesus did in you when He saved your soul!

— 186 —

If you have ever been near the flames of fire, you will always remember the warmth and you will long for it when your heart grows cold.

As Peter turned and went away weeping, and he remembered what Jesus predicted about the rooster and his denial. This could have cause him to think about the teachings and the parables Jesus taught. After all Peter was there when Jesus shared the parable of the Sower. Maybe he missed the point of how the kingdom of God is to begin. Matthew 13 records the events of a crisis day in the ministry of Jesus and reveals to us some kingdom truths that shows us what we are to do with the gift of evangelism. Jesus knew that the growing opposition of the religious leaders would lead to His crucifixion. This is a truth that He had taught His disciples on many occasions. But their logical question would be, "What will happen to the kingdom of God?" In fact, John the Baptist must have wondered what would happen next. John had announced that the kingdom of heaven was at hand. He told his audience that Christ would baptize with the Holy Spirit and fire. John had the highest expectations as he anticipated the coming of Jesus. When Jesus began His earthly ministry, John Identified Jesus as "the Lamb of God, who takes away the sins of the world" (John 1:29 NKJV). The question the disciple of Jesus and John the Baptist was asking; is answered by Jesus through the teachings used in parables. He first explained the truth concerning the kingdom, and then later explained to them the facts about the cross.

THE METHOD OF JESUS' TEACHING

Jesus used parables to teach His disciples and us, about the kingdom of God. Jesus, up to this point, had already used parables in His ministry, and yet on one particular day He ends up teaching eight parables to His disciples (Matt. 13). The word "parable" means "to cast alongside." (Concise Oxford English Dictionary Eleventh Edition, 2004) A parable is a story, or comparison, that is put alongside something else to help make the lesson clear. According to Matthew 13:10-17, we know why Jesus taught in parables. First, "Therefore I speak to them in parables, because seeing they do not see, and hearing they do not hear, nor do they understand" (Matt. 13:13 NKJV). His reason reminds me of the time God called Israel a stiff neck people (Deut. 31:27). Then Jesus gives His second reason for speaking in parables, which was to fulfill a prophecy concerning the Messiah. "I will open my mouth in a parable; I will utter dark sayings of old, which we have heard and known, and our fathers have told us" (Ps. 78:2-3 NKJV). Of course, Jesus quotes from Isaiah 6:9-10 and then Matthew tells us again why Jesus used parables in Matthew 13:34-35. Jesus was not trying bring about confusion nor did not teach parables to confuse nor judging the people. He was trying to encourage them about who He was and about the kingdom of heaven. He was, for a lack of illustration, trying to wet their appetite for the things of God. These parables would give light to those with trusting, searching hearts. But they would bring darkness to the unconcerned and unrepentant of hearts.

THE MYSTERY OF JESUS' TEACHING

In Matthew 13:3-9, the parable of the Sower describes for us how the kingdom of heaven begins. It begins with evangelism, the preaching of the Word of God, which plants the seed (the gospel) into the hearts of people. When we say, "Let me run something by you" we are expressing the idea of this parable. Yes, we would like to get the seed to their hearts, but they have to make a decision on their own and that is done in their mind. Once they decide to accept the seed, then the seed moves to their heart. Both the mind and the heart play a role in the decision, and as the Holy Spirit tugs on their heart, their heart will impact the decision made in the mind.

But why use the seed to teach us about God's Word? "For the word of God is living and powerful, and sharper than any two-edge sword, piercing even to the division of soul and spirit, and of joints and marrow, and is a discerner of the thoughts and intents of the heart" (Heb. 4:12 NKJV). There was a preacher that once said, "I sometimes wish that Jesus had given us the parable of the bomber. But He did not!" Well, Jesus gave us the parable of the Sower, because God works by sowing seeds, not by dropping bombs. Jesus is telling us that the will of God gets done in people's lives not by earth-shattering explosions but by the quiet teachings of the Word of God. It will be like a gardener sowing seed. The seed will not grow everywhere, but where it is received, it will produce an abundant harvest.

Unlike the words of men, the Word of God has life in it; and that life can be imparted to those who will believe. The truth of God must take root in the heart, be cultivated, and permitted to bear fruit.

Please understand we are to behave as church members and use the gift of evangelism to reach a lost and dying world with the seed (the gospel of our Lord Jesus Christ). The parable of the Sower teaches us some great lessons as to why it is hard for us to see any fruit to our labor. Nevertheless, regardless of the outcome of sowing the seed, we are still to behave as church members and do evangelism.

THE SEED

In the parable of the Sower, the seed represents the Word of God, the Sower who went forth to sow is like a preacher preaching the Word of God, and the sower is like a church member who is going out and sharing the gospel. Now when the Bible calls itself seed, that is remarkably interesting, because seed has life, therefore the Word of God has life. Jesus said, "It is the Spirit who gives lie; the flesh profits nothing. The words that I speak to you are spirit, and they are life" (John 6:63 NKJV). There is such power in the Word of God It has life to transform; the Word of God is not dead words; it is not merely philosophy, or history, or good ideas, but it is power.

When we go forth and bear the precious seed of the gospel, we are caring the most important message the world has ever heard. It is a living, powerful message! It is a message that the world needs to hear. The message of the gospel has tremendous power. Just as seed can transform a barren field into a place of live and blessing, the gospel can transform a dead and dry life into something that can bless men and glorify God. Anyone who hears the gospel and meets the Master will be forever changed. When the gospel seeds lands in good soil, it will work. It will change every life it touches. It will work for every man.

THE SOWER

In the parable of the Sower, Jesus is the sower of the seed. Everywhere Jesus went He was sowing the seed. The Bible says Jesus came preaching

(Mark 1:14), and He scattered this seed everywhere. Peter knew this, but he was not behaving as though he believed this. Jesus is throwing seed as if He had seed to spare. He throws the seed in thorns, on the wayside, on the stony ground, and in the good ground. He is just scattering seed everywhere. That should be a lesson for us to behave as church members, because "Jesus said to them again, "Peace to you! As the Father has sent Me, I also send you""" (John 20:21 NKJV). If we are going to behave as church members, then we must be seed-sowers. Everywhere we are to scatter the seed. You see, you cannot tell by casual observation what soil will be productive, because you were not called to be a soil analyst. All soil looks alike, and it is hard to tell the difference between the hard, stony, weeds, and good soil.

When I get up to preach before the congregation, it is hard for me to tell who is receiving and who is not. Some have their eyes closed and some do not. Those who have their eyes closed and say, "Well, pastor I am meditating," and I think no you were probably asleep. There was this one man who was trying to impress his pastor. He said, "Pastor, give me a good prayer that I might pray when I enter the church." The pastor knew the habits. He said, "How about this, 'Now I lay me down to sleep...'" It is hard sometimes, though, to be able to tell what the attitude of the heart is. You cannot tell, you do not know the soil, all you can do with the gift of evangelism is just scatter the seed. The Sower just scattered the seed everywhere he went.

THE SOIL

There are four types of hearts that a person could have in their heart. The first soil is the hard ground. "And as he sowed, some seed fell by the wayside; and the birds came and devoured them" (Matt. 13:4 NKJV). The wayside is the pathway through the field, and it has been packed down and hardened by traffic. The traffic of the world has trampled over the ground, over and over again and has made it hard and unyielding, and the seed cannot get in. This represents the hard hearts of the secular hearer, their minds have been so beaten down by the things of this world, that their minds have become such a footpath for materialism. The old saying goes, "It rolls off them like water off a duck's back." The seed does not get in,

"When anyone hears the word of the kingdom, and does not understand it, then the wicked one comes and snatches away what was sown in his heart. This is he who received seed by the wayside" (vs. 19 NKJV).

The next soil is the stony ground. "Some fell on stony places, where they did not have much earth; and they immediately sprang up because they had no depth of earth. But when the sun was up, they were scorched, and because they had no root they withered away" (vs. 5-6 NKJV). The superficial hearer are people who hear the Word of God and the seed got in, but it could not get down because it did not have any root. The dirt layer in the stony places is approximately one inch thick, give or take. In other words, it is a very thin layer of dirt which sits on top of solid rock, and they sprang up. Now, while the soil looks good on the outside and looks fertile, the sower cannot see beneath the surface. These so-called church members that spring up, they do not have any depth to their walk; they are just superficial Christians. These superficial Christians hear the preaching of the Word of God, their chin will quiver, tears will come to their eyes, they will get a lump in their throat, but they never receive the Word of God. They seem to and sometimes they even come down the aisles and join the church; they even make emotional statements about Jesus, but they are not fully trusting in Christ.

Another soil where the seed was planted is the ground of thorns. "And some fell among the thorns, and the thorns sprang up and choked them" (vs. 7 NKJV). Jesus explains this soil to us; He says, "Now he who received seed among the thorns is he who hears the word, and the cares of this world and the deceitfulness of riches choke the word, and he becomes unfruitful" (vs. 22 NKJV). Here in this soil, we see that the seed did get in and got down deep, however, there was a rival crop that was undisturbed. There in the soil was the good seed and thorns, and they were growing together and the thorns never got dealt with. As they continued to grow together, the thorns began to choke out the seed to the point that the seed never became fruitful. So how does the gift of evangelism apply this to the church? The hearer hears the Word of God, and receives it, but the hearer never repents of his sin. There is a division inside the heart of the sinful hearer. He wants the good seed, and he wants the thorns and brambles at the same time, however, you cannot have it both ways. Jesus said, "I tell you, no; but unless you repent you will all likewise perish" (Luke 13:3).

These are the people who say, "Well, I tried Christianity for a while and it did not work for me. I gave my heart to Jesus, I trust in Him to save me, and now I am back just like I was before; it just did not work." The reason why it does not work for these individuals is because they are trying to hold on to Jesus with one hand and the world with the other. What has happened is the fact that they have a divided heart and do not know what being a Christian truly is. A Christian is somebody who has let go of the world with both hand and taken hold of Jesus.

The last soil where the seed was planted is the good ground. "But others fell on good ground and yielded a crop: some a hundred-fold, some sixty, some thirty" (Matt. 13:8 NKJV). It is shocking to realize that three of the four soils did not bear fruit. Jesus did not describe an age of great harvest, but one in which the seed would be rejected. He was not impressed with the great multitudes that followed Him, for He knew that most of the people would not receive His Word within and bear fruit. I have been pastoring and preaching the gospel long enough to know that if I keep scattering the seed, some of it is going to fall on good ground. Because it is in the sincere heart that fruit is produced. Fruit is the test of true salvation, because Jesus said, "You will know them by their fruits. Do men gather grapes from thorn-bushes or figs from thistles? Even so, every good tree bears good fruit, but a bad tree bears bad fruit" (Matt. 7:16-17 NKJV). This fruit would include behaving as follower of Christ, behaving as a fisher of men, behaving as a church member, sharing what we have with others, worshiping God, living holy lives, and doing good works. If a plant is to bear fruit, it must be rooted in soil and exposed to the Son. We are called to "go" and "make". When we go, we sow the seed and reap the harvest we are to take the harvest and make disciples. We are to keep on sowing and "he who continually goes forth weeping, bearing seed for sowing, shall doubtless come again with rejoicing, bringing his sheaves with him" (Ps. 126:6 NKJV).

ROAD MAP FOR RESCUERS

As church members, who have the gift of evangelism, God has called us to rescue. As a matter of fact, Jude reminds us of that call to rescue, he writes, "but others save with fear, pulling the out of the fire, hating even the garment defiled by the flesh" (Jude 23 NKJV). Therefore, we are to behave as church members rescuing sinners from the fires of hell. People will tell me, as an excuse, "Well, I do not have the gift of evangelism." Yes, it is true that God gave the gift to be an evangelist to some believers (Eph. 4:11). However, as stated earlier in this chapter, God has given the responsibility for presenting the gospel to every believer, gifted or not. The Great commission is a command for every child of God; and we are His ambassadors (2 Cor. 5:20) to share the message of reconciliation to a lost and dying world.

Another excuse that I have heard is, "Well, I am not that type of person who can just talk to people." Somewhere down the line we have come up with the idea that an ambassador for Christ has to be someone who is out going, a good talker, or a salesman. Paul recognized that Apollos was a servant just like him (1 Cor. 3:5). God uses different kinds of servants to reach different kinds of people, just as a craftsman uses a wide variety of tools to build what he is building. In His recue "tool kit," God has some church members who are His forceful "hammers", some who are His rough "sandpaper", some who are His quiet but relentless "screwdrivers", and others who are His fine "finishing tools." Each of us are a special tool in His hand to help lost people come to believe. The Master Builder will decide when He needs a tool like you for a life He want to build, you just need to always be ready.

Thankfully, someone has blazed a trail for us to follow. Jesus Himself has become for us an excellent model of how to reach across insurmountable obstacles to bring someone to God. There are at least six lifesaving actions to rescue the perishing. Here is the road map starting in John 4.

ENTER THEIR WORLD

According to John 4:4, Jesus had to go through Samaria. This raises a lot of questions especially for Jews of that day. Why would a Jew have to go through Samaria? A Jew would have found a different way if all possible to avoid going through Samaria. But Jesus considered it important to get there. The reason being is because if you want to reach Samaritans, then you have to go to Samaria. When you follow Jesus's recue roadmap you cannot expect people to come to our turf. We have to take the risk of going to theirs. Being in Samaria would have been an uncomfortable place for a Jew to be in, but when is comfort an issue when dealing with someone's salvation? No one was ever rescued by a comforter in a comfortable spot! The fire fighter has to go into a burning building. After an earthquake, the rescuer has to go into the rubble of a collapsed building. The life guard has to go into the surf where the drowning person is. We have to go into the world where the lost people are. You cannot save them if you do not seek them.

GO AFTER ONE

"Now Jacob's well was there. Jesus therefore, being wearied from His journey, sat thus by the well. It was about the sixth hour" (John 4:6 NKJV). Jesus did not go directly into the Samaritan village and start preaching on the streets. His strategy was not to initially try to reach the whole village. He simply focused on one, and because of that one, much of the village did ultimately come to faith in Him. In the same way, Jesus is not asking you to go reach your whole office, neighborhood, or school; He may just want you to do what He did and that is to focus on one. That is what Andrew did (John 1:41-42) and that one later preached to three thousand people where they would be saved. Only God knows the long-term series of miracles that could result from you praying a simple prayer: "Lord, please put on my heart, one person You want me to reach for you. Lord, open a door for your message, so that we may proclaim the mystery of Christ, Amen." Your "Peter", your "woman at the well" becomes a person you pray for by name every day, asking God to give you those natural opportunities for you to show them and tell them about Jesus.

CREATE SPIRITUAL CURIOSITY

"Jesus answered and said to her, "If you knew the gift of God, and who it is who says to you, 'Give Me a drink,' you would have asked Him, and He would have given you living water"" (John 4:10 NKJV). Jesus did not start by talking about her sinful relationship or by introducing Himself as the Savior. He just threw out some "bait" that would make a fish start nibbling. He said something that would create spiritual curiosity. Jesus told us to do the same, "Let your light so shine before men, that they may see your good works and glorify your Father in heaven" (Matt. 5:16 NKJV). The gift of evangelism enables you to do just that, but how can we do that? When we behave as church members, we can start building some bridges or relationships with them. We can show them random acts of kindness. We can invite them to church services, events, Sunday School, or anything where you are actively engaging them, presenting and sowing the seed.

START WITH THEIR STARTING POINT

"Jesus answered and said to her, "Whoever drinks of this water will thirst again"" (John 4:13 NKJV). What has happened in the past, when it came to evangelism, believers started making it man's sin problem their starting point. Yes, sin is a problem, however, praise God, Jesus already dealt with the sin problem when He died on the cross. Today, people do not understand the wrong of sin, because sin has been neutralized by a culture that rejects the "absolute" idea that there is a right and wrong. Therefore, if people around us do not understand the spiritual peril they are in, because of their sin, then how do we introduce the Savior to people to who sin is not an issue? Jesus started talking about a need the woman at the well cared about. According to verse 13, Jesus turns the corner to reveal the problems with every well this woman has ever gone to for her satisfying love. While many of the lost people we need to rescue do not care much about the disease of sin, they care deeply about the symptoms of sin in their lives. They probably do not know it is sin which is causing those symptoms in their lives, but they are experts on the damage sins does.

Here are a few symptoms you can look for. Loneliness is a symptom where a person feels empty on the inside and broken within. Another symptom is restlessness, this is where a person does not have inner peace, no personal peace about things, or they are always wanting more. Then there is the dark side symptom. This symptom is where a person feels troubled, bothered by their bondage and tempter. They are a person who is selfish, or someone who is depressed. This symptom can be seen because this person can have a filthy language, or they display behavior of being insecure. Then next symptom is that of uncertainty and insecurity. The person who displays the behavior of insecurity reminds me of the *Peanuts* character, Linus and his security blanket. This person is always looking for life's anchors. One last symptom is that of pointlessness. These are people who are always wondering why do bad things happen to good people? What about life after death? What is the purpose of life? These are just a few examples of lost people that you have to figure out what symptom they have and start from there if you want to move them towards accepting Jesus Christ as their personal Lord and Savior. Jesus did not start with the issue of sin, but He did not avoid it either. We may know the history of the person's sin like Jesus, but we need to move them from the symptom to the disease, and then the cure.

AVOID RELIGIOUS TRAPS

So, as the lesson of what Jesus is saying to the woman at the well starts penetrating her heart, she tries to change the subject (John 4:20). Jesus refuse to fall into the trap of arguing religion with this woman (vs. 21). The issue is not religion; it is a relationship with God Himself. Many of us fall into the trap that Jesus so skillfully avoided. Our rescue mission is not to prove that our religion is better than someone else or defend our religious beliefs of practices. It is not even to convert a person to our denomination. Our mission is to present Jesus Christ and Him crucified (1 Cor. 2:2). A discussion of religion differences is bound to obscure the central message and polarize a conversation that could have been redemptive. When you understand what a person does with Jesus is a life-or-death situation, and you should always bring the conversation back to Jesus.

EMPHASIZE THE RELATIONSHIP

For church members, whether they have the gift of evangelism or not, to succeed in their life-or-death mission we have to stay on target. Talking about religion is a detour. Talking about a relationship with God is the main road. As Jesus modeled the effective rescue in Samaria, He quickly steered the conversation away from religion and back to a relationship. He refused to talk about how their different religions worshipped, instead He talked about, "But the hour is coming, and now is, when the true worshipers will worship the Father in spirit and truth; for the Father is seeking such to worship Him. God is Spirit, and those who worship Him must worship in spirit and truth" (John 4:23-24 NKJV). Again, it is how you relate to God that matters. Using the gift of evangelism is not really all that complicated. You are to take Jesus by one hand and someone you care about by the other hand and bring them together forever!

Tragically, church members tend to spend most of their relationship time with others who are already in the Jesus lifeboat. We will be in heaven with those folks forever, but we have only a few years here on earth to help some people outside the lifeboat get to heaven. It is easy to fill up our lives with other believers because it is comfortable and natural. However, it is hard work to build a relationship with someone outside of Christ, someone with whom we have less and less in common. But your relationship with a lost person may be the only road that will take that person to the cross. That lost person probably will not get there by the road marked "church" or "Christian media" or "evangelist". He or she will get to the cross because he or she was loved there by a friend of Jesus who paid the price to become their friend too. Use the gift of evangelism and behave as a church member.

CHAPTER FIFTEEN

ROYAL AMBASSADORS

Now then, we are ambassadors for Christ, as though God were pleading through us: we implore you on Christ's behalf, be reconciled to God. (2 Corinthians 5:20 NKJV)

The gift of apostleship is another gift that helps us behave as church members, because this gift motivates the church to get out of their comfort zone, which is inside the walls of the building, in order to fulfill the Great Commission. In Paul's list of gifts, found in 1 Corinthians 12:28-30, we find apostles and prophets are listed first. They are listed first because they are the one who laid the foundation for the ministry of the church. If I was to assign theme verses to this book, Ephesians 2:19-22 would probably be my top pick. "Now, therefore, you are no longer strangers and foreigners, but fellow citizens with the saints and members of the household of God, having been built on the foundation of the apostles and prophets, Jesus Christ Himself being the chief cornerstone, in whom the whole building being fitted together, grows into a holy temple in the Lord, in whom you also are being built together for a dwelling place of God in the Spirit" (Eph. 2:19-22 NKJV). We are to behave as church members working together, growing in our walk with Christ in unity and harmony thanks to the gifts of the Holy Spirit.

The word "apostle" means "one who is sent", or "a messenger." (Strong's Concordance, 1984) What is unique is the Latin equivalent which is the word "missionary" (Dictionary, 1828) Whether it is a gift or not, every Christian is called to be an evangelist, missionary or an apostle, because we have been given the message of reconciliation (2 Cor. 5:18) to be a testimony to a lost and dying world. The reason for the message of reconciliation, is because man had rebelled against God and therefore became an enemy of God and was out of fellowship. Because of Jesus Christ's work on the cross, God and man has been reconciled together. God has turned His face back towards the lost world in love. The word "reconcile" means "to change thoroughly" (Strong's Concordance, 1984) It gives us the idea that there has been a change in the relationship between God and man. Please understand God does not have to be reconciled to man, Jesus accomplished that on the cross, but it is sinful man who must be reconciled back to God. Therefore, the person who reconciles us back to God is Jesus Christ, which He accomplished that upon the cross.

When Jesus died on the cross, all our sins were imputed to Him. The word "impute" means to place on one's account" (Strong's Concordance, 1984) Basically, all our sins have been paid in full and God no longer holds them against us, if we have placed our faith in Jesus Christ. When we accept Jesus as our personal Lord and Savior, our sins are forgiven, we are reconciled back to God, and He has placed on account the righteousness of Christ (2 Cor. 5:21). The work of reconciliation is based upon imputation, because the demands of a Holy and Just God and His law have been paid in full by Jesus upon the cross, and God can be reconciled to sinners. Therefore, those who place their faith in Jesus Christ, will never have their sins imputed, held, against them. When you place your faith in Jesus your records are cleansed and they share the righteousness of Jesus.

How does this wonderful doctrine of reconciliation motivate church members to behave and serve Christ? We are Christ's ambassadors with a message, for God had given us the ministry and the work of reconciliation. The title ambassador comes from having a personal relationship with Jesus

Christ. By definition, an ambassador is a person assigned by the highest authority to represent him in a specific place. Usually, a nation's president or prime minister appoints the ambassador. The impression people in that place have of the ambassador's country depends on how the ambassador lives and behaves. Whether or not they understand the mind and heart of the one who assigned you depends on how clearly you communicate it by word and deed. We are Christ's ambassador, appointed by the highest Authority in the universe to represent Him! He has committed to us the message of what He did on the cross. He commanded us to represent what He is like by the way we live and behave, to communicate clearly the message He gave His life for us. Now, you may not want the responsibility of Christ's ambassadorial appointment. It appears you have no choice; you already have the assignment known as the Great Commission. Therefore, since we are Christ's ambassadors, you are His man or woman in your circle of influence, people will be forming their opinions of Jesus based on you, for better or for worse. They will either understand His life-saving message or miss His message based on what you do or say. You may be an effective ambassador for Jesus or you may be a disastrous one; but you will be Christ's ambassador. You have a life-or-death assignment from Jesus; to be His ambassador, to deliver His message. You have a life-or-death mission from Jesus, to be His rescuer, to reach someone who is dying without Him. You are probably thinking, "I cannot do this," and you are right. You cannot by yourself, but with Jesus you can (Phil. 4:13). All God is asking is for you to show up, be ready, and be available; and He will take care of the rest.

Now Satan is out there trying to do his best to tear everything apart, but Christ and His Church are involved in the ministry of reconciliation, working to bring things back together. Ministry is not easy, and if we are going to succeed, then we must behave as church members and motivated by the love of Christ, the massage He has given us, and the commission to be His ambassadors. That is where the gift of apostleship comes into play. It is there to aid us in doing the work of reconciliation.

There are some great examples in the Bible of missionaries that we can learn from. Epaphroditus serves as an illustration of an apostle. Paul to told the church at Philippi that he was their messenger (Phil. 2:25). Then there are the unnamed brothers involved in the collection Paul was taking for the saints in Jerusalem (2 Cor. 8:23). Of course, there were the Twelve and a few others like Paul (Rom. 1:1), Barnabas (Acts 14:14), and James (Gal. 1:19). All of these were gifted to lay the foundation of the church. However, there is a missionary in the Old Testament and his name is Jonah. Jonah is a great missionary book. As you begin to study the book of Jonah you can tell right away that this is a missionary story, because God said to Jonah, "Arise, go to Nineveh, that great city, and cry out against it; for their wickedness has come up before Me" (Jonah 1:2 NKJV). Nineveh was a Gentile city and God was telling Jonah, a Hebrew, to go to this city. So, as you understand this, you begin to understand this intriguing story of Jonah as one of the most interesting stories found in the Word of God.

This book is more than a whale of a story, it is a story with a message, a missionary message which we can use the gift of apostleship and behave as church members. Now people have tried their best to figure out if this story is a literal story or a parable, whether it could happen or whether it could not have happened. I believe this is one story, that we are to take by faith, and because of faith I believe it happened just as it is written in the Word of God. Some theologians and biologist have searched high and low to find out if there is indeed a whale big enough to swallow a man and keep him alive. However, trying to find a fish big enough to swallow a man causes you to miss the point. God prepared a great fish to swallow a man and keep him alive. What all that entails, God knows better than we do. In the Old Testament it is called a fish; in the New Testament it is called a whale, but the Hebrew word in the Old Testament is "ketos" which means "sea monster." (Strong's Concordance, 1984) What it was I do not really know. Maybe you have never seen one like it and probably never will; but God, the same God who made the world, prepared a great fish. I do not worry about the possibility; I just believe that God is able. Because you see, the question is now how great a fish, but how great a God? Therefore, we just simply accept that God is able to do everything far better that we can ever imagine. But again, we get so wrapped up and confused about the fish story that we forget that this is a missionary story.

THE MISSIONARY MANDATE

Now when God told Jonah to go to Nineveh, it was a great city. This large city had been established well before Jonah had arrive, however, it was a city with a huge sin problem. When God said to go to that city, God was showing that He is the God of missions. Jonah was a prophet, but he was a prophet to his own people. He was a patriot and loved his own people and his home, but he had nothing but contempt and hatred for the Ninevites because of their wickedness. He really had no desire to preach the gospel of God to these people because he thought they did not deserve it. Plus, he wanted God to judge them and so he was afraid that God might bless them. But when God said go to Nineveh, we see right away the heart of God. God wants to lift, to love, to bless all the nations of this world, and that includes the cruel nations, the oppressive nation, Iran, Iraq, China, North Korea, and Russia. It includes Muslims living in the United States who want to destroy this great nation. All of the people of the world: the ignorant people, the downtrodden people, the misguided people, the sick people, the suffering people, the perishing people of the world till all the earth shall be filled with the knowledge of the glory of the Lord as the waters cover the sea.

God told Jonah to go, but Jonah did not want to go. Please understand this, Jonah did not get into trouble because he went; he got into trouble because he did not go. Jonah got in trouble because he had the wrong behavior towards the will of God. Obeying the will of God is important as a missionary. There are parents who do not want their children to be missionaries, because they do not want them to go into places where there is danger. Jonah's behavior towards God's will comes from a deep feeling that God was asking him to do the impossible. Do you know where the safest place is? It is right in the middle of the will of God. Peter was safer on the waves with Jesus than he was in the boat without the Lord Jesus. The safest place and the happiest places are in the center of the will of God. That does not mean there will not be any difficulties. It does not mean there is going to be all honey and no bees. But if Jesus is there that is the place you need to be. There is not a higher place than to be in the middle of the will of God. It was when Jonah refused to listen to God and answer God's call that is where he got in to trouble.

Jonah had a bad behavior towards God's word as well. When he received God's command, he thought, "Well, the choice is up to me." That is not how that works, because when God commands us to do something we must listen and obey. Disobedience is not an option. Jesus said, "But why do you call

Me 'Lord, Lord,' and not do the things which I say?" (Luke 6:46 NKJV). Jonah forgot that it was a great privilege to be a prophet of God, to hear His Word, and know God's will. So, are you willing to do what God says if He tells you something to do? You might be thinking, "Well, He is not calling me because I do not have the education." That is not the question; the question is, are you willing? Jonah thought that he could hand in his resignation as a prophet. He knew that he could not run away from God, but he ran anyways. At one time or another, Moses, Elijah, and Jeremiah felt like quitting, but God did not let them. We need to stop offering up reason why we cannot come to church, why we cannot serve in the church, why we cannot share the gospel, why we cannot give our tithes and offering, why we cannot pray for someone, teach a class, become a preacher or missionary. What we need to do is start saying, "Here am I, Lord. Send me." So, what is the missionary mandate? "And He said to them, "Go into all the world and preach the gospel to every creature."" (Mark 16:15 NKJV). We need to arise and go to Nineveh, wherever your Nineveh is.

THE MISSIONARY MESSAGE

Here in the book of Jonah, we can see the gospel of Jesus Christ presented clearly and plainly. What is the missionary message? The missionary message is the gospel of Christ. What is the gospel of Christ? "For I delivered to you first of all that which I also received: that Christ died for our sins according to the Scriptures, and that He was buried, and that He rose again the third day according to the Scriptures" (1 Cor. 15:3-4 NKJV). We can find that message tucked away here in the book of Jonah. Listen to what Jesus says, "For as Jonah was three days and three nights in the belly of the great fish, so will the Son of Man be three days and three nights in the heart of the earth. The men of Nineveh will rise up in the judgment with this generation and condemn it, because they repented at the preaching of Jonah; and indeed, a greater than Jonah is here" (Matt. 12:40-41 NKJV). Jesus said that Jonah was a picture, a prophecy, a type, an illustration, a glimpse of Himself.

How does Jonah picture the Lord Jesus Christ, if he was disobedient and sinful, and ran from the Lord? Easy, Jesus became sin for us. "For He made Him who knew no sin to be sin for us, that we might become the righteousness of God in Him" (2 Cor. 5:21 NKJV). Jesus was not a sinner, but He took our sin. Jonah is a picture of Jesus and here is how. First, there is the vicarious death of Jesus. Those people aboard the ship represents a lost humanity. The vessel humanity is plunging in that storm through the waves of judgment, destined for eternal destruction on the reefs of judgment. Here is where Jonah becomes a picture of Jesus. There is a storm and something has to be done with the storm or else they are going to perish. The only way that the storm can be quieted, is by a substitutionary death. One person must die for all.

Notice Jonah 1:10-13. "Then the men were exceedingly afraid, and said to him, "Why have you done this?" For the men knew that he fled from the presence of the Lord, because he had told them. Then they said to him, "What shall we do to you that the sea may be calm for us?" for the sea was growing more tempestuous. And he said to them, "Pick me up and throw me into the sea; then the sea will become calm for you. For I know that this great tempest is because of me." Nevertheless, the men rowed hard to return to land, but they could not, for the sea continued to grow more tempestuous against them" (NKJV). So, do you see it? They are trying to bring the ship ashore by rowing harder, but there is nothing that can be done. There is only one way that the storm of judgment would be stopped and that is for the men to throw Jonah overboard. Now understand, Jonah had to be willing, and that is why he volunteered the information. Furthermore, it had to be done by their hand. Jonah could not jump overboard. Jesus Christ was not a suicide, nor was He a martyr; He was a substitutionary sacrifice. Yet, Jesus's death was done according to the will and plan of God. The last part of verse 14 says, "For you, O Lord, have done as it pleased you" (Jonah 1:14 NKJV). It has pleased the Lord to bruise the Lord Jesus Christ with the wicked hands we have taken Him and crucified Him. His guilt is upon us. Willingly Christ went to the cross, thrown into the sea of judgment to be devoured for us. That is a picture of the substitutionary death of our Lord and Savior Jesus Christ.

A second way Jonah is a picture of Jesus is the victorious resurrection of Jesus. "Now the Lord had prepared a great fish to swallow Jonah. And Jonah was in the belly of the fish three days and three nights" (vs 17 NKJV). Do you think that was by coincidence? The answer is no, because

Jesus was in the grave for three days and three nights (Matt. 12:40). This is a picture of the resurrection of our Lord and Savior Jesus Christ. That is the reason why I do not have any difficulty with the story of Jonah. If I can believe in the resurrection of Jesus Christ, I can believe in a whale swallowing a man and keeping him down for three days. If I can believe in God, the God who flung out the stars, the God who scooped up the seas and heaped up the mountains and made man from the dust of the earth, the God who painted the rainbow in the sky, the God who fashioned the wings of the butterfly, the God of heaven and earth is the God I worship, then He is the God of resurrection. What is the missionary message? The missionary message is this to the people of this world: Christ died for you sins. He was buried, raised again on the third day by the power of God; there is not another message like that in this world. Jesus is all this world needs today, and we need to behave as church members and use the gift of apostleship.

THE MISSIONARY MIRACLE

Do you know what the greatest miracle was in the book of Jonah? The greatest miracle was not Jonah staying down three days and three nights and being alive in the belly of that fish. The greatest miracle was the transformation of Nineveh. The greatest miracle is the miracle of grace when God forgave and when God saved. "Now the word of the Lord came to Jonah the second time, saying "Arise go to Nineveh, that great city, and preach to it the message that I tell you." So, Jonah arose and went to Nineveh, according to the word of the Lord. Now Nineveh was an exceedingly great city, a three-day journey in extent. And Jonah began to enter the city on the first day's walk. Then he cried out and said, "Yet forty days, and Nineveh shall be overthrown!"" (Jonah 3:1-4 NKJV). Did you miss God's calling the first time? Well, God is not finished with you, "Arise and go." For Jonah it took three days to walk across the city of Nineveh. Scholars tell us it was a city of perhaps a million people, the largest city at that time on the earth. Jonah walked across this large city and he was not preaching a bed of roses nor a message that was scratching their itching ears. No, Jonah preached the message that God told him to preach. It was a message of judgment. Listen, you will never understand the message of grace till you preach the message of judgment. The healing balm of the gospel means nothing to a man until he has been wounded by the sword of the law. So, Jonah preached the judgment of God, and the people of Nineveh repented of their sins (vs. 5-10). That is a great miracle of God's grace where God saves and God forgives, even people as vile and wicked as Nineveh. We are Christ's ambassadors given the message of reconciliation, with the aid of the Holy Spirit in us, to take to a lost and dying world.

THE EXPANDED PROGRAM OF MISSIONS

Jesus said, "Most assuredly, I say to you, he who believes in Me, the works that I do he will do also; and greater works than these he will do, because I go to My Father" (John 14:12 NKJV). Are we going to do greater works that Jesus? Since Jesus fed the five thousand with two loaves and two fishes, then does that mean you are going to do better than that? Since Jesus walked on water, then are we going levitate like Him? Since Jesus raised the dead, then how are we going beat that? Understand, Jesus is not saying we are going to do greater miracles than He did, but He is telling us that we will do greater works. For example, over in John 5:20 Jesus said, "For the Father loves the Son, and shows Him all things that He Himself does; and He will show Him greater works than these, that you may marvel" (NKJV). God the Father will show God the Son greater works than the miracles that we read about, that is what Jesus is talking about we will do. Jesus continues, "For as the Father raises the dead and gives life to them, even so the Son gives life to whom He will" (vs. 21 NKJV). God the Father is saying that God the Son will raise up the physically dead; God the Son gives spiritual life to those who come to Him. Jesus claimed to be one with His Father in His works. So, if healing a man on the Sabbath was a sin, then God the Father was at fault. Because God the Son did nothing of Himself, He only did what God the Father was doing. God the Father and God the Son work side by side, doing the same works the same way (John 10:30). Jesus was totally dependent upon God the Father and the power of God the Holy Spirit.

"For the Father judges no one, but has committed all judgment to the Son, that all should honor the Son just as they honor the Father. He who does not honor the Son does not honor the Father who sent Him" (John 5:22-23 NKJV). Because God the Father loves God the Son, the Father shows Him His works. The blind religious leaders could not see what Jesus was doing, because they did know God the Father or God the Son. In fact, even greater works were a part of God the Father's plan for God the Son, works that would cause the religious leaders to marvel. Now watch the greater works that Jesus is doing greater than raising the dead literally. "Most assuredly, I say to you, he who hears My word and believes in Him who sent Me has everlasting life, and shall not come into judgment, but has passed from death into life. Most assuredly, I say to you, the hour is coming, and now is, when the dead will hear the voice of the Son of God; and those who hear will live" (vs. 24-25 NKJV). Here Jesus is talking about salvation, hearing the gospel. This is the greater work, greater than raising the dead. The greatest work that you and I can ever do is leading a soul to Jesus Christ. Giving a person eternal life, through the gospel of Jesus Christ is greater than raising the dead. This is the greater Jesus is referring to when He tells us that we are going to do greater works than He did (John 14:12).

Why did Jesus come to earth and what was the work He had to do? "Jesus said to them, "My food is to do the will of Him who sent Me, and to finish His work"" (John 4:34 NKJV). Jesus did not come to be a miracle worker, someone who walks on water, raise the dead, nor to feed the multitudes; even though He did those things. Jesus's food was to finish the work of Father, which is to bring salvation to a lost and dying world. There is no way possible we could ever do greater works than Jesus did; even if we had the miracle working power which Jesus had, we still would not be able to do greater than Jesus. However, Jesus came to seek and to save that which is lost. Therefore, Jesus tells us that we are going to do a greater work than He did. We are going to able to bring in many more people to Jesus Christ than He did. So, when Jesus said that His food was to do the will of Him that sent Jesus, and to finish His work, Jesus now begins to talk to us. Here is where the mission gets expanded for those with the gift of apostleship. Jesus said, "Do you not say, 'There are still four months and then comes the harvest'? Behold, I say to you, lift up your eyes and look at the fields, for they are already white for the harvest! And he who reaps receives wages, and gathers fruit for eternal life, that both he who sows and he who reaps may rejoice together" (vs. 35-36 NKJV). Who is the one who is sowing the seed? The Lord Jesus. Who is the one who is going to do the reaping? Church members, and we are going to rejoice with Jesus. "For in this the saying is true: 'One sows and another reaps.' I sent you to reap that for which you have not labored; others have labored, and you have entered into their labors" (vs. 37-38 NKJV). It all started with Jesus planting the seed, others have cultivated; now is the time for us to behave as church members and with the gift of apostleship go out and reap. We are to be out there in the world reaping the harvest that Jesus began. Jesus is just simply saying that greater works than these is what church members, His children will do. More people were converted in one day at Pentecost than Jesus saw converted in all His ministry.

THE EXPLOSIVE POWER OF MISSIONS

If we are going to do greater works that Jesus, then how are we going to do that? We do not have what it takes. Do we have what Jesus had? The answer is yes, because Jesus goes back to the Father (John 14:12). This does not mean that we are going to upstage Him, nor does it mean that we are going to know a better way than Jesus did. What it means is that Jesus was doing these great works while here on earth, then He leaves, goes back to the Father, and sends the Comforter, the Holy Spirit who in turns gives great spiritual gifts so we can behave as church members (vs. 13). Therefore, the gift of apostleship is part of that explosive power to do greater works. The work that Jesus has begun is being completed through His church. Jesus did not leave us alone here and give us the great commission to do His work by ourselves, He sent His Spirit, the Holy Spirit, to live inside us to help us to do greater works.

THE EXPECTED PRACTICE OF MISSIONS

What is the expected practice of a missionary or someone with the gift of apostleship? Jesus says, "If your love Me, keep My commandments"

(John 14:15 NKJV). Later Johns writes, "Jesus answered and said to him, "If anyone loves Me, he will keep My word; and My Father will love him, and We will come to him and make Our home with him"" (vs. 23 NKJV). The person who does these greater works is the person who is filled with the Spirit (Eph. 5:18), who knows how to pray, and who is obedient, and keeps His commandments. Let me remind you again of what He has commanded us: "But you shall receive power when the Holy Spirit has come upon you; and you shall be witnesses to Me in Jerusalem, and in all Judea and Samaria, and to the end of the earth" (Acts 1:8 NKJV). Jesus has programed the whole church, for the whole age, to bring souls to Jesus. We are to be a witness for Him, and if we are not witnessing then we are not behaving as a church member. The royal ambassador's program has not failed, is just has not been tried. Remember, Jesus said, "And whatever you ask in My name, that I will do, that the Father may be glorified in the Son. If you ask anything in My name, I will do it" (John 14:13-14 NKJV). One theologian said, "Witnessing is a necessity for a truly saved soul. A light does not shine, a spring that does not flow, a seed that does not grow is no more a strange thing than a life in Christ that does not witness for Christ." Are we going to play church, or are we going to behave as church members and get serious about bringing souls to Christ.

CHAPTER SIXTEEN

BECOMING A PEOPLE OF THE TOWEL

After that, He poured water into a basin and began to wash the disciples' feet, and to wipe them with the towel with which He was girded. (John 13:5 NKJV).

One of the most intriguing people in the New Testament is a man by the name of Epaphroditus. His story can be found in Philippians 2:25-30. Epaphroditus is interesting because he was a rare individual who was a servant. In that text, it tells us Epaphroditus served the Apostle Paul (vs. 25), and was very sick. Yet, he still was concerned about the Philippians because he knew they were concerned about him (vs. 26). Epaphroditus is a church member who has the gift of service and or helps. Typically, those with the gift of service recognize the practical need in the church and they behave with an attitude of joy as they give assistance in meeting those needs. Those with the gift of serve and or help are usually those Christians that work behind the scenes, much like Epaphroditus.

Paul explains to us that the sickness Epaphroditus suffered came about because he was a servant. Paul writes, "Because for the work of Christ he came close to death, not regarding his life, to supply what was lacking in your service toward me" (Phil. 2:30 NKJV). The phrase "not regarding his life" is interesting, because it is a gambling term meaning "to recklessly expose one's life to danger." (Concise Oxford English Dictionary Eleventh Edition, 2004) In gambling terminology, it means "to risk everything on one roll of the dice." (Strong's Concordance, 1984) Epaphroditus willingly placed his life on the line to serve Paul. He gambled everything for Jesus Christ so that the man of God would be served and the Philippian church, who sent him, would be well represented.

In ancient Carthage, around 250 A.D., there was a group of Christian who called themselves "The Gamblers." (Unknown, 2015) They named themselves after Epaphroditus. The Gamblers would go into the city of Carthage, during the height of the plagues and at a time when the bodies were stacked head high along the streets, and carry the dead outside the city and bury them. They risked their very lives to serve the citizens of Carthage even though there was many in the city that hated them because they were Christians. The Gamblers possessed the same spiritual gift that dwelt in Epaphroditus, the gift of service. Did you know that the desire to serve and help others is not a natural desire. That is the reason the Holy Spirit gives you a gift of service so we can behave as church members. However, it is more than that, this gift mirrors the same selfless service that is seen in our Lord Jesus Christ.

On the eve of His death, Jesus assumes the place of a slave and serves His disciples. While they were eating the Passover, Jesus gets up from the table and dons a towel. He poured a basin of water, and He begins to wash the disciples' feet. When Jesus did this, He took the place of a slave before His men. He took the place of the lowest kind of slaves, who were called "the people of the towel." They were called this because it was their job to wash the feet of those who were superior to them. Jesus did this to call His disciples to become people of the towel as well. He said, "For I have give you an example, that you should do as I have done to you" (John 13:15 NKJV). Jesus wants every child of God, who follows Him, to be a servant. He wants us to become a people of the towel. If we are going to exercise our gift of service, then we must develop a heart for others like that which beat in the chest of Jesus. We can become people of the towel, but to do so, we should learn the lessons Jesus teaches His disciples in John 13:1-17.

WE MUST LEARN FROM HIS LABOR

Jesus "rose from supper and laid aside His garments, took a towel and girded Himself. After that, He poured water into a basin and began to wash the disciples' feet, and to wipe them with the towel with which he was girded" (John 13:4-5 NKJV). Washing feet was slave's work. Even Jewish servants could not be forced to wash their master's feet. It was a task reserved for the lowest Gentile slaves. Sometimes, a child would wash a parent's feet; a wife would wash the feet of her husband; or a friend would wash a friend's feet in a display of extreme affection. So, here we see Jesus as He took the place of a slave before His disciples. He willingly humbles Himself to meet a need in the lives of His men.

Jesus washed the feet of His disciples without being asked to do so. In fact, they were probably shocked when Jesus began to wash their feet (vs. 6, 8). Understand, in those days, it was a breach of hospitality to fail to wash a guest's feet (Luke 7:40-50). The disciples should have been falling all over one another to what the feet of Jesus, but it never entered their minds to serve Him. After all, for many of them, they probably were not accustomed to the proper edict of hosting and dining in society. However, they knew enough that they were all waiting for someone to serve them. Jesus served with no expectation of reward. No one even said thank you. He did what He did just because He wanted to do it. Jesus served others with a willing heart. No one had to twist His arm, He voluntarily took the place of a slave and served His men. Jesus had already told His men, "Just as the Son of Man did not come to be served, but to serve, and to give His life a ransom for many" (Matt. 20:28 NKJV). Therefore, when Jesus performed this service, it should have reminded them of what He was teaching them.

Jesus served those who did not deserve to be served. Think about it, because we as church member should behave the same way Jesus did. Take for example, Jesus washed the feet of Simon Peter and before the night would end those feet would stand at a Roman fire as Peter denied Jesus three times. He washed the feet of Judas Iscariot. His feet had already carried him to the Jewish leaders where he bargained away the life of Jesus for a few pieces of silver. Before this night would end, those same feet would carry Judas back to the Jews where he would completely abandon Jesus to His enemies. Jesus also washed the feet of the other ten and before the night would end, all of those feet would run away in fear. Jesus knew all of this, yet He served them anyways. What is impressive is the fact that He continued at the task until every dirty foot had been cleansed and the job was completed (John 13:5).

Jesus did what He did for a very specific purpose. While He and His men were celebrating the Passover, the disciples were occupied with other matters, while Jesus was occupied with the weighty matters of eternity. He knew that before the night ended, He would go to Gethsemane where He would labor in prayer before His Father. He knew that Judas would betray Him to the Jews (John 13:21-27). He knew that the Romans would arrest Him and put Him on trial. He knew that before twenty-four hours passed, He would be condemned, rejected by His people, beaten, crucified, and buried. He knew that He would bear the sins of His people on Calvary and die in their place. His mind carried all these burdens, still He wanted to serve His men. While Jesus carried the burden of the lost on His heart, His men were worried about far more trivial matters. According to Luke 22:24-30, they were arguing about who should be the greatest among the disciples. Jesus used the washing of His disciples' feet to teach them what being a true servant was all about.

We are not behaving as church members when we behave like the disciples behaved that night. There are very few who truly possess a servant's heart. Most are willing to be served, but not too many are willing to serve others. Like Jesus, we should be willing to serve others regardless of the cost. We must be willing to humble ourselves and do whatever is necessary to serve others. Paul stressed this to the church at Philippi, "Let each of you look out not only for his own interests, but also for the interests of others (Phil. 2:4 NKJV). He also points this out to the church at Rome, as he is telling them how to behave like a Christian. "Be kindly affectionate to one another with brotherly love, in honor giving preference to one another; not lagging in diligence, fervent in spirit, serving the Lord; rejoicing in hope, patient in tribulation, continuing steadfastly in prayer; distributing to the needs of the saints, given to hospitality" (Rom. 12:10-13 NKJV). Listen, someone has to do the grunt work! We must learn to serve without having to be asked. We must learn to serve others willingly, with no thought of reward (Matt. 6:2-4). Whose praise would you rather have? The praise of men or the blessings of the Lord? We must learn to serve those who are selfish and refuse to serve. We must teach the next generation how to serve. Teach them by encouraging them to be more involved in service. Teach them by example. There is much we can learn from our Lord's labor. He served others and set a standard for us that we should strive to reach in our own service.

WE MUST LEARN FROM HIS LORDSHIP

Jesus said, "If I then, your Lord and Teacher, have washed your feet, you also ought to wash one another's feet" (John 13:14 NKJV). When you look at what was going on that night, when Jesus was washing the feet of His disciples and compare it to who He is; something amazing is revealed. First, there in John 13:4 it says, that Jesus "rose from supper" (NKJV). Jesus had already risen from His fellowship with God the Father and God the Holy Spirit in heaven to come to earth. Second, Jesus laid aside His outer garments (vs. 4). Jesus had already laid aside His heavenly glory to be born in human flesh. "Let this mind be in you which was also in Christ Jesus, who being in the form of God, did not consider it robbery to be equal with God, but made Himself of no reputation, taking the form of a bondservant, and coming in the likeness of men. And being found in appearance as a man, He humbled Himself and became obedient to the point of death, even the death of the cross" (Eph. 2:5-8 NKJV). Third, Jesus girded Himself with a towel (John 13:4). The word towel refers to a "knotted cloth", or a slave's service apron (Strong's Concordance, 1984) Jesus had already robed His deity in humanity when He came to this earth as a man. Next, Jesus poured water into a basin to cleanse the dirty feet of His men (vs. 5). Jesus would soon pour out His precious blood to cleanse the dirty souls of His people. Finally, Jesus washed and dried the feet of the disciples (vs. 5). Jesus would wash away the awful stains of sin from the souls of all who call upon His name. Jesus was and is God in human flesh (John 1:1, 14; Col. 1:15; John 14:9). This was and is the Lord of glory. This is the Creator of all things (Col. 1:16). This is the Savior, Redeemer, and Deliverer of lost sinners (1 Pet. 1:18-19). This is the King of kings and the Lord of lords (Rev. 19:16).

If the Lord Jesus Christ would condescend to serving the disciples, then we have no excuse for not serving others. If He would wash the feet of Peter and Judas, then how much more should we seek to find ways to serve those around us? The fact is serving others is not an option; it is a command (John 13:14). The word "ought" in verse 14 is in a tense that suggest we should always be washing feet (Strong's Concordance, 1984) The word "ought" has the idea of "the good will due to another" (Concise Oxford English Dictionary Eleventh Edition, 2004) In other words, the Lord is saying that we should always be looking for ways to serve others for His glory. We should continually be searching for ways to demonstrate the love of God to those around us! Some people are especially gifted to serve others (Rom. 12:8). Those people are easy to identify, however, regardless of whether we have the gift of service or not, we all can and should behave as church members actively serving others for the glory of God.

We are never more like Jesus than when we are serving others. In Luke 6:40, Jesus says, "A disciple is not above his teacher, but everyone who is perfectly trained will be like his teacher" (NKJV). When we humble ourselves and assume the position of a slave before others, we demonstrate true Christ likeness. When we behave as a church member serving one another, we glorify Him and honor Him in His way for His glory (Jam. 4:10; 1 Pet. 5:5-6). Serving others is a recipe for happiness. Jesus put it this way, "If you know these things, blessed are you if you do them" (John 13:17 NKJV). When we can come to the place where we stop worrying about who is doing what and we simply serve who we can, where we can; we will live a more blessed victorious Christian life. If we could ever come to the place where it does not matter who does what job; who gets the glory for what is done; or even why the task needs to be accomplished, we would be developing into a people of the towel.

WE MUST LEARN FROM HIS LOVE

As we study this event of Jesus washing the feet of His disciples, notice the reason for all of this: "Now before the Feast of the Passover, when Jesus knew that His hour had come that He should depart from this world to the Father, having loved His own who were in the world, He loved them to the end" (John 13:1 NKJV). This verse tells us why Jesus did everything He did. It tells us why He came into this world in the first place. It tells us why He became a man. It tells us why He laid aside the riches of heaven to embrace poverty on earth. It tells us why He died for us on the cross. It tells us why He willingly assumed the place of a slave to serve His men. It is very simple reason as to why. Verse 1 tells us that Jesus knew His time with His men was at an end. He knew He was leaving, and even at the end of His earthly ministry, His heart was filled with love for His men. Before He leaves them, He is determined to teach them a much-needed lesson of humanity. Before He leaves, He is determined to demonstrate the depths of His love for them. So, He assumes the place of a slave and He washes their feet. He served them because He loved them!

His love for us explains everything He did for us. His love for us explains 2 Corinthians 8:9, which says, "For you know the grace of our Lord Jesus Christ, that though He was rich, yet for your sakes He became poor, that you through His poverty might become rich" (NKJV). His love for us explains it all; from Bethlehem to Calvary, through the tomb and back to glory. He did it all because He loved us!

THANK GOD FOR GUYS LIKE HUR

In Exodus 17:8-13, we meet a man who behaved as though he had the gift of service. Before we meet this man, let me give you a little bit of background on what is going on to bring this man to a willingness to serve others. It was a very important time in the life of the nation of Israel. As they journeyed toward the Promised Land, they are faced with their first encounter with an enemy army. The Bible tells us they came face to face with the armies of Amalek. These people were a nomadic tribe that was a constant thorn in the side of the people of Israel. In this first encounter, they proved their nature by conducting an unprovoked attack against the Israelites. This prompts the Lord to promise the total annihilation of the Amalekites. This promise would later be fulfilled.

In these verses, we find the Moses mentioned, along with Aaron, and the first mention of Joshua, Israel's future leader. All of these men were great leaders in the history of Israel and all played a very important role in the early history of Israel. However, there is another man mentioned in these verses that deserves our attention: his name is Hur. This a man who steps out of nowhere, demonstrates the gift of helps and then disappears into the same shadows from which he came. It is understandable that people have long looked to Moses and Joshua as great leaders and as role models. Both men are classed as true hearos of the faith. However, in this particular story, the real heroes are Aaron and Hur.

Here in these verses, we see how Hur demonstrated the gift of helps. When Moses held his hands up, it was a sign of intercession and Israel prevailed in the battle. When Moses put his hands down, Amalek prevailed. After a while, Moses became weary to hold his own hands up and Aaron and Hur stepped up and held Moses's hands up until the battle was finished. These two were true heroes, however, of the two, Hur seems to stand out. Here is a man about whom we know next to nothing, yet he enabled an entire nation to see a great victory. Let me just add, that we need to behave as church members and give thanks for those in our church who are the people of the towel, those who are just like Hur. These people of the towel are those who are willing to take the second seat; those who are willing to make up the second line; people who are often unnoticed, un-thanked, and underappreciated, people just like Hur. People who perform a function in the Body of Christ are so vital, but who never get the recognition they deserve. People who enable the rest of us to do what the Lord has called us to do.

PEOPLE LIKE HUR ARE INVALUABLE

"But Moses' hands became heavy; so, they took a stone and put it under him, and he sat on it. And Aaron and Hur supported his hands, one on one side, and the other on the other side; and his hands were steady until the going down of the sun" (Ex. 17:12 NKJV). Moses is unable to hold his hands up, and if they fall, then the Amalekites will certainly win the battle. However, Aaron and Hur step forth and held the hands of Moses up until the battle is won. The task Hur accomplished that day does not sound like a lot to you and me, however, had it not been for the service of this man, Moses would not have had the strength to do his job, and Joshua would never have been able to lead Israel to victory in the battle. The help he performed was absolutely invaluable!

Things have not changed in the church today. In the church, there are still leaders like Moses, Aaron, and Joshua. These are those who get the credit, those who get seen, those who do the headline grabbing work of the ministry, but behind every one of those leaders, there is an army of people of the towel, just like Hur. There are a vast number of people who are praying, fasting, and carrying the load so that the leaders are able to do their work. People who pray and seek the Lord's face and lift up the hands of those who are weary in the Lord's work are absolutely indispensable.

As a pastor, there are times when I preach a message that really touches someone's heart. After the worship service, people will come up and tell me they really enjoyed that message, it really helped them, they were blessed. People will try to give the preacher credit for the message; however, I know that anything good that came out of my mouth and mind came from the Lord. Now as a pastor the most valuable thing I have as I stand behind the pulpit, is knowing that God's precious people are holding my hands up in prayer. Those are the ones who are behaving as church members. Those are the ones who are using their gift of service. Those are the ones who are standing in the gap for those who are out front. The world may never know your name, but if the battle is ever to be won it will be won by the saints of God who are winning the victory in the closet of prayer as they lift up the hands of God's servants. Even Jesus had some who held up His hands as He ministered, who were people of the towel. "There were also women looking on from afar, among whom were Mary Magdalene, Mary the mother of James the Less and of Joses, and Salome, who also followed Him and ministered to Him when He was in Galilee, and many other women who came up with Him to Jerusalem" (Mark 15:40-41 NKJV). If the aid of others helped the Lord, then how could anyone think that they could get by without it? The Body of Christ, the church, would be nothing if were not for those who spent time lifting the church up in prayer. Our pastors would be nobody if it were for the people of the towel behaving as church members. May God bless everyone who stands in the gap for God's servants! No price could ever be placed on what people like Hur are worth to the church!

PEOPLE LIKE HUR ARE INVOLVED

Hur was not a great leader like Moses. He was not a great general like Joshua. He was not priest like Aaron. He was not even in the army. He was just Hur. The Bible does tell us later that Hur was a man of influence among the people, which indicates that he was someone with the gift of helps (Ex. 24:14). On this day, there was one thing Hur could do and he did it willingly, actively, and faithfully. He could hold up the hands of Moses, and he did the best job he could.

That should be a lesson for us as church members. Not everyone can preach great messages, not everyone can sing solos or play instruments. Not every can be an effective evangelist or missionary. Not everyone can do the visible jobs. We need to remember that the Lord has gifted us spiritual gifts, and has placed us in His body in the place that you can be the most effective (1 Cor. 12:4-27). Therefore, whether we are a highly visible part of the body, or an obscure, unnoticed part, we are all essential to the proper function of the Body of Christ and we need to behave as church members. The whole idea is that while we cannot do everything, we can do what we can do. Jesus said about Mary, "She done what she could. She has come beforehand to anoint My body for burial" (Mark 14:8 NKJV). It is not important if you can do what others can do, it is important that you do what you can do. Be what the Lord has saved you to be and He will bless your life!

Thank God for those people who know they cannot do everything, but are determined to do something! Thank God for the people of the towel who behave as a church member. There is always a place in the Lord's work for people who want to be involved (1 Cor. 15:58; Eph. 2:10).

PEOPLE LIKE HUR ARE INVISIBLE

Up to this point in the book of Exodus, Hur is not mentioned and there are only a couple of others afterward. This is a man who lived in the shadows while others around him received the glory. He was invisible to the crowd, who could only see Moses, Aaron, and Joshua. After the battle, can you imagine Joshua as he led the victorious Israelite army back into camp? I am sure there were congratulations all around, slaps on the back and shouts of "Way to go!"; "Good work, Joshua!" I can see the people as they received Moses back into the camp with shouts and expressions of gratitude. I can hear Aaron as he led the congregation in a prayer of thanksgiving to the Lord for giving them the victory. Then I can see a fellow named Hur as he walks wearily towards his tent to rest. No one pat him on the back; no one tells him that he did a good job. In fact, only a couple of people know what he did that day. To the people, he is invisible, but in his heart, he is overjoyed because he knows God knows! While no one in the camp is telling Hur that he did a great job that day, the Father in heaven makes note of Hur's sacrifice and Hur hears a voice whisper, "Well done, good and faithful servant."

There are many in churches today who are just like Hur. They are invisible to the crowds. The preacher, the teachers, and the singers all get their pats on the back and hear the people say, "Well done!" People like Hur remain invisible. I am convinced that the people of the towel while they are here on earth will one day receive the greatest acclaim in heaven. Furthermore, I believe that those who are on the front line will have the greater judgment (Jam. 3:1). If the Lord has called you to be a people of the towel and asks you to perform a quiet, godly ministry, rejoice in the call He has extended to you and let Him use your life as He sees fit. After all, it is His kingdom and He knows where we are needed far better than we ever could!

PEOPLE LIKE HUR ARE INVESTORS

As Hur lived his life and performed his God-given ministry, others were watching. Sometime later, God needed someone to build the Tabernacle and provide a place where the Lord could meet with His people. When the Lord looked down at those millions of Israelites, His eyes settled on one man. It was a fellow by the name of Bezalel (Ex. 31:2). This man just happened to be the grandson of a man named Hur. Bezalel was watching as his grandfather served the Lord. He watched as he took the backseat while others got all the credit. He watched as the Lord used Hur time and again for His glory. He probably remembered an evening when Hur returned to the hilltop, tired, and drained from holding up the arms of Moses. While the rest of the camp was excited about the great victory that Joshua and Moses had worked, Bezalel probably took note of the fact that it was his grandfather, a man who was willing to serve God in a quiet fashion that helped bring the great victory to pass.

If you have the gift of service, you may not have a high-profile position. You may think that cleaning the church, praying for the services, or teaching your little class is unimportant function. Just remember that others are watching you. There are people who are not saved who are watching how you serve the Lord in your position. There are little ones who will see whether mom or dad is faithful in the little things. There are no unimportant duties in the church. To behave as church member means that your life is an investment. As we do the little things God gives us, we are telling all those around us that God's work is important in every detail. That is why we ought to be on time and ready for the Lord's work on Sunday and Wednesday. That is why sermon preparation is vital, why the church building should be kept clean, because people are watching. When we behave as a church member using our gift of service, we are showing a lost and dying world that God's business is the most important business in the world.

When we serve the Lord as we should, we are making an investment in the lives of others. We are making a grand statement about the greatness of our God. Just as love compelled the Savior to serve, our love for others should compel us to serve others for His glory. When we love as we should, we will place the needs of others ahead of our own needs. 1 Corinthians 10:24 reminds us of our obligation to others, it says, "Let one seek his own, but each one the other's well-being" (NKJV). True love manifests the heart of Epaphroditus and Hur. True love lays everything on the life for the glory of God and for the good of others. True love always fulfills the two greatest commandments (Matt. 22:37-40). The bottom line is this behave as a church member and serve or help others.

CHAPTER SEVENTEEN

LOVE MERCY

Jesus wept. (John 11:35 NKJV)

The prophet Micah tells us of the character of the next spiritual gift; the gift of mercy. Micah writes, "He has shown you, O man, what is good; and what does the Lord require of you but to do justly, to love mercy, and to walk humbly with your God" (Mic. 6:8 NKJV). When we behave as a church member, we are to love mercy, demonstrate mercy, show mercy. There is not a better example of what the gift of mercy means than our Lord Jesus Christ. The gift of mercy is the "cheerful acts of compassion characterize those with the gift of mercy. Person with this gift aid the body by empathizing with hurting members. They keep the body healthy and unified by keeping others aware of the needs within the church" (LifeWay Christian Resources, 2003) The shortest verse of the Bible says, "Jesus wept" (John 11:35 NKJV). According to the Greek word for the word "weep", and is only used one time in the Bible (John 11:35), it was more of a silent weeping. While everyone else was moaning and crying aloud Jesus was weeping silently with tears.

But why was Jesus weeping at all? For He knew, according to John 11:11, He was going to wake up Lazarus. The weeping of Jesus does show us the humanity of our Savior, plus His weeping represents what mercy should look like. Jesus is the perfect God-Man, however, Jesus experienced situations, human emotions, and human behavior in a deeper way that we do. His tears assure us of that our Lord and Savior can show sympathy; for He is indeed "a Man of sorrows and acquainted with grief" (Isa. 53:3 NKJV). Today, we can find all the mercy we need from Him. "Seeing then that we have a great High Priest who has passed through the heavens, Jesus the Son of God, let us hold fast our confession. For we do not have a High Priest who cannot sympathized with our weakness, but was in all points tempted as we are, yet with out sin. Let us therefore come boldly to the throne of grace, that we may obtain mercy and find grace to help in time of need" (Heb. 4:14-16). But that is what makes Jesus so awesome! As He was ministering here on earth, He experience what we experience but in a deeper way. Therefore, since He know what we go through, we can come boldly into His presence and get the help we need. There is no trial too great, no need too small, no temptation too strong that our High Priest cannot handle for us! He will give us mercy and grace when we need it. If we fail to hold fast to our confession of Jesus Christ, we are not proving that Jesus Christ has failed. We are only telling a lost and dying world that we have failed to behave like Christ, because we have failed to draw on His grace and His mercy when it has been freely given to us as a spiritual gift from the Holy Spirit.

Jesus indirectly taught us how to behave as a church member having the gift of mercy in the Beatitudes (Matt. 5:7-10). This is the way we are designed to relate to others; meaning we are to do so with mercy and peace, with pure motives, and patience. There are many people who will tell me "I will try to behave." Please understand our behavior is a fruit of the Spirit, it is not an effort that you put forth. We just do not merely apply the teachings of Jesus onto the surface of our lives. We must keep His commandments, and if we want to be merciful then we must love mercy.

A SIDE OF MERCY

"Blessed are the merciful, for they shall obtain mercy" (Matt. 5:7 NKJV). Let me just say, that mercy is not an easygoing, open-mined, wishy-washy attitude that winks at sin. In our postmodern culture has embraced the idea of tolerance to argue that everyone has the right to do whatever he wants. The reason for this is because mercy and tolerance are such close cousins in our world's way of thinking to the point that the two terms have become almost interchangeable. However, biblical mercy and tolerance are not the same thing. God is merciful, but He is not tolerant. He does not let sin slip by unnoticed or unpunished. Some people have a hard time understanding this principle, they believe the gospel message itself is a picture of God's tolerance. But it is not, God has not overlooked our sin; He has merely arranged payment for our sin through the precious blood of Jesus. Furthermore, mercy is more powerful than tolerance. Tolerance cost its giver nothing, while mercy will always cost its giver something, perhaps even everything.

Mercy is not pity, because pity is what the priest and the Levite showed in the parable of the Good Samaritan. The two felt sorry for the man who had been beat up by the robbers and left for dead. But it was only the Samaritan who was moved, beyond feelings and emotions of pity, into a merciful action. The gift of mercy helps us to identify with the needs of those around us, respond in compassion, and seek to give more than they deserve.

A SIDE OF PURITY

We experience God's mercy when we put our trust in Jesus (Eph. 2:4-7), and He gives us a clean heart (Acts 15:9), and peace (Rom. 5:1). After receiving mercy from God, we then behave as a follower of Christ and a church member by sharing His mercy with others. We are to also seek to keep our hearts pure that we might see God in our lives. "Blessed are the pure in heart, for they shall see God" (Matt. 5:8 NKJV). Our culture does not provide us an easy environment for maintaining purity of heart. But is it any wonder that our world is confused about the standard of purity these days, when the modern-day church seems to be sending out mixed signals about sin? For example, several denominations have suggested that responsible cohabitation should be seen as a recognized option to marriage. Another example is, other denominations have split or are at the point of splitting over the issues of homosexuality and transgenderism.

The "pure in heart" are few and far between these days. Purity of heart refers to more than the avoidance of sinful behaviors. It is a singleness of mind and purpose. The reason the "pure in heart" or those who are given the gift of mercy can behave as a church member is not because they have more self-control that others, but it is because they have only one master, only one King. They do not have conflicting loyalties. The Holy Word of God comes down hard on those who have a divided heart. It says for example, serving God and money is worse than serving money alone because the divided heart pulls us in two directions (Matt. 6:24). Another example, being lukewarm is worse than being either hot or cold. Better to be cold than to be a tasteless, repulsive lukewarm drink that is trying to be hot and cold at the same time (Rev. 3:15-16). All behavior comes from the heart. Jesus said, "Brood of vipers! How can you being evil, speak good things? For out of the abundance of the heart the mouth speaks. A good man out of the good treasure of his heart brings forth good things, and an evil man out of the evil treasure brings forth evil things" (Matt. 12:34 NKJV). So, when our hearts are pure and undivided, kind words and responsible actions just naturally flow out through our lives. That is why the gospel is about the heart of man, about being cleansed from and given a new nature, a new heart that desires to be holy "as He who called you is holy, you also be holy in all your conduct" (1 Pet. 1:15 NKJV).

A SIDE OF PEACE

Those with the gift of mercy will often be those who are peacemakers. "Blessed are the peacemakers, for they shall be called sons of God" (Matt. 5:9 NKJV). Jesus is the supreme example of being a peacemaker. Paul marveled at how God had reconciled two irreconcilable groups into one kingdom community, by tearing down the dividing wall of hostility that separated Jews and Gentiles and making both groups one through the she blood of Jesus Christ, our peace (Eph. 2:14-18). Therefore, since Jesus is our peace, peacemaking should be a behavior of every child of God, especially those with the gift of mercy. We are to be active and persistent in our efforts to resolve conflicts, restore relationships, and repair broken walls. We must refuse to retaliate when wronged (Matt. 5:39), but love our enemies (Matt. 5:44), even to the point of genuinely praying for the good of those who persecute and belittle us.

Paul gives us clear directions on how to behave as a church member and be a peacemaker in Romans 12:17-21. Never get revenge, never pay back evil for evil. Do what is honorable in everyone's eyes. Make every effort to live at peace with everyone. Refuse to avenge ourselves when harmed or threatened. Instead, we should conquer evil with good and as a result we will resemble our Father so others will know us as the sons of God. I know it is not easy to behave like a peacemaker, but our hearts should never stop seeking peace and doing everything we can to be used of God, to advance His kingdom work, and edifying the church all by simple behaving as a church member.

It is hard being a peacemaker, because part of having the gift of mercy is the ability to forgive. Forgiving someone who has wronged you is not easy. Take David for example. David was man after God's own heart (1 Sam 13:14). How is it possible that David was a man after God's own heart when he was guilty of adultery, deceit, and murder? David was a good man, a godly man, but he was still human. When he excelled, he rose to the top; when he failed, he plummeted to the very bottom. However, David was quick to get things straightened out with God. When he was confronted with his sin, confession was quickly offered and repentance was swift. David was a man after God's own heart because David kept short accounts with God.

David was also a man who kept short accounts with his fellow man as well. In 2 Samuel 19:16-23, David is returning to Jerusalem after the rebellion of his son Absalom. As David nears the city, he is met by a man name Shimei. Shimei had wronged David and if anybody deserved David's hatred and wrath it was Shimei. However, when David came face to face with Shimei, he did not react in anger or malice. David actually reached out to Shimei with compassion, mercy, and forgiveness. David is a picture of someone who loves mercy by offering forgiveness. This is how we should behave as church members.

THE ATTACK DAVID SUFFERED

To understand what is going on in 2 Samuel 19, we need to know what events took place several months earlier. Over in 2 Samuel 16:5-23, David was attacked by Shimei, who had some harsh words for David as he fled the city of Jerusalem during the rebellion of Absalom. "Now when King David came to Bahurim, there was a man from the family of the house of Saul, whose name was Shimei the son of Gera, coming from there. He came out, cursing continuously as he came" (2 Sam. 16:5 NKJV). The word "cursing" refers to things that were "worthless and vile; disgraced; and brought low." (Concise Oxford English Dictionary Eleventh Edition, 2004) Shimei is revealing the fact that David has been disgraced and calls him a "bloodthirsty man" (vs. 7 NKJV), and a murder. Basically, what Shimei is shouting is, "Get out of here you murderer! Get out of here you fool, you are a nobody!" These words of Shimei must have cut into the heart of David like a knife. We have all had people say hurtful things to us and about us. When it happens, it hurts, it makes us angry.

Now, not only did Shimei use his words to attack David, but he also threw stones. Apparently, he did not only want to harm David with his words, but Shimei wanted to do physical harm too. But notice where Shimei is doing all of this cursing and throwing stones; in public. Shimei is trying his best to publicly humiliate David. It is one thing to be attacked by one person but to be attacked by many people, the hurt is magnified. When people hurl words in our direction, or when they attack us publicly, or even behind our backs, it rips us open to the bone. Some of what Shimei was true. David was guilty of murder, though I am not certain how many people knew about his deed. Regardless, David remembers. While the "bloodthirsty man" part was true, the rest of Shimei's words were lies. Dave was not a vain, worthless man. He was God's chosen King of Israel. In spite of his failures and his foolishness, he was God's anointed and was to be respected for that fact alone (1 Chron. 16:22). In fact, David had more integrity than Shimei. When given the opportunity to kill Saul, David had refused to lay His hand on God's man (1 Sam. 24:6, 11).

The words of Shimei in 2 Samuel 16:8, are nothing but blatant lies. In fact, there is a total of three lies in this one verse. Shimei said that God is getting revenge against David for murdering Saul and his family; that is a lie! Saul committed suicide and his sons were killed in battle. Shimei said that David stole the throne; that is a lie! The throne was given to David by a sovereign act of God. Shimei said, that God has given your throne to Absalom; that is a lie! Absalom took the throne of his father by rebellion. The bottom line here is the fact that Shimei is the kind of person who would kick another man when he was down. This was indeed the lowest time for David. His kingdom and his family are in shambles. He is an outcast and on the run from his own son. Here is Shimei attacking David when he is at a vulnerable moment in his life.

David's reaction to Shimei and his attack is worth noting because it shows us how to apply the gift of mercy. David's nephew Abishai offers to kill Shimei, but instead of allowing Shimei to be put to death, David responds with calm words (2 Sam. 16:10-12). He basically says, "Let him alone. Maybe the Lord has told him to do this. Maybe he is right! If he is, so be it. But, if he is wrong, the Lord will work it out in His time and in His way." To do what and say what David did, takes grace, love, and mercy. David may have been at one of his lowest points in his life, but this was a high-water mark of self-control.

How are we supposed to behave as a church member when we are attacked? Is a child of God to behave by getting even? By getting our "pound of flesh"? When someone hurts us, we want to hurt them back twice as bad as they hurt us. Is that not how church members, followers of Christ supposed to behave? Certainly not! We are supposed to behave just like David behaved. We are supposed to place the matter in the hand of the Lord and leave the results up to Him. He knows what was said, what was done, and the motive behind the attack, therefore, He knows how to settle the score if it needs to be settled (Rom. 12:14-21; Lev. 19:18; Prov. 24:29). He knows how to give you strength so you can show mercy. God's design for His children is that we become and behave like Jesus (1 Pet. 2:23; Isa. 53:7). So, the next time you are cursed, attacked, threatened, lied about, etc., what are you going to do? There two choices, you can step outside of God's will and handle it yourself. Or, you can take the high road and leave it in the hands of God. By the way, if you are determined to behave as a church member and be like Jesus, you had better keep a tender heart of mercy ready to forgive, and you had better have a skin as thick as that of a rhinoceros because you are going to be attacked. Learn to deal with these kinds of matters like David did at the very moment of offense. If you do not, that hurt is going to fester into something far worse and far more dangerous. If we are not diligent in handling these matters the right way, that offense will grow into resentment. From there, it is just a short step into hatred. That hatred will produce bitterness; and bitterness will find a way to seek revenge. It is wise to learn to place our hurts in the hands of the Lord and walk away from them. He can handle the matter far better than we can!

THE ADMISSION DAVID SECURED

When we come to 2 Samuel 19:16-20, months have passed and the rebellion of Absalom has been suppressed. Now, David is returning home and as he and his men cross the Jordan River, several people are gathering to meet the returning king. Among them is Shimei and one thousand of his men. Here is what happened, "Now Shimei the son of Gera fell down before the king when he had crossed the Jordan" (2 Sam. 19:18 NKJV). Shimei's behavior is that of humility, which is far different than what he displayed the last time his path crossed with David. Perhaps Shimei has had time to contemplate his mistakes. After falling at David's feet, he makes his confession of his wrong in his attack on David, and uses three of the hardest words known to man to say: "I have sinned" (2 Sam. 19:20 NKJV). Shimei hopes that David will not hold the past against him (vs. 19), and by his actions and behavior Shimei seems to be genuinely sorry for what he has done. There is a hope on Shimei's part for David to offer him forgiveness.

It took a real man to do what Shimei did! There is some debate among scholars as to whether his confession was sincere, or whether it was just an attempt to save his hide. The truth of the matter is, we cannot know his heart nor his motives, but it does seem like he was sincere. After all, the Holy Spirit does not call his confession into question. Now, before we get into David's display of mercy, he shows to Shimei, we should think about our own hearts and see if we could behave as David behaved here. The truth is we have all been hurt, but what is a sadder truth is, we have all been on the Shimei and hurt others ourselves. We are all guilty of saying things out of turn; talking about someone else, doing hurtful things, and even telling lies on another person. When life find us in this position, what are we supposed to do? We are to do exactly what Shimei did. We are to go to the person we have offended and we are to confess to them, what we have done and we are to seek their forgiveness. "Therefore, if you bring your gift to the altar; and there remember that your brother has something against you, leave your gift there before the altar, and go your way. First be reconciled to your brother, and then come and offer your gift" (Matt. 5:23-24 NKJV). "Confess your trespasses to one another, and pray for one another, that you may be healed. The effective, fervent prayer of a righteous man avails much" (Jam. 5:16 NKJV).

THE AMNESTY DAVID SUPPLIED

When David hears this, he responds to Shimei in grace and not in retaliation. Notice what David said to him, "Therefore the king said to Shimei, "You shall not die." And the king swore to him" (2 Sam. 19:23 NKJV). What he did is a lesson to those of us who get hurt from time to time. But why did he have to say that he would not die. Again, in this second meeting, Abishai wants to kill Shimei, but David prevents his violent nephew from killing the humbled man. In other words, David stood as a protector of the very person who had wronged him. That is what grace looks like. That is what it means to use the gift of mercy and behave as a church member.

When David heard this confession of Shimei, David knew that this was a day of rejoicing and a day of forgiveness. He also perceived that it was a day of grace in his own life. He was returning to glory to reclaim his throne and it was because God has forgiven him and had given him grace and not what he deserved. Therefore, David promised forgiveness and amnesty to Shimei. Why? It had not been many days since David himself had sinned against Uriah, Bathsheba, the nation of Israel, and the God of heaven. When David had bowed before the Lord and confessed his sins, God had freely forgiven him. Now, David extends that same grace to the one who had wronged him greatly.

David's response to Shimei demonstrates what our own response should be when we are faced with an opportunity to forgive. The gift of mercy will help you with this opportunity. First, we need to remember that even at our very best none of us are perfect. We have all sinned against God and we have all sinned against others. Still, we have been forgiven many times. We have a responsibility to forgive others when they sin against us (Matt. 18:15-35; Luke 17:1-5; Eph. 4:32). Second, just as we should be quick to forgive, we should learn to express that forgiveness. In other words, do not just think it, say it! When something happens, we may pray about the matter and leave it with the Lord, but the offending party needs to know that they have been forgiven. We need to reach out to those who reach out to us! Some church members have asked me, "What if someone hurts us and they do not deal with it? Can we hold a grudge then? Is it alright to be angry with them until they come around begging our forgiveness?" Certainly not! Regardless of what they do to us or say about us we should have the same spirit Jesus displayed when He was on the cross and "then Jesus said, "Father, forgive them, for they do not know what they do" (Luke 23:34 NKJV).

DIGGING OUT THE ROOT OF BITTERNESS

David may have forgiven Shimei, but did David forget what Shimei did. Forgiveness like that, is not forgiveness at all! David's last requestion before he dies is found in 1 Kings 2:8-9. On his death bed, David commands Solomon to be sure that Shimei pays for the evil he had done. Solomon eventually carries out this command and Shimei is executed (1 Kings 2:36-46). David's forgiveness was not perfect, was it? Now are you not glad that God does not forgive like man does? When God forgives, He also forgets (Jer. 31:34). If you never forget after forgiving someone, have you really forgiven that person?

Do you know what bitterness is? The word bitterness is an adjective and it has several meanings: first it means strong and sharp in taste, having a sharp strong unpleasant taste. Second, it means resentful, angry. Next it means difficult to accept or painful or very hard to accept. It also means expressing intense hostility. Finally, it means very cold, penetratingly and unpleasantly cold. (Concise Oxford English Dictionary Eleventh Edition, 2004) I want us to take a look at that second definition: resentful. Resentful has the idea of brooding anger over something that has happened in your life. This anger produces a bad behavior with a bad spirit within a person. It is a spirit of hostility and coldness towards God and others.

Where does this bitterness come from? Bitterness can come about as the result of what others do to us or say about us. Sometimes, bitterness can result from the events of life themselves, as we blame God or others for our troubles. Bitterness will affect every relationship within your life, but it will affect your relationship with the Lord most of all. The Bible talks about the "root of bitterness" that is possible in our lives. "Looking carefully lest anyone fall short of the grace of God; lest any root of bitterness springing up cause trouble, and by this many become defiled" (Heb. 12:15 NKJV). "So that there may not be among you man or woman or family or tribe, whose heart turns away today from the Lord our God, to go and serve the gods of these nations, and that there may not be among you a root bearing bitterness or wormwood" (Deut. 29:18 NKJV). Theses verses refer to "root of bitterness" because it begins hidden within the soil of your heart. From there, its roots will entwine themselves around your heart and mind, until they choke the life out of you emotionally and spiritually. If allowed to grow unchecked, this "root of bitterness" will spring up into a plant that will cast a shadow over everything you are and do. A "root of bitterness" in your life will literally come to dominate your very existence and you will not behave as a church member, neither will the gift of mercy come through.

TESTIMONY OF AHITHOPHEL

"Now when Ahithophel saw that his advice was not followed, he saddled a donkey, and arose and went home to his house, to his city. Then he put his household in order, and hanged himself, and died; and he was buried in his father's tomb" (2 Sam. 17:23 NKJV). Ahithophel met a tragic end because he allowed a root of bitterness to flourish in his life. His was a sad fate, but thankfully, there are lessons about mercy we can learn from his tragedy.

Ahithophel was a saved man and there are many indications that he was saved. First, he worshipped God. Over in 2 Samuel 15:12 is the first time we meet Ahithophel and when we meet him, he is engaged in the act of worship. This indicates that he was a keeper of the law and a worshiper of the Lord. Second, he spoke for God. Ahithophel had the reputation as a man who gave good, godly counsel. In fact, 2 Samuel 16:23 says, "Now the advice of Ahithophel which he gave in those days was as if one had inquired at the oracle of God. So was all the advice of Ahithophel both with David and with Absalom" (NKJV). Since Ahithophel was a saved man, he therefore served God by serving others. He was a great counselor to David. Great leaders surrounded themselves with good counselors and David was no exception. Ahithophel was one of the men David trusted for advice and direction as he governed the nation of Israel. David trusted him so much that he called him a familiar friend (Ps. 41:9). In that psalm, which looks back on the treachery of Ahithophel's life, David still refers to him a familiar friend. These men were at peace with one another and they were as close as men could be.

In spite the fact that Ahithophel gave outward indication that all was well between himself and the Lord and between himself and David, there was something working in his heart that would destroy everything. Even during these times of his life, Ahithophel was being eaten alive, from the inside out, by an event that had happened years earlier. The lesson is clear, what you see on the outside does not always show you the true condition of the heart! This reminds us of the word hypocrite. Jesus used this word "hypocrite" to describe the scribes and Pharisees (Matt. 23:13-15, 23, 25, 27). The word "hypocrite" is an interesting word that originally referred to "an actor, or one who plays a part." (Holman Illustrated Bible Dictionary, 2003) In the famous Greek tragedies, one actor would often play many parts. This actor would have a different mask for each part he was to play. As he transitioned from part to part, he would simply switch on mask for another. Hence, hypocrisy came to refer to someone who "plays different parts by hiding behind different masks" (Concise Oxford English Dictionary Eleventh Edition, 2004) In the church there are some who will wear their church face on Sunday and live like the world on Monday that person is a hypocrite. However, by the same token, someone who loves you to your face, but secretly despises you in their heart is also a hypocrite.

They are merely playing a part and hiding behind a mask. What is the bottom line? What you see is not always what you get. People tend to try and hide a lot of themselves from others. But we all need to remember, God sees it all, even that which you have hidden (Heb. 4:13).

THE TRAGEDY OF AHITHOPHE'S LIFE

The bitterness that was hidden within the heart of Ahithophel finally came out. How this bitterness manifested itself in his life can be seen in his behavior and actions. First there was a conspiracy, which as Absalom rebelled against his father, Ahithophel saw his chance to enact his revenge upon King David. Ahithophel joined the rebellion and stood against God's anointed (2 Sam. 15:31; Ps. 41:9). Next, Ahithophel was giving bad advice to Absalom because of his hatred for David. His first recommendation he made was designed to disgrace King David (2 Sam. 16:20-23). By having Absalom go into his father's concubines, he publicly disgraced David and created a rift between father and son that could never be healed. The second recommendation was designed to destroy King David (2 Sam. 17:1-4). Had this second piece of advice been followed, it is possible that David would have been defeated.

The last sign that bitterness had manifested itself in the life of Ahithophel is the conclusion of his life. David had a true friend in Absalom's court, a man by the name of Hushai. Hushai had originally planned to go with David when he fled from Absalom, but at David's request, he stayed behind in the city to try and overthrow the counsel of Ahithophel (2 Sam. 15:32-37). Hushai comes to Absalom and professes his loyalty (2 Sam. 16:16-19). After he has gained Absalom's confidence, Hushai contradicts the wise counsel of Ahithophel (2 Sam. 17:1-22), which resulted in Absalom accepting Hushai's counsel and David being warned of what is about to take place and thus David is spared. Of course, the key verse is 2 Samuel 17:14 which says, "So Absalom and all the men of Israel said, "The advice of Hushai the Archite is better than the advice of Ahithophel." For the Lord had purposed to defeat the good advice of Ahithophel, to the intent that the Lord might bring disaster on Absalom" (NKJV). God was behind all this intrigue, because David, not Absalom, was the king of Israel! When Ahithophel saw that his counsel was rejected and his plans to defeat and destroy David failed, he returns to his house, puts everything in order and commits suicide! What a tragic end to what had been a good life.

Ahithophel did all these things because there was a root of bitterness in his life. He hated David and had merely pretended to be his friend all those years. As that root of bitterness grew in his life, Ahithophel lost sight of his former friendship with David. He lost sight of his walk with the Lord. Everything of value in his life had been choked out and he was left with nothing but bitterness and hatred. The root of bitterness had utterly consumed this man.

As tragic as these events may be, I would like to point out that there are many in our churches who are also afflicted with the root of bitterness and it is keeping them from behaving as a church member. The reason you have this root of bitterness is because some event in your past, because of someone said something to you or about you, because you did not get your way at some point and your feelings are hurt and nothing means as much to you as getting your revenge. You are angry at someone else; you are hurt and you want them to hurt. You are offended and so you give them the cold shoulder, purposely go out of your way to avoid having to speak to them. You think you are hurting them, but in reality, you are hurting no one own but yourself. How? Your bitterness will kill no one but you! When you and I allow bitterness over hurts, slights, and events of life to take control of us; we are committing slow, spiritual suicide. We are allowing our very spiritual life be strangled right out of us! When we allow our hurts to linger, they will grow into a root of bitterness that will stifle anything spiritual within our lives. It is a tremendous tragedy when church members, saved people, spiritual people stop behaving like they should and allow their lives to be consumed by hate, anger, and bitterness! The best thing you can do is build a bridge and get over it before it kills you!

THE TEACHING OF AHITHOPHEL'S LIFE

As we look at Ahithophel's life, I think you would agree with me that his life is a tragedy. Ahithophel's life is a lesson in foolishness. This man truly lives up to his name which means "brother of folly; or brother of ruin" (Holman Illustrated Bible Dictionary, 2003) Knowing what happened to him, we would have to confess that we do not want the same thing to happen to us. Let me give you a couple things that you can should take away from his life to help you behave as a church member.

Now, I have told you a lot about Ahithophel's bitterness, however, I have not really told you what it was that made him bitter. There are two passages that reveal the reason behind Ahithophel's bittern and hatred towards David. They are found in 2 Samuel 11:1-27 and 2 Samuel 23:34. When you look at these two passages of Scripture together you can see that Bathsheba was the granddaughter of Ahithophel. David had treated Ahithophel's granddaughter like she was a plaything and had arranged the murder of her husband Uriah the Hittite. Considering what David did to Bathsheba, it is no wonder that Ahithophel was angry. However, he allowed his anger to burn within his heart from close to nine years, all the while feigning friendship towards David, biding his time until he could exact revenge. This bitterness that Ahithophel had was eating him alive until he was brought to the point of intrigue and murder (2 Sam. 17:1-4). Then, when he saw that his plans had failed and the man he hated would return to the throne, Ahithophel took his own life rather than face David.

With all this in mind, what can we do to avoid being consumed by the root of bitterness so we can behave as a church member and use the gift of mercy? First, you must acknowledge your own sin in your life which allows a root of bitterness to flourish. When you harbor resentment in your heart and fail to extend mercy and forgiveness to those who hurt you, then you are just as guilty as they are in the eyes of the Lord. "If we confess our sins, He is faithful and just to forgive us our sins and to cleanse us from all unrighteousness" (1 John 1:9 NKJV). Second, people must be forgiven! When it comes to using the gift of mercy forgiving people is not an option; it is a necessity (Matt. 18:15-17, 21-35; Luke 17:1-5; Eph. 4:32). It is better to confront those who have offended you and get things settled than it is to allow bitterness to consume you from the inside out! Next, your past must be forgotten! What happened yesterday can never be changed, but you do hold the key to tomorrow. You should never allow the hurts of yesterday to control your life today. It is a shame when we drag around the baggage of what someone said, what someone did or how we were hurt.

It does nothing but strangle the spiritual life right out of you! You say, "I cannot forget it!" Jesus says, "Come to Me, all you who labor and are heavy laden, and I will give you rest" (Matt. 11:28 NKJV). "And He said to me, "My grace is sufficient for you, form My strength is made perfect in weakness." Therefore, most gladly I will rather boast in my infirmities, that the power of Christ may rest upon me" (2 Cor. 12:9 NKJV). The gift of mercy will give you the grace to forgive and Jesus give you the grace to forget it, if you will bring it to Him (1 Pet. 5:7). Finally, hatred and anger must be forsaken! Over in Ephesians 4:26-27, Paul gives us serious warning concerning anger within our lives. Anger allows our adversary, the devil, to take a foothold in our lives from which he can attack every area of our lives. You must bring your bittern to the Lord!

How much mercy have you been giving lately? How pure is your heart? Are there relationships you need to be the peacemaker? Are you using the gift of mercy? Are you behaving as a church member?

CHAPTER EIGHTEEN

GOD'S JUBILEE

So let each one give as he purposes in his heart, not grudgingly or of necessity; for God loves a cheerful giver. (2 Corinthians 9:7 NKJV)

To behave as a church member, we should "be filled with Spirit" (Eph. 5:18 NKJV). The early church was filled with the Spirit and because they were showing love one to another, they were demonstrating what it means to behave as a follower of Christ. They demonstrate for us the next spiritual gift, the gift of giving. Here is what was said about the early church, "Then fear came upon every soul, and many wonders and signs were done through the apostles. Now all who believed were together, and had all things in common, and sold their possessions and goods, and divided them among all, as anyone had need" (Acts 2:43-45 NKJV). The gift of giving is the ability to give freely and joyfully towards the work of the mission of the church. The early church members were cheerfully and liberally giving to each other as someone had a need. There was no one in the early church that said, "What is mine is mine." Neither did they say,

"Well, I gave that to the church, and since I am leaving the church, I am taking it back." No, what they were saying and proving it by their behavior is, "Lord, if you want it, then you can have it, it is Yours." What we need to remember is that during the days of the early church is the fact they were facing an emergency, there was persecution going on. Therefore, they gave with cheerful heart, because of the gift of giving to everyone. Everything they owned was at the disposal of the Lord Jesus Christ.

Is everything you own at the disposal of Jesus? Honestly, if Jesus asked you for your last penny, would you give it to Him? After all, it all belongs to Him, therefore, do not get the idea that one-tenth belongs to God and the rest is yours for your pleasure, for your squandering. It all belongs to God. One-tenth is only a sign that it all belongs to God. The same can be said about the week. Do not get the idea that one day belongs to God and six are for you. Every day belongs to God, and He is to be the Lord over it all. There are so many church members that think they are going to over-give. Listen you cannot out give God. You shovel out; He shovels in, He has got a bigger shovel. We can only give to Jesus what He has first given to us, because everything we have comes from Him. David said, "But who am I, and who are my people, that we should be able to offer so willingly as this? For all things come from You, and of Your own we have given You" (1 Chron. 29:14 NKJV). In the book of Exodus, we find the people of Israel giving materials for the building and furnishing of the tabernacle. Not only did God create all the material that was given, but He also worked in the hearts of the people and gave them a willingness to give cheerfully. In fact, Moses had to tell them to stop giving, because they had given so much materials (Ex. 36:6-7). What is unique is the fact of where all the Israelites wealth came from. Before the Jews left Egypt, they had spoiled the Egyptians (Ex. 12:35-36), and there were also the spoils from the battle against Amalek (Ex. 17:8-16). God saw to it that they had everything they needed to build the tabernacle just as God had planned it. The Israelites and the early church were giving from cheerful hearts and in the process, they were worshipping God who had given them so much.

Worship is not a business arrangement with God by which we agree to praise Him if He will agree to bless us. Our primary purpose in worshipping God is to please and glorify Him, but one of the spiritual by-products of true worship is that of behaving like Christ. "But we all, with unveiled face, beholding as in a mirror the glory of the Lord, are being transformed into the same image from glory to glory, just as by the Spirit of the Lord" (2 Cor. 3:18 NKJV). When Moses came down the mountain, he did not know he had a shining face (Ex. 34:29). In the same manner, we do not always recognize the transformation the Lord makes in our hearts and lives, because when you are spending time with Jesus then you are focused upon Jesus. Worship is our highest priority and our greatest privilege.

In Deuteronomy 14-16, Moses explains Israel's worship and tells us the kind of people they are. Today, we should behave as a church member who belongs to the true and living God. In these chapters, the new generation stood on the verge of entering into the Promised Land and claiming their inheritance. However, there is a great underlying question they were not thinking about, "How are they going to behave when the intoxicating effects of sudden prosperity overwhelms them?" Financial security has a subtle way of sucking the spiritual life right out of you. Success brings its own subtle test which can dull your spiritual passion. The book of Deuteronomy has more to say about the spiritual dangers of living in a prosperous society than any other book in the Bible. Deuteronomy is God's hand book on maintaining spiritual health in a materialistic culture. God called His people to develop a culture of kindness in which they practiced giving, exercising restraint, and demonstrating their love for God and their neighbors when it came to handling money. The overall event that these chapters are referring to is called God's Jubilee.

God's Jubilee is a time of great joy, rejoicing, and celebration. Isaiah calls it "the acceptable year of the Lord" (Isa. 61:2 NKJV), and he is referring to the both the day that Jesus was born and when Jesus steps out, "for the Lord Himself will descend from heaven with a shout, with the voice of an archangel, and with the trumpet of God" (1 Thess. 4:16 NKJV). The name "jubilee" is derived from the Hebrew word "*jobel*" meaning "the joyful shout or clangor of trumpets", by which the Year of Jubilee was announced (Holman Illustrated Bible Dictionary, 2003) Moses is teaching the new generation of Israelites about God's Jubilee and he has some interesting things for them to learn.

PRACTICE GIVING

"You shall truly tithe all the increase of your grain that the field produces year by year" (Deut. 14:22 NKJV). What is a tithe? Back in Deuteronomy 12, Moses teaches us that God commanded His people to give ten percent of their produce, (grain, fruits, vegetables, and animals), to Him as an act of worship and an expression of gratitude for His blessing. The land was God's gift, and from it they were able to earn a living. Every year, each family had to go to the sanctuary with their tithes, enjoy a feast there, and share the tithe with the Levites who, in turn, would share it with the priests. Moses repeats this commandment here in Deuteronomy 14:22, because when it comes to giving to the Lord, some people need more than one reminder (2 Cor. 8:10-11).

In addition, every person in Israel had to attend three festivals. "Three times a year all your males shall appear before the Lord your God in the place which He chooses: at the Feast of Unleavened Bread, at the Feast of Weeks, and at the Feast of Tabernacles; and they shall not appear before the Lord empty-handed. Every man shall give as he is able, according to the blessing of the Lord your God which He has given you" (Deut. 16:16-17 NKJV). The people were to be generous with their tithes and gifts to the sanctuary and enjoy a thanksgiving feast, it would teach them to fear the Lord (Deut. 14:23), because if the Lord had not blessed them, they would have nothing to eat and nothing to give. As David said, "O Lord our God, all this abundance that we have prepared to build You a house for Your holy name is from Your hand, and is all Your own" (2 Chron. 29:16 NKJV). When we cease to fear God and behave as church members, then we fail to appreciate His bountiful provisions He has given us. When we become proud church members, then we start taking His blessings for granted. That is when the Lord has to discipline us and remind us that He is the Giver of every gift.

God's principles of giving heve not changed. In the New Testament, the strongest emphasis is on the spirit in which we give. "So let each one give as he purposes in his heart, not grudgingly or of necessity; for God loves a cheerful giver" (2 Cor. 9:7 NKJV). This the behavior of a church member who has the gift of giving. However, every Christian who is enjoying all the blessings that God gives us each and every day, we ought to do far more than the Jews did who lived under the Mosaic Law. The New Testament does not command us on how much we should give, but it does urge us to give in proportion to the blessing we have received from the Lord (1 Cor. 16:1-2). I have heard it said, "The calculation Christian will always be the biggest loser, while the generous Christian will enjoy the blessings of God." Another old saying that I have heard is, "If you give because it pays, it won't." Listen, our motive for giving and tithing must always be to please the God and glorify Him (1 Cor. 10:31). So, when you write that check or offering envelope with money in it supporting your local church, let it be an act of worship! Let it be an expression of your joy in what God has given you. The more the Lord prospers you, the larger your tenth will be, and great will be your joy in giving.

Restrain Greed

When it comes to the practice of giving, it does not always have to be about money; it also can include the giving of your time. God had established the principle of the Sabbath in fourth commandment of Ten Commandments (Ex. 20:8-10). The Sabbath day was holy to the Lord, it was a day for worship and for the family; a day to be renewed in body, soul, and spirit. The Sabbath law still remains even in our twenty-four hours a day, seven days a week culture. God commands us that we are to keep one day in seven Holy, and on that day, we are to stop working. We are to give this day to God and we are to use it to be renewed, restored, and refreshed. People will make different choices about what is appropriate on this day, but whatever we do; we must not make it like another work day.

Now if you think that it is challenging to keep the Sabbath holy and rest, you have not heard anything yet! You see, not only did God say that the people were to rest on the Sabbath day, but the land was to lie fallow for one year in seven (Lev. 25:1-5). God gave a special promise in connection with this law. He would send a bumper crop during harvest time in the sixth year so there would be enough food to sustain the people through the seventh year and during the planting season of the eighth year (Lev. 25:20-22). So, how would you have reacted to the Sabbath year? Perhaps you would look at your fields and say to yourself, "What a waste!

This Sabbath law is costing me a whole year of income. Just think of the money I could make if I had planted this seventh year." The Sabbath Law placed a restraint on greed. God's people were to learn how to say "no" to something good in order to say "yes" to something better. Thus, one year in every seven they passed up an opportunity for significant income in order to learn again that there is more to life than work and money. In a world of greed, we need to behave as church members practicing restraint.

CANCELING DEBTS

The Sabbath Year involved much more than rest for the land. It also meant canceling debts and setting free servants who had served for six years. "At the end of every seven years you shall grant a release of debts" (Deut. 15:1 NKJV). The whole nation descended from one family, and so Moses said, "If there is among you a poor man of your brethren, within any of the gates in your land which the Lord your God is giving you, you shall not harden your hearts nor shut your hand from your poor brother, but you shall open your hand wide to him and willingly lend him sufficient for his needs, whatever he needs" (vs. 7-8 NKJV). This is how we should behave as a church member using the gift of giving. We are to give with an open hand, lending freely (Lev. 25:36-37). According to this law, the Israelites were not to charge interest among their brethren, however, they could charge interest to a foreigner. Of course, the purpose of the interest was to motivate the borrower to pay the loan back as quickly as possible.

Today Christians are under an obligation to repay their debts, Paul writes, "Own no one anything" (Rom. 13:8a NKJV). We honor God as we plan on repaying our loans. If you have benefited from someone else's generosity through a loan without interest, do not take advantage of the kindness by failing to repay it. Understand the Sabbath Year and the Year of Jubilee were part of God's wise plan to balance the economic scales in the nation so the rich could not exploit the poor or the poor take advantage of the rich. However, the Lord knew that there would always be poor people in the land because Israel would not consistently obey these laws. The nation of Israel would have been the most prosperous nation on earth if they had followed the instructions God gave them, but they rejected His will and adopted the methods of the nations around them. They did not observe the Sabbath Year every seventh year or the Year of Jubilee every fiftieth year and for this failure they paid a great price.

There is an underlying principle to this practice of canceling debt. It is called forgiveness. Along with the gift of mercy and the gift of discernment, the gift of giving teaches us that giving is more than just money. Just as we are to cancel loans or debts we are to forgive, even if the debt has not been paid in full. No matter the amount we are to forgive the debt.

Debt can also include those who have wronged us. Think about it, if someone has wronged you, you would say, "They owe me an apology." Owing someone is a debt. Yes, it can be hard to forgive, that is where the gift of mercy and gift of giving come in to aid in the giving of forgiveness. Jesus taught us to pray for forgiveness and the ability to forgive, when He taught the disciples the Model Prayer in Matthew 6:9-13. Jesus said we are to pray this, "And forgive us our debts. As we forgive our debtors" (Matt. 6:12 NKJV). If we ask God to forgive us our debts we owe Him, which our sins we commit, then we should forgive those who have sinned against us, wronged us, owes us an apology, and have built up a debt with us. If we cannot then we are like the man in Jesus's parable of the unforgiving servant (Matt. 18:21-35). Basically, the man had asked to be forgiven of his debt that he owed, which he receives forgiveness for. Then he goes and finds the man that owed him, which that man could not repay his debt and begs for forgiveness. Man did not offer forgiveness to the man who owed him, so he throws him into prison. Matthew 6:12, reminds me of the master's question that he asked the man he forgave. He said, "Should you not also have had compassion on your fellow servant, just as I had pity on you?" (Matt. 18:33 NKJV). To behave as a church member means that you are willing to give forgiveness to those who are indebted to you, just as Jesus has.

TESTING HEARTS

What is unique about the parable of the unforgiving servant is the fact that Peter asked Jesus about forgiveness. "Then Peter came to Him and said, "Lord, how often shall my brother sin against me, and I forgive him?

Up to seven times?" Jesus said to him, "I do not say to you, up to seven times, but up to seventy times seven" (Matt. 18:21-22 NKJV). Something that is implied here in giving forgiveness is testing of one's faith. The Sabbath year was a test of faith, but it was also a test of love. Suppose you have fifty thousand dollars in the bank, and your brother has come on hard times and needs a loan of five thousand. You look at the calendar and you notice that it is year six in the cycle, and the year of canceling debts begins in just a few months! So, you think to yourself, "If I give him money now, I do not have much chance of getting it back before the year of canceling debts begins." But God says, "Beware lest there be a wicked thought in your heart, saying, "The seventh year, the year of release, is at hand", and your eye be evil against your poor brother and you give him nothing, and he cry out to the Lord against you, and it become sin among you" (Deut. 15:9 NKJV).

These laws tested the hearts of the lender and the borrower. The lender should ask himself, "Am I willing to help my brother even if it proves to be costly?" The borrower should ask himself, "If I receive from my brother, am I the kind of person who will abuse his kindness?" Moses was teaching these principles to a group of people who owned no property and had no means of generating income. But God was about to bless them with significant wealth. When that happened, they were to give generously, practice restraint, and demonstrate grace in the way they used their money and possessions. These laws were given specifically to Israel, but we need to search our hearts. Even though we are not bound by these laws, they point to the kind of behavior God calls us to display.

For the people of Israel, each new year opened with the blowing of the trumpets on the first day of the seventh month, and ten days later, the people celebrated the Day of Atonement by fasting, repenting, and offering the required sacrifices. But every fiftieth year at the close of the celebration of the Day of Atonement, the horns were blown again to announce that the Year of Jubilee had begun (Lev. 25:9-10). It would require a great deal of faith for the people to celebrate this special year, because the previous year, the 49th year, would have been a Sabbath year when the fields, vineyards, and orchards would not have been cultivated. The Jews had to trust God to provide for them for the 49th year, through the 50th year, and also through the 51st year, while they waited for the harvest. God certainly would not fail them, but their faith might fail them. In fact, there is no evidence in Scripture that the nation of Israel ever celebrated the Year of Jubilee.

After the years passed, people must have wondered if the nation would ever have a leader who would have the authority and the will to sound the trumpet and proclaim a Jubilee Year. There was one king who got close. The prophet Jeremiah wrote that King Zedekiah proclaimed a year of freedom for the captives, but later changed his mind, and it never happened (Jer. 34:8-20). Then after the exile, when Jerusalem was rebuilt, the people established the new community and made a commitment to observe the Sabbath of the land and cancel all debts on the seventh year (Neh. 10:31), but it never happened. Then Jesus came into the world, and Luke tells us about the day Jesus began His public ministry. Jesus went to Nazareth, where He had been brought up and, on the Sabbath Day, He went int the synagogue, took the scroll of the prophet Isaiah that was handed to Him, unrolled it, and read. "The Spirit of the Lord is upon Me, because He has anointed Me to preach the gospel to the poor; He has sent Me to heal the brokenhearted, to proclaim liberty to the captives and recovery of sight to the blind, to set at liberty those who are oppressed; to proclaim the acceptable year of the Lord" (Luke 4:18-19 NKJV). Jesus rolled up the scroll and gave it back to the attendant and then sat down. Everybody was watching Him, "and He began to say to them, "Today this Scripture is fulfilled in your hearing" (vs. 21 NKJV). Jesus has proclaimed God's Year of Jubilee, and we are still living in that year of the Lord's favor.

The Sabbath laws were a great blessing for the debtor, but was costly for the creditor. This pales in comparison to the cost to God of canceling all our debts and restoring our inheritance with the death of His Son, Jesus Christ. The only way to write off a debt is to suffer the loss of the amount of the debt personally, whether it be money, pride, or possessions. If you owe me one thousand dollars, and I write it off, then I incurred a loss of one thousand dollars. If God is to write off all our debts to Him, it means that He has suffered the total cost of that debt in Himself. That is why Christ went to the cross. He bore the loss, and in this way canceling our debts, restoring the inheritance of everlasting life, and giving forgiveness. Understand this is good news for the poor! The people were looking to their political leaders to implement the Jubilee and it never happened because it was too costly. But God did something even better for them and for us, He anointed Jesus to come and to preach the gospel to the poor. God will cancel all debts; God will restore the lost inheritance; and God will give forgiveness. Jesus says, "Come to Me, all you who labor and are heavy laden, and I will give you rest" (Matt. 11:28 NKJV). Jesus completed His work upon the cross. Shouldn't we behave as church members?

CHAPTER NINETEEN

THE LOST ART OF HOSPITALITY

Be hospitable to one another without grumbling. (1 Peter 4:9 NKJV)

We have come to our final spiritual gift, the gift of hospitality. "Those with this gift have the ability to make visitors, guest, and strangers feel at ease. They often use their home to entertain guests. Persons with this gift integrate new members into the body" (LifeWay Christian Resources, 2003) In the day and age in which we live, hospitality has become a lost art. Could it be that we place hospitality and service to one another in the same category? Maybe the reason hospitality is not thought about is because we been overcome with so much social media at our fingertips, we have forgot how to interact with others in person. Teenagers will be sitting in the same room and communicate not with their word from their mouths, but with words from their phones. Another possible reason could be that we do not behave as church members is because when we are at potlucks or fellowship meals, church members tend to be cliquish. Members just want to sit with only their little group and not get to know one another.

Did you know that there are over eighty-four hundred examples of hospitality in the Bible? The Bible provides for us example after example of friendship and generosity towards other people. As a matter of fact, believers are encouraged to behave by showing hospitality towards other believers, even strangers. Here are some examples from the Old Testament. Abraham entertains three men (Gen. 18:2-5); Lot hosts visitors from God (Gen. 19:1-3); Abraham's servant is welcomed in Rebekah's home (Gen. 24:22-25); hospitality is shown to David and his men (2 Sam. 17:27-29); the widow of Zarephath cares for Elijah even though she lived in poverty (1 Kings 17:7-16); and Nehemiah shows hospitality to fellow Jews (Neh. 5:17). There are more I could list but these will suffice. When we come to the New Testament, Hospitality is demonstrated many different ways: at the house of Levi (Luke 5:29); Peter's mother-in-law house (Matt. 8:14-15); in Bethany where Jesus is anointed (Matt. 26:6-7); Mary and Martha (Luke 10:38); Zacchaeus (Luke 19:5-7); and even on the road to Emmaus (Luke 24:29). However, Jesus sets the example for biblical hospitality and how we are to behave as church member using the gift of hospitality. He even holds us to a higher standard of hospitality. While Jesus was here on earth there is even records of Jesus participating in hospitality (Mark 1:29; 5:40; 7:17, 24; 9:28; Luke 7:36; 8:51; Matt. 8:14; 9:28; 13:36). These were not isolated incidents this was His normal practice of hospitality.

PROPER ETIQUETTE

In Luke 14:7-14, Jesus took the time to teach His disciples about the proper etiquette of hospitality. He urged them to practice hospitality with the less fortunate and not to expect anything in return. This is another reason that hospitality has become a lost art. Experts in management tell us that most people have this invisible sign which reads, "Please make me feel important", and therefore if we do, then we can succeed in human relations. What is sad is the fact this concept has crept into the church, even among pastors. We have changed the name of hospitality to networking, and have ignored what Jesus is teaching in this passage of Scripture.

However, we fail when we say or do things that makes a person feel less adequate. Which cause the person to become angry or resentful, because everybody wants to feel important.

In Jesus day, there was the status quo symbols that identified people of importance. If a person was invited to the right house, and seated in the right place then people knew that person was important (Jam. 2:2-3). Back then, the closer you sat near the host, the higher you were in the social standing, which would give you more attention. They were placing more emphasis on reputation than they were having the right character or living the right kind of life. Jesus said, "When you are invited by anyone to a wedding feast, do not sit down in the best place, lest one more honorable than you be invited by him" (Luke 14:8 NKJV). Then He says, "But when you are invited, go and sit down in the lowest place, so the when he who invited you comes, he may say to you, 'Friend, go up higher.' Then you will have glory in the presence of those who sit at the table with you" (vs. 10 NKJV). Jesus was not giving them a gimmick that would produce a guaranteed promotion, instead He was warning them against false humility. Later when Jesus sent the twelve out on a mission (Mark 6:7-13), He told they were to accept the hospitality of the local people and were to abide in whatever house they were invited into. They were not to seek out better accommodations. They were not to look for more comfortable lodging. They were to take what they were given and they were to be happy with. God is not impressed by our status in society or in the church. He is not impressed by what other people think about us, because God sees our heart, He knows our thoughts and motives. God still humbles the proud and exalts the humble (Jam. 4:6).

Jesus also told His disciples what the one who does the inviting should do. He tells them that when they give a lunch or a dinner, not to just invite those friends, family, or rich neighbors that might invite you to their events. But He encouraged them to invite those who were poor, maimed, lame, or blind. If they would do this they would be blessed, because those people cannot repay you but you would be repaid at the resurrection of the righteous (Luke 14:12-14). When we behave as a church member using the gift of hospitality, our motives should not be for the praise of men, but for the glory of God.

In the days of Jesus, it was not proper etiquette to invite poor people and the handicapped to dinner. However, Jesus commands us to invite the needy people because they cannot pay us back. If we are behaving as church members then God will see it and will reward us properly, although getting a reward should not be what motivates us for our hospitality. When we serve others from an unselfish heart, we are laying up treasures in heaven. Now, I understand that our modern world is quite competitive, and it is easy for church members to be more concerned about money and cost. However, we must behave in such a way the we are maintaining the unselfish attitude that Jesus had and share what we have with others.

THE LOVE FEAST

In the early church, they had a custom that all believer would eat together (Acts 2:42, 46). What this created was an opportunity to fellowship with one another, and sharing their food with those who were a little less fortunate. At the end of this agape feast the church members celebrated and participated in the Lord's Supper. This agape feast was part of the worship service in the church of Corinth. However, this agape meal or love feast eventually did more harm than good. As matter fact, Paul even pointed this out, "Now in giving these instructions I do not praise you, since you come together not for the better for the worse" (1 Cor. 11:17 NKJV). Here is what was going on in the church at Corinth. The church members had developed a bad behavior of developing various cliques. People ate with their own crowd. Paul pointed that out as well. He says, "For first of all, when you come together as a church, I hear that there are divisions among you, and in part I believe it" (vs. 18 NKJV). Instead of fellowship with as the whole family they would only sit and eat with those they liked. The result was the fact the poor and weak Christian church members were left out.

The Corinthian mentality surrounding the Lord's Supper service was, at least for them, a time of gluttony and selfish excess. They had lost the true meaning of the Lord's Supper and were taking the whole thing lightly. The rich people brought a great deal of food for themselves, while the poorer members went hungry. Remember, the original idea behind the agape meal is that of sharing, but they had lost their focus. There were even some members in the church that were getting drunk. What is sad about this is the fact that this weekly agape meal was the only decent meal the poorer church members regularly would have. While the poorer members enjoyed that decent meal, the rich had the audacity to scorn them, which not only would hurt their stomach but their pride.

The divisions or cliques at dinner were only evidence of much deeper problems that were going on in the church. Paul is not saying they should abandon the agape meal, but they should restore the meal back to its original purpose. Paul basically says, "Let the rich eat home if they are hungry, because when you abuse your fellow believers how do not have very much what you are doing is despising the church!" (1 Cor. 11:22). The love feast should have been an opportunity to edify the church, but the rich were using it for a time of embarrassment.

HOSPITALITY IS A LIFESTYLE FOR THE LAST DAYS

Hospitality is a virtue that commanded and commended throughout the Bible. It is included in the law (Ex. 22:21; Deut. 14:28-29), and Jesus enjoyed being hospitable as did the disciples in their ministry (Acts 28:7; Phile. 22). When we are showing hospitality, we are reflecting God's hospitality to us (Luke 14:16). Church members, especially leaders, should be given to hospitality (1 Tim. 3:2; Titus 1:8). Over in the book of James, he tells the "twelve tribes which are scattered abroad" (Jam. 1:1 NKJV), that they need to beware of showing personal favoritism when being hospitable (Jam. 2:1-13). When we use the gift of hospitality and open our homes to God's servants, we are helping to promote the truth of God's Word and the sudden return of Jesus Christ. In fact, we when we share with others, we share with Christ (Matt. 25:35. Furthermore, hospitality prepares us for the return of the Bridegroom. In Jesus parable of the ten virgins, five virgins were wise and got prepare for the bridegroom's return, and five were foolish and were unprepared for his return (Matt. 25:1-13). So, when we open homes and show hospitality, we are glorifying God by behaving as church members and preparing for Christ's return.

Peter writes, "But the end of all things is at hand; therefore, be serious and watchful in your prayers" (1 Pet. 4:7). Jesus may come at any moment, if the end of all things is at hand, then how should we be living? Hospitality is a lifestyle and we are to behave as church members living in the last days, perilous times, or the end times. Yes, Peter wrote that verse 2,000 years ago, and no, Peter was not wrong for writing it. He said exactly what he should have said, because from the Day of Pentecost right up until this present day we are living in the end times. For example, in Acts 2:17, Peter, on the Day of Pentecost, described what was happening. He said, "And it shall come to pass in the last days, says God, that I will pour out My Spirit on all flesh" (Acts 2:17 NKJV). Peter called Pentecost a part of the last days. Paul told the Corinthian church, "Now all these things happened to them as examples, and they were written for our admonition, upon whom the ends of the age have come" (1 Cor. 10:11 NKJV). Paul said that 2,000 years ago as well. The writer of Hebrews says, God "has in these last days spoken to us by His Son" (Heb. 1:2 NKJV). All of the Bible writers speak of the times in which we are living as the end times, last days, or perilous times. Why? Because ever since Pentecost until this present time, Jesus Christ, Our Bridegroom, could come at any moment. Every Christian is living in the last days. If Jesus can come at any moment, then for every one of us, in any age, the end is at hand.

The question is are you prepared? Paul said, "The Lord is at hand" (Phil. 4:5 NKJV). James says, "Behold, the Judge is standing at the door" (Jam. 5:9 NKJV)! Jesus has His hand on the door know, rattling it ready to come in; are you prepared? John says, "Little children, it is the last hour" (1 John 2:18 NKJV); are you prepared? Every Christian ought to behave and live as though Jesus could come at any moment. Hospitality is the gift that helps up be prepared by sharing with others. When you host a party, do you usually like to make you are prepared for the event. When you get ready for a dinner and invite people over, are you not making sure all the food is prepared? Since Jesus can back at any moment, we should be living a lifestyle that is preparing us and others for His return. Peter says, "the end of all things is hand" (1 Pet. 4:7 NKJV), then what should our lifestyle be for the last days? What is the lifestyle of the child of God? There are five things I would like to show you how the gift of hospitality is a lifestyle to behave as a church member.

WE SHOULD BE LEARNING OF HIS COMING

Again, Peter says, "But the end of all things is at hand; therefore, be serious and watchful in your prayers" (1 Pet. 4:7 NKJV). Peter is saying, "If Jesus is coming, you get in the right from of mind." You need to get serious in your thinking. You need to learn more about the Second Coming of Jesus Christ. There is a lot of studying we need to do, and we need to get serious about it. There are people today who are doing a lot of serious thinking, but they are just thinking seriously about the wrong thing. For example, you can go to the zoo and see a monkey with a serious look on his face, but it is because he has an itch. We need to be serious and not frivolous when it comes to hospitality and promoting the coming of Christ. Because you are not going to understand anything, you are not going to be able to make sense out of anything, if you leave the missing key out of the whole thing; which is the Second Coming of Jesus Christ. As I said earlier, hospitality is a dying art, just as the teaching of Christ's return is a dying art. When we have people over, we want to have a great time, fun, laughter, and joy; we do not really want to talk about serious things. Hospitality is a lifestyle and when you do, you have the opportunity to promote and prepare the church family for the His return. The Bible says that the kingdoms of this world will become the kingdoms of our Lord and His Christ (Rev. 11:15); and you cannot make sense out of history until you understand the Second Coming of Jesus.

Here is the connection between the gift of hospitality and the Second Coming of Christ. Peter was talking to saints who were suffering and sometimes people get the idea that if we go down the aisle, and we give our hearts to Jesus, and we get baptized, then our troubles are over. Listen, if you have never met the devil, then it is because you and the devil have been going in the same direction. When you repent of your sin, you turn from sin, that is when you are going to meet the devil head-on. In many ways, your troubles are going to begin when you give your heart to Jesus. Jesus tells us that world is going to hate us, and in Peter's day many Christians were being persecuted. They were being lied about, they were being slandered, they were being passed over for promotions, and their goods were being confiscated. When you are showing hospitality, you are demonstrating and showing what Paul said, "For I consider that the sufferings of this present time are not worthy to be compared with the glory which shall be revealed in us" (Rom. 8:18 NKJV). The reason we need to behave as church members, the reason we need to be more hospitable, the reason we need to know more about the Christ's return, is because if you do not know about His return, if you do not do some serious thinking, then the devil is going to discourage you, and lead you down blind alleys, and get you off base. Nothing makes sense unless you live in light of His Coming and the gift of hospitality gives you that opportunity.

WE SHOULD BE LONGING FOR HIS COMING

Peter says that we are to be "watchful in your prayers" (1 Pet. 4:7 NKJV). We are to be longing for Jesus to come. Have you ever had a guest, or a friend, who was coming, and it was somebody who you just anticipated coming, and you kept going to the window to look out to see if they were there? Maybe you hear a car go pass, and you got to the window, and you pull back the drapes, or maybe you did not even hear a noise, but you find yourself just going and looking out the front door. That is the way we ought to be living and behaving. We ought to be just watching for Him to come. I believe in the imminent return of Jesus Christ. He is coming at any moment. Peter would not have told these people to watch, if the coming of our Lord Jesus Christ had not been something that was imminent. Are we watching? Are you prepared?

Peter said that this watching should be in your prayer. What kind prayer are we to pray? We are to pray for Jesus Christ to come. When you long for Him to come, you start praying for Him to come. Did you know through your prayers you can cause Jesus to come more quickly than He would have come? But do not get the idea that the Second Coming of Jesus Christ is a time cut in stone that can never be changed. Peter writes "Looking for and hastening the coming of the day of God" (2 Pet. 3:12 NKJV). Notice that phrase, "hastening the coming of the day of God", here is the transitive Greek meaning of that phrase: causing the day of the Lord to come more quickly by helping to fulfil those conditions without which it cannot come. (Holman Illustrated Bible Dictionary, 2003) Think about it, we are causing the Second Coming to come more quickly today when we fulfill the conditions without which the day of the Lord will not come. That day, which is not a day unescapably fixed, but one the arrival of which it is free to the church to hasten on by faith and by prayer. After thinking about the Greek meaning of this verse, that makes a lot of sense. For example, we have been taught that the kingdom is going to come. But how did Jesus teach us to pray in Matthew 6:10? We are to pray, "Thy kingdom come." We are told to pray for the coming of His kingdom. We know that, one day, there will be peace in Jerusalem, and there will not be peace in the world, until there is peace in Jerusalem. However, there will not be peace in Jerusalem until Jesus, the Prince of peace, rules upon the throne of David. When is that going to be? When He comes. What does the Bible tell us to do? "Pray for the peace of Jerusalem" (Ps. 122:6 NKJV). When you pray for the peace of Jerusalem, then you are really praying for the Second Coming of Jesus Christ. John prayed, "Amen. Even so, come, Lord Jesus!" (Rev. 22:20 NKJV). Are you praying that prayer? You ought to be.

Hospitality is a lost art. Learning about the Second Coming is a lost art. Praying for His return is a lost art. Peter says it is the last time, that we are to be learning of His coming; we are to be serious minded; we are to be looking for His coming; and we are to watch. We are to be longing for His coming, we are to pray "thy kingdom come", we are to pray "Let there be peace in Jerusalem, that there might be peace on Earth", even so, come Lord Jesus! This is a reality, Jesus Christ is coming at any moment, and we are to be sharing with others that longing for Jesus, "whom having not seen you love" (1 Pet. 1:8 NKJV). Hospitality is a lifestyle, we are to behave as a church member because one of these days we will see Him, not as He was, but as He is, in all of His majesty, power, and glory.

WE SHOULD BE LOVING AT HIS COMING

The reason why the gift of hospitality promotes the coming of Jesus is the fact that, when He comes, He should find us with hearts filled with love. "And above all things have fervent love for one another, for love will cover a multitude of sins. Be hospitable to one another without grumbling" (1 Pet. 4:8-9 NKJV). It is very interesting that Peter would say, "Above all, have love." Why? Because He is talking about the last days. The reasons he says this is, because Jesus taught Him concerning the last days. Jesus said, "And because lawlessness will abound, the love of many will grow cold" (Matt. 24:12 NKJV). What this means is, in the last days there is going to be a tidal wave of lawlessness, which means there is going to be crime, immorality, and depravity in the last days. Therefore, since there is going to be great lawlessness in the world, then there is going to be a great lovelessness in the world.

Let me ask you a question: Have you ever found yourself, in these days where we see so much crime, being suspicious of almost everybody, afraid to go to the door and open the door? So, you double-lock your door. You lock your car door as soon as you get in. You try to walk to the other side of the parking lot just to avoid someone who looks like he is trying to sell you something, or ask for money. Have you ever felt that way? It seems that we are almost paranoid about every little thing. Because lawlessness is ever growing, the love for others grows cold. Peter says, do not let that get to you. Do not let the devil keep you from loving, in these last days (1 Pet. 4:8).

But why is love so important in the gift of hospitality? Because love is the greatest virtue you can have. "And now abide faith, hope, love, these three, but the greatest of these is love" (1 Cor. 13:13 NKJV). The greatest commandment is love. "Jesus said to him, 'You shall love the Lord your God with all your heart, with all your soul, and with all your mind'. This is the first and great commandment. And the second is like it: 'You shall love your neighbor as yourself.'" (Matt. 22:37-38 NKJV). Since, these are the first and second great commandments then we need to behave as church members and learn how to do them, the gift of hospitality helps with this. Love is so important in the gift of hospitality, because love is the greatest testimony. How is the world going to know we are part of the Bride of Christ? Is it the size of the church you attend? The size of the budget? The way the yard looks? Is your church on FaceBook, YouTube, or on the radio or television? Jesus says, "By this all will know that you are My disciples, if you have love for one another" (John 13:35 NKJV). Hospitality is a lifestyle. Love should be a great motivation to serve the Lord, to give above and beyond, to give sacrificially; to be faithful to Sunday School, Sunday Night services, Wednesday night, anytime the doors are open. Love should cause us to share and be hospitable (2 Cor. 5:14). Nothing should motivate you like a heart full of love for Jesus and, especially, His love for you.

But what kind of love is Peter talking about when we are talking about the gift of hospitality? There are three things that Peter points out. First, love that cost, just like hospitality cost. The word "fervent" in 1 Peter 4:8 means "stretched out" (Holman Illustrated Bible Dictionary, 2003) Why would he say, "Have stretched out love?" The idea is of an athlete who is stretching his muscles to reach the finish line, to cross the goal line, to make a slam-dunk, or hit that baseball. Whatever he is doing, his muscles are taut and tense, and he is stretching and yearning for the goal. This is the same practice in getting ready for a dinner event, even so, the gift of hospitality gets us prepared for Christ's return. There is a price to pay, athletes pay the price to win, Peter is saying there is no such thing as cheap love. Love cost and according to James if you are showing partiality then you are trying to show hospitality on the cheap (James 2:1-13). If you are being cheap, where love does not cost you something, they you are not using the gift of hospitality nor are you behaving as a church member.

Secondly, love covers, and Peter says, "love will cover a multitude of sins" (1 Pet. 4:8 NKJV). Peter is quoting from Proverbs 10:12 which says, "Hatred stirs up strife, but love covers all sins" (NKJV). Peter, being the good preacher, is contrasting hatred and love. Hatred takes joy in exposing the weakness of others. There are some people in every church, in every fellowship, that just seem to have the ability to find out something bad about somebody. Their ears are like garbage cans. They just gather up all the bad. They just go around picking all the scabs and sores and finding fault. When they find it, they take great delight in exposing it. That is no way for a church member to behave, that is not love. Love does not rejoice in iniquity. Love wishes that it never happened, and love tries to cover it up. That does not mean we condone sin; we just cover it; there is a difference. However, let me point out that if we only invite those who will invite us back, if we only invite the rich and not the poor or handicapped, if we are cliquish, then are we in danger of showing hatred and exposing the weakness of others (Luke 14:12-14)?

Finally, because Jesus is coming, we need to have a love that cost, we need to have a love that covers, and we need to have a love that cares. Peter gets personal and says, "Be hospitable to one another without grumbling"

(1 Pet. 4:9 NKJV). In those days, there were very few motels, very few inns and the ones they did have were filthy, immoral, and expensive. Therefore, they would have churches in homes, and the homes had to be open to the preaching of the gospel. There were some who might gripe, "Why are they going to use my home today?" Peter said, "Do it without grudging." Or, maybe there is a travelling evangelist, a missionary, a pastor, or maybe there was a saint that needed to be taken care of, to which Peter is saying, that real love is very practical, it is more than words; it is a love that cost, that covers, that shares. There in the upper room, "He took the cup, and gave thanks, and said, "Take this and divide among yourselves; for I say to you, I will not drink of the fruit of the vine until the kingdom of God comes." And He took the bread, gave thanks and broke it, and gave it to them saying, "This is My body which is given for you; do this in remembrance of Me"" (Luke 22:17-19 NKJV). Paul writes, "For as often as you eat this bread and drink this cup, you proclaim the Lord's death till He comes" (1 Cor. 11:26 NKJV). The gift of hospitality is a lifestyle and we should behave as church members. Because when Jesus comes, is He going to find our hearts filled with love?

CHAPTER TWENTY

WHY ATTEND CHURCH?

And let us consider one another in order to stir up love and good works, not forsaking the assembling of ourselves together, as in the manner of some, but exhorting one another, and so much the more as you see the Day approaching. (Hebrews 10:24-25 NKJV).

The Holy Spirit gives us these spiritual gifts for a purpose, which is to exalt Christ, edify the church, and equip the saints. Each gift given to church members are to work together in love, harmony and unity for the purpose of fulfilling the Great Commission. However, the church in the 21st century has a genuine problem. The problem is lagging and sagging church attendance. Church members today have the idea that perhaps they are doing God a favor when they come to church on Sunday morning and on Sunday night. What is sad is that pastors often feel as though they have to beg church members to come to church. That should never be the case. To behave as a church member, you should have a desire within your heart to be in the presence of your Lord and Savior. There should be need to worship Him and fellowship with fellow church members.

The problem of attendance is getting so bad in some churches that pastors are tempted to exaggerate their attendance, by saying, "Well, ministerially speaking we had this many on Sunday." There were two pastors talking about the numbers. The first pastor said, "We had more in Sunday School than you have this Sunday!" The second pastor said, "Oh yeah. Prove it!" The first pastor said, "Well look, If I lie about my statistics, and you know that I am lying, and I know you know, isn't that like telling the truth?" We get embarrassed sometimes because people stay away from church. In some churches, people go to church about three times: when they are born or christened, when they are married, and when they are buried. Basically, people go to church; when they are hatched, when they are matched, and when they are dispatched. The first time they throw water, the second time rice, and the third time dirt. That is about the only time some people attend services today.

In the New Testament, if you willingly, deliberately missed the assembly, the coming together as a church, they would assume that you had never been saved. They assumed that you had gone back into the world and demonstrated that you never had a personal, genuine relationship with the Lord Jesus Christ. They wondered if you had ever been saved at all, if you ceased from attending the worship service. They saw worship not only as a privilege, but they saw worship as a solemn duty. Over in the book of Hebrews, the writer uses the phrase "let us" three times in Hebrews 10:22-24 to show us the importance of coming together as church members using our spiritual gifts. For example, in verse 22, he says, "Let us draw near" (NKJV). Then in verse 23, "Let us hold fast the profession of our faith" (NKJV). Finally, in verse 24 he says, "Let us consider one another and to provoke unto love and to good works" (NKJV). Three times he uses this phrase "let us", and each time he is talking to the congregation, to the assembly. He is not talking to individuals; he is talking corporately. The first time, he is talking about let us worship together. The second time, he is saying let us witness together. The third time, he is saying let us work together. Ideally, if we are going to behave as a church member, then we are to put these three teaching into practice as we do the work Christ has called us to as we attend church.

EXALT THE SAVIOR

Why do we attend church? "Therefore, brethren, having boldness to enter the Holiest by the blood of Jesus, by a new and living way which He consecrated for us, through the veil, that is, His flesh, and having a High Priest over the house of God, let us draw near with a true heart in full assurance of faith, having our hearts sprinkled from an evil conscience and our bodies washed with pure water" (Heb. 10:19-22 NKJV). We attend church to draw near to the Lord Jesus Christ. You do not come to church, primarily, to hear a sermon. You come to church, primarily, to hear music. Yes, that is part of it, but the overriding purpose of attending church is to draw near to Jesus. Someone might say, "Well, that is something I can do alone at home, or in a boat, or wherever." Yes, you should do that alone, but corporate worship is taught in the Bible, and together, as the Body of Christ, the bride of Christ, we should draw near to Him.

The writer of Hebrews says that we are to "enter the Holiest by the blood of Jesus" (vs. 19 NKJV). The Holiest is the Holy of Holies in the temple according to the Old Testament. It was the innermost room of the temple or the tabernacle. The Holy of Holies is where the Shekinah glory of God sat upon the Ark of the Covenant. The writer of Hebrews says we are to come through the veil into the Holy of holies, however, in the Old Testament, the high priest could only go into the Holy of Holies once a year. He would go in there with a basin of blood and sprinkle the blood upon a piece of furniture called the mercy seat, and he would not dare go in there without the blood. He would not dare go in there without permission of God. No one else other than the high priest would dare to go in there. But writer of Hebrews tells us to enter the Holy of Holies by the blood of Jesus. Up until Jesus's death on the cross no other person besides the high priest could go in, but praise be to Jesus! Because of Jesus every church member, genuine child of God can go in. The high priest would only go in once a year, but because of Jesus we can come to Him every day! Not only as individuals, but we also can go in as a church body all at the same time; into the holiest by the blood of Jesus.

The writer of Hebrews also tells us to go "through the veil" (vs. 20 NKJV). The veil was a great woven curtain that separated the holy place from the Holy of Holies, and it was a curtain wall. The veil was a picture of the Lord Jesus Christ. The veil, which symbolically represents Jesus's body, was made of colors. Exodus 27 tells us that the veil was made of white linen, sky blue thread, blood red or crimson thread, and royal purple thread; these colors represent the Lord Jesus Christ. Had we seen it in its day, it would have been shimmering in all those colors. The veil separated the holy place from the Holy of Holies. When the priest went in, he would lift up the corner of the veil and slip under. Tradition tells us that they tied a rope around his leg in case he was stricken dead in there, because no one could go in there to get him out. They would have to pull him out.

The reason, in my opinion, why there were four colors, is because there are four gospels: Matthew, Mark, Luke, and John. Matthew speaks of Jesus Christ as King. Matthew would then be represented by the color purple. Mark speaks of Jesus as the suffering servant, as the Son of man who shed His blood. Mark is represented by the color blood red or crimson. Luke speaks of Jesus Christ as the virgin-born Son of God from heaven. Luke is represented by the color sky blue. White speaks of Jesus Christ in His absolute deity, His sinlessness. This is what John speaks about in his gospel. The veil is a picture of Jesus, the colors represent the gospels, and the gospels is a portrait of Jesus Christ our Lord. But, how are you going to come through the veil? When Jesus hung on the cross, when He hung His head and died in agony shedding His blood; the Bible says that the veil of the temple was torn from top to bottom, and the way into the Holy of Holies is now made clear and open by the sacrificial death of the Lord Jesus Christ. Just as the writer of Hebrews says, we come "through the blood" (vs. 19 NKJV). There is no other way to go into the Holy of Holies except through Jesus Christ.

Some people will say, "Well, I just believe that I am going to be saved by living a life like the Lord Jesus Christ." If that is what you are counting on to get you to heaven, then you are not going. Nobody can live a more perfect life that Jesus. That veil did not say, "Come in!" That veil said, "Stay out!" His absolute royalty, His deity, His sinless humanity, His absolute pure-white purity, does not say, "Come in." It says, "This is what I demand of you, and you cannot get in here, because this perfection keeps you out." It was only when Jesus died, and through His death, a way was made into the Holy of Holies. If you do not get anything else from this book, *Behave as a Church Member*, learn this: Salvation is not learning lessons from the life of Christ; it is receiving life from the death of Christ.

Now, what the writer of Hebrews is talking about in Hebrews 10:19-25 is for us to behave as a church member through attendance. He is saying the climax of the whole thing is, "Let us not forsake the assembling ourselves together, as is the manner of some" (Heb. 10:25 NKJV). Do you know what we are doing when we gather together? We are behaving as church members put those spiritual gifts to use. We are exalting the Savior when we worship Him in the Spirit. We worship God in spirit and truth. We exalt the Savior when we just enter in through the veil into the Holy of Holies that is what we are doing when we enter the sanctuary of the church. We do not attend just one service once a year, but every time we meet, as a congregation, we are exalting the Savior. The writer of Hebrews is saying, "Let us draw near with a true heart in full assurance of faith, have our hearts sprinkled from an evil conscience and our bodies washed with pure water" (vs. 22 NKJV).

This brings up a question. Why does God want us to worship Him? Is God some cosmic egotist who has to be constantly told how good He is, how glorious He is, how great He is? Is that what you think God is like? Listen, God does not need our worship, He does not need our gifts because they do not enrich Him. God owns everything. Our fellowship with Him and others does not improve God. He does not learn anything from us. Our praise does not make God any more glorious. God wants us to worship Him for what worship does for us. When we worship, we become like what we worship, whether it be individually and/or corporately. Have you ever been in a boring worship service? If you said, "yes," you are wrong. There is no such thing as a boring worship service. You may have been in a boring church service, but you have never been in a boring worship service. Worship is one of the most exhilarating things that there is, because in a worship service you behave as a church member by exalting the Savior.

EVANGELIZE THE SINNER

"Let us hold fast the confession of our hope without wavering, for He who promised is faithful" (Heb. 10:23 NKJV). Did you know that when you attend church, you are professing your faith? When you attend church, it is your way of saying, "I believe in Jesus!" In the early church, as I have already stated, if people ceased from coming to church and joining the assembly, the other church members would assume that they have gone back to the world. Forsaking the assembly was an indication to the early church member that people had forsaken the Lord. "Now the just shall live by faith; but if anyone draws back, My soul has no pleasure in him. But we are not of those who draw back to perdition, but of those who believe to the saving of the soul" (Heb. 10:38-39 NKJV). When people join the church and you see them for a while, and then they disappear, as one pastor put it, "They are Alka Seltzer Christians." In other words, you dip them in water, they fizzle a little bit, and then they disappear; they draw back. Why do they draw back? They never were truly saved. That is the way John puts it, "They went out from us, but they were not of us; for if they had been of us, they would have continued with us; but they went out that they might be made manifest, that none of them were of us" (1 John 2:19 NKJV). Let me say this in love: if you are willing to forsake the assembling of yourself together, you cannot claim to be true to Jesus Christ. It that is the case then you are not behaving as a church member.

When you go to church it is a witness, it is a profession of faith. When you go to church you are saying, "I belong to that group." When you back out of your driveway on Sunday, you, spouse, and your children; does your neighbors know where you are going? Do they know you are going to church? Attending church is your profession of faith in Jesus Christ, because your actions speaks louder than words.

ENCOURAGE THE SAINTS

"And let us consider one another in order to stir up love and good works, not forsaking the assembling of ourselves together as is the manner of some, but exhorting one another, and so much the more as you see the Day approaching" (Heb. 10:24-25 NKJV). Here is where those spiritual gifts and behaving as a church member comes in to focus. We have a responsibility not only as believer, church members, but has brothers and sisters in Christ. When we come to church, we come to encourage one another. As a pastor I am encouraged by the church members of the church where I pastor. I cannot tell you how many people have encouraged me, as I have seen them going up and down the hallways. Some will say, "Pastor, we are praying for you. We love you." I need that, because that strengthens me. You need that, we need one another. The Bible says, that we are exhorting one another. The word exhorting means "encouraging" (Concise Oxford English Dictionary Eleventh Edition, 2004) There are several "one another passages in the Bible that tells how to behave as church members toward one another. Here is a list:

1. Wash one another's feet (John 13:14).
2. Prefer one another (Rom. 12:10).
3. Be of the same mind toward one another (Rom. 12:16).
4. Do not judge one another (Rom. 14:13).
5. Do not speak evil of one another (Jam. 4:11).
6. Receive one another (Rom. 15:7).
7. Admonish one another (Rom. 15:14).
8. Care for one another (1 Cor. 12:29).
9. Minster gifts one to another (1 Pet. 4:10).
10. Greet one another (1 Cor. 16:20).
11. Serve one another (Gal. 5:16).
12. Bear one another's burdens (Gal. 6:2).
13. Submit to one another (Eph. 4:21).
14. Comfort one another (1 Thess. 4:18).
15. Edify one another (1 Thess. 5:11).
16. Exhort one another (Heb. 3:13).
17. Confess your faults to one another (Jam. 5:16).
18. Pray for one another (Jam. 5:16).
19. Use hospitality one to another (1 Pet. 4:9).
20. Fellowship with one another (1 John 1:7).

Do you think God is trying to tell us something? God is telling us that in order to behave as a church member, Christianity is not some sort of lone ranger behavior. You do not attend church for what you can get out of it. So, how do we encourage one another? We can first be encouraging to one another, by our presence when we gather together. When you come to church, you are saying two things: "God is important to me" and "people are important to me." Probably what you are thinking right now is: "Pastor, you are getting legalistic. You are trying to tell me I have to be at church every time the doors are open." No, that is not what I am trying to tell you, however, you ought to be at church Sunday morning, Sunday night, and Wednesday night unless you are providentially hindered. I understand that not everyone can attend every service. There are some who cannot attend every service due to some physical ailment. Some people cannot get out at night. I understand that. There are some, because of their work schedule and other things keep you from attending church. I understand that as well. But if you are a church member of a church somewhere, then you ought to behave as a church member of that church. You are a part of a church family. Let me ask you a question: "When your family has a birthday party, or a celebration, or a regular meal, is that your family? When it is mealtime, do you not think you ought to come and sit down at the table with the rest of the family? That goes for the church family as well. When the church meets together on Sunday the church family is assembling itself together. Should you not be there?

Obviously, if you are sick, you cannot come to the family meal. Obviously, if you are out of town, you cannot come. Obviously, if you are at work, you cannot come. Everybody cannot be here for every service. But listen, we do not need to be carelessly, lazily, and thoughtlessly staying away from the house of God as a habit. There was a church that was built in the year 1500 A.D. in Europe. In that church building they had no candelabra. They did not have any lights. The mayor of the town told everybody to bring his or her own lantern to church. When it came time for the people to come in, each person brought their lantern to church and hang it on the end of the pew. The more the people that would come in the brighter the church house became. If no one came, the church house would be in darkness. Every time you come to church, you are bringing the love, the light of the Lord Jesus Christ. If you stay away, then it would be tragic for the house of God to be dark. The writer of Hebrews tells us, "Not forsaking the assembling of ourselves together, as is the manner of some, but exhorting one another, and so much the more as you see the Day approaching" (Heb. 10:25 NKJV). We are living in the end times; do you not see the day approaching? The Day, the writer of Hebrews is talking about, is the consummation of the age. He says, as the night gets darker, the saints ought to get brighter. We need one another. We owe to one another a fearful loyalty in these days. We are to behave as a church member by exhorting one another, firing up one another. These are wicked days, lascivious days, evil days with all kinds of mayhem and wickedness in the world. That is all the reason we need to be faithful, loyal, and to behave. God has given us some great spiritual gifts. Use what God has given you, look for opportunities to grow our gift, and you may discover that you have other spiritual gifts that you did not know you had. My prayer is that God will help you use these gifts for His purpose and glory, and may He help us behave as a church member.

REFERENCES

2019. *Evangelism Conference.* Little Rock.

1986. *Hoosiers.* Directed by David Anspaugh.

Barna, George. 1997. In *Leaders on Leadership*, 18. Venture Books.

2004. *Concise Oxford English Dictionary Eleventh Edition.* New York: Oxford University Press.

Dictionary, Merriam-Webster. 1828. "Merriam-Webster Dictionary." In *Merriam-Webster Dictionary.* Merriam-Webster Dictionary.

2003. *Holman Illustrated Bible Dictionary.* Nashville: Holman Bible Publishers.

LifeWay Christian Resources. 2003. *Spiritual Gifts Survey.* Accessed 2022. https://youngadults.lifeway.com/wp-content/uploads/downloads/SpiritualGiftsSurvey.pdf.

Powers, Dr Christopher. 2021. *Behave as a Fisher of Men.* Bloomington: WestBow Press.

Powers, Dr. Christopher. 2021. *Behave as a Follower of Christ.* Maitland: Xulon Press.

1984. *Strong's Concordance.* Nashville: Thomas Nelson Publishers.

2000. *The Baptist Fatih and Message .* Accessed August 30, 2021. https://bfm.sbc.net/bfm2000/.

Unknown. 2015.

n.d. "Webster."

Wood, D.R.W., I. Howard Marshall, and A.R. Millard. 1996. *The New Bible Dictionary, Third Edition.* Intervarsity Press.

Printed in the United States
by Baker & Taylor Publisher Services